MILTON MOORE

How much price competition?

The prerequisites of an effective Canadian competition policy

McGILL-QUEEN'S UNIVERSITY PRESS
MONTREAL AND LONDON · 1970

© McGill-Queen's University Press 1970
International Standard Book Number 0-7735-0083-9
Library of Congress Catalog Card No. 71-135415

This book has been published
with the help of a grant from
the Social Science Research
Council of Canada, using funds
provided by the Canada Council.

Design by
Kari Nordby

Printed in Canada by
John Deyell Limited

To Helen, Graeme, and Jennifer

Contents

Preface

With the exception of the Preface and Introduction, this study was written for the general reader, not for the economist. The Introduction is intended for readers who have enough familiarity with the writings of Canadian and American economists on competition and trade policy to be able, from a summary statement of my position, to identify the parts of the book they may wish to examine in detail. The general reader may find the remainder of the Preface and some parts of the Introduction too cryptic to be entirely intelligible. It is suggested that he start his reading at chapter 1.

The study is not intended as a "scholarly work" in the narrow sense of the term. Thus the omission of a bibliography is deliberate, and notes are kept to the minimum required for adequate documentation of quotations and explicit references to published works. More important, minimum use is made of the language of the economist, and only oblique references are made to important controversies that have enlivened the journals in recent decades. Consequently, the university economist is likely to be disturbed by my sometimes summary treatment of theoretical issues. Since the book is addressed to another audience and purpose, I hope that my fellow economists will not complain that it is neither a textbook nor a scholarly study.

I have been engaged intermittently for several years in a study of the pricing and other competitive behaviour of modern industries. My practical experience and unsuccessful attempts to build a bridge for students between textbook models and market behaviour have induced me, on the grounds of realism and relevance, to join the growing body of instructors and students who have rejected the standard theory of the firm. Only the pure-competition model is adequately developed in the standard textbook exposition. Appropriately handled, that model meets the tests of predictive and explanatory power. The main defects of the standard exposition result from the assumption that the firm varies output by varying factor ratios, and therefore the law of diminishing marginal productivity is operative and short-run marginal cost increases monotonically over the relevant range of outputs. In fact, over a wide range of operating rates, output is typically varied by changes in the number of hours of operation in the plant per period, factor inputs being held in a fixed ratio. Only when output approaches or exceeds capacity, in the engineer's meaning of that term, are factor ratios varied.

However, the industries that fit the pure-competition model sufficiently well to yield validated predictions constitute only a small proportion of the private sector of our economy. All other models, and especially oligopoly, are inadequately developed in the standard exposition and, partly as a consequence, fail to meet the test of predictive power.

University economists prefer that theoretical issues be resolved by argument in the learned journals before any policy-oriented study based on unorthodox assumptions is addressed to an audience other than themselves. However, like the poor, controversies over the theory of the firm and how well markets work will always be with us, partly because much of the dispute is coloured by incompatible ideologies.

As long ago as 1966, I completed most of a first draft of what was to be a scholarly study of the theory of the firm. In the process I discovered an encouraging number of problems to be resolved, and the study has become something of a labour of love. Since the received theory had to be questioned, I expected my study either to be stillborn or to receive searching and hostile criticism. Consequently, it was the part of wisdom not to try to rush the study to completion but rather to proceed cautiously, meeting criticism in advance and paying due homage to the literature. It was with some misgivings, therefore, that in 1967 I accepted an invitation from the Economic Council of Canada to write an overview study of some of the issues involved in Canadian competition policy, for whatever assistance it might provide to those responsible for carrying out the work required to respond to the federal government's Reference to the Council concerning (a) consumer affairs, (b) combines, mergers, monopolies, and restraint of trade, and (c) patents, trade marks, copyrights, and registered industrial designs. Mine was only one of the several research studies commissioned, and a number of the studies of particular problems are being published by the council to provide information additional to that contained in its *Interim Report on Competition Policy*, issued in July of 1969. From the outset, however, since it was a study of policy, I considered it preferable that my study be published by a university press. I wish to thank the council for its cooperation in readily granting a release of their rights to the study and permission to publish elsewhere.

Although those who were to read the study in manuscript form were experts, I addressed myself to the wider audience to whom my study might be of interest: businessmen, lawyers, accountants, civil servants, and members of parliament and of the general public who are well informed about business activities but who are not professional economists. I considered that the value of the study to the Economic Council would not be diminished if I did not write in the crabbed language of the economist and, in any event, a technician's study addressed to technicians with the wide scope of this study could not have been completed within the time allowed by the council for completion of the studies under the government's Reference.

Although addressed to a lay audience, the study, especially chapter 1, may strike the reader as being quite textbookish. This was not intentional; for the reason explained in the first pages of that chapter, I could not avoid it. To consider changes that might improve conditions, one must start with a statement of the existing conditions. So it was unavoidable that I describe in considerable detail my understanding of the state and nature of business competition in Canada in the 1960s. It was also required that I state my case in justification of changes in the rules governing business behaviour, and that case can only be that there exists avoidable economic waste. So this matter is examined in chapter 2. It was also appropriate that some attention be paid to past efforts to increase the productivity of the Canadian economy by imposing rules upon competitive behaviour. Therefore, this third necessary preliminary forms chapter 3.

The heart of the study appears at the end as chapter 4. To a considerable extent the validity of the arguments presented there in support of radical changes in the laws regulating business activities depends upon the correctness of the first three chapters.

Since ideological issues unavoidably intrude at every turn of the argument, it is appropriate that the author state his ideological leanings. The particular value judgement that infuses the study is that the public good takes precedence over the right of the individual to pursue his economic self-interest. Lurking in the background are two primary assumptions. The first is that there is no ground on which an individual can rest a claim to any natural economic rights or economic privileges;

all his economic rights are conferred on the individual by the community, including the right to retain the income earned by participating in the vast, cooperative, communal endeavour that constitutes the economy of a modern industrial state. The second is that political, economic, and social stability cannot be long sustained in a democratic state in which political power is widely diffused unless there is an acceptance by most members of the community of the ethical rule that the welfare of each has equal weight.

I wish to thank several of my colleagues for helpful criticisms of parts of this book while it was in manuscript. They may be puzzled to discover that their comments have not resulted in many changes in the wording of the book. They may be assured that the reason is not that their comments were treated lightly; their influence will be discernible in the larger study which I hope will someday appear. In particular, I wish to acknowledge helpful comments from Ronald Shearer, Gideon Rosenbluth, Paul Bradley, David McQueen, and Frank Roseman and to express special thanks to Edwin Black, without whose help the study would probably never have appeared in print.

An introduction
addressed to economists

The term *competition policy* is used to replace the usual, cumbersome, descriptive phrase *anticombines and restrictive trade practices policy.* The former term has considerable currency in Britain and was adopted by the Economic Council of Canada in its *Interim Report,* on the government's reference concerning consumer affairs, patents, combines, mergers, and restrictive trade practices.[1] *Competition policy* is preferable not only because it is shorter but also because it places the emphasis on the positive rather than the negative aspects of the problems of public regulation of business behaviour.

The prerequisites of an effective competition policy consist of the set of hard decisions which the federal government must take concerning several fundamental issues that involve conflicts of interest. Few of the problem situations have ever been squarely faced in Canada; when an agency of government has been confronted with any of them, it has rarely taken an unequivocal position. No Canadian government has ever been forced to realize that it must decide what kind of free enterprise system is wanted. None has ever had to declare itself concerning (*a*) the type and severity of price competition that is a necessary condition for the efficient working of the price system in a market economy; (*b*) whether companies have acquired rights to the privileges they enjoy—to merge, to engage in price discrimination, to follow conventional pricing practices such as delivered pricing systems, and to refuse to sell; (*c*) whether a market economy works efficiently without government direction or a complex set of rules of behaviour must be imposed (as in the United States); or (*d*) how roughly companies should be allowed to play the competitive game, that is, what protection of the relatively weak companies should be afforded by explicit rules of fair play.

Unless politically courageous decisions are made concerning these policy issues, no improvement in the working of the Canadian economy will be induced and our competition policy will continue to be the

1

charade that it now is. And the honest course for a government to take would be to admit that nothing of substance stood behind the imposing facade of regulation.

Most of the policy decisions that must be made concern the severity of price competition to which Canadian industries should be exposed, and most of the conflicts of interest arise from the privileged position that the modern corporation possesses. Difficult though it may be for companies to live with it, severe *price* competition that forces the inefficient company to the wall is the sine qua non of an efficient market economy, and the inducement of severe price competition is a necessary condition for the elimination of the considerable waste of resources which results from the prevalence of nonprice competition. On the surface this contention appears to be no more than the standard doctrine of the academic economist. However, the similarity is only apparent. It is well known that the neoclassical theory of employment and inflation has been on the ascendant during the past two decades and has all but become the *received theory*—the conventional wisdom of the day. According to neoclassical theory in its simplest extreme form, a market economy would perform very well when measured against the criteria of rapid economic growth, sustained high employment, and a stable price level, provided only that wages were flexible downward, the supply of money increased at the appropriate rate, and the economic role of governments were minimal. It is less well realized that there is a similar apology of the existing state of affairs at the micro level. There is a school of neoclassical economics which purports to have discovered that, despite appearances to the contrary, the North American economy operates very much as an economy of purely competitive industries would because most oligopolies act in disregard of their mutual dependence, and therefore the performance of the North American economy approaches tolerably well the best of all attainable worlds—and the approach would be closer were it not for the errors of commission by governments. Although less extreme than the neoclassical view, it is nevertheless the received theory of the day not less than Canadian restrictive trade practices policy which made it appropriate a decade ago for Rosenbluth and Thorburn to refer to Canadian combines law as a cops-and-robbers game.[2] The implicit assumptions of the Canadian law are not greatly at odds with those of contemporary theory of the behaviour of the firm. It is assumed by both that so long as the number of firms in an industry is greater than "a few" (for example greater than ten) and there is no formal collusion, competition among the firms in an industry will satisfy the requirements of efficiency.

Rosenbluth and Thorburn's critique aroused considerable interest in part because it alleged a lack of concern by both major political parties for the implementation of orthodox combines policy. But these authors did not press their critique deeply enough. Apparently they would have been content to see Canadian competition policy operate within the framework of analysis developed in the United States. But United States policies reflect neoclassical theory. And the neoclassical theory of the firm still rests upon a polarity of two models, with (bad) monopoly at one pole and (good) pure competition at the other. The task is seen to be one of moving most industries toward the competitive model. In contrast, the dissenting view is that the two polar models are of little significance. For one thing, monopolies do not behave as assumed. But, much more important, most industries are oligopolies, and they are a class unto themselves. The key assumption in the analysis of their behaviour is that most oligopolies engage in conventional pricing practices that are indistinguishable from the tacit collusion that is almost universally disapproved. One can readily discover on which side of the chasm that divides these two views of the modern economy a person stands by finding out his reaction to the protests of the convicted executives of the giant electrical companies of several years ago.[3] The executives alleged they were being sent to jail for activities that were the norm. This protest is in accord with the dissenting view. But the conventional view required *Fortune's* contributor to turn upon these odd men out and deny their allegation. At whatever cost, the myth of the competitive system had to be sustained, so the executives who were caught out had to be censured. In this sense, United States policy, no less than Canadian, is a cops-and-robbers game.

Given my conviction that most industries are oligopolies, including some consisting of well over a score of independent firms, the usual prescription for improving performance is precluded. It is usual to reason that a firm with a small market share, say 5 percent, cannot detect the effects upon its sales of a competitive move, such as a price reduction, undertaken by another firm of equal size. Consequently a firm of that "small" size does not take into account the effects that any of its own competitive moves may have upon the behaviour of its competitors. It need not worry that it will provoke a reaction. This reasoning is irresistibly appealing and dominates nearly all the model building of oligopoly behaviour, because the *symmetry assumption* creeps in undetected. The symmetry assumption is that each firm is an equally close competitor of all others in its industry. But, excluding the retail level, every buyer is some firm's customer, and no firm can take away another's customer without the latter knowing about it, because the prevalent mode of business stresses close customer-supplier relations. One of the primary functions of sales agents is to ensure that customers are not successfully courted by rivals. If sales were effected with the anonymity of organized markets such as the stock exchange, this would not be so. But the organized market is the rarity.

Since marketing holds the key to success, the typical firm even in industries of relatively large numbers of firms keeps watch upon the competitive moves of all its rivals. Consequently, the firm is acutely aware that it must take account of the reactions of all others whenever it plans a competitive move. And if there is one lesson that all Canadian oligopoly firms have learnt beyond forgetting, it is that price cutting by a few usually results in a lower level of prices, to the detriment of all and the benefit of none. This is why elaborate pricing systems have been built up to guard against a break in price. The final result is that price competition in any sensible meaning of the term is wholly absent, and nonprice competition is the prevalent form of intraindustry rivalry.

The conventional remedies of the North American economist, as distinct from the actual United States regulation of business behaviour, are increased numbers of competitors, the prevention of formal collusion, and freedom of entry. These are the stock-in-trade of the "structural school." I find myself in the anomalous position of agreeing with most of the criticisms of the "performance school" levied by the adherents of the structural view while at the same time being in the behavioural camp when it comes to designing remedial regulations. The three structural prescriptions are quite sound as far as they go. But they do not go nearly far enough.

Increasing the numbers of competitors has already been discussed, indirectly. Since over a score of firms may act on the recognition of their mutual dependence and, in particular, accord the avoidance of uncontrolled price competition among them top priority in their competitive strategy, increasing the number of firms is not a promising avenue to the inducement of price competition. In any event, given the prevalence in the Canadian economy of overlapping regional markets, not many markets are sufficiently large to absorb the output of even half a dozen plants of minimum optimal size. Bans upon collusion suffer from an equal defect. Formal collusion is susceptible to regulation, but conscious parallel action is extremely difficult to detect and even more difficult to prove, and it is impossible to prevent independent action on the recognition of mutual dependence. But the effects of all three are similar. Finally, preventing the erection of artificial barriers to entry additional to the natural barrier of minimal optimal scale must certainly form part of any effective competition policy. But it is difficult to distinguish predatory conduct from aggressive competitive behaviour, and entry is not likely to be so open (except in the industries characterized by excessive ease of entry) that price competition would be induced even if predatory behaviour were successfully banned. Even if all three measures were pressed with great vigour, therefore, Canadian competition policy would not result in a substantial increase in price competition.

What is more important, since price competition is only a means to desired ends, the waste of resources resulting from the absence of price competition would not be significantly decreased. There is little hope of a significant improvement in productivity until our conception of the waste resulting from imperfect competition is entirely reconstructed. It may be assumed that the major objective of existing competition policy is that the consumer should be accorded the presumed benefits of competition. To the economist this statement usually means that output and price should be "right," so that the consumer will be protected from the loss suffered when prices are "too high" and output "too low." It is argued in chapters 2 and 4 that the loss of consumers' surplus attributable to such imperfect prices and outputs is minute in relation to the substantial waste that results from excessive nonprice competition free from the constraint of price competition. These substantial wastes are high costs due to short runs of multiple designs and styles, and plants too small to realize most of the economies of scale; chronic excess capacity in many service industries, particularly retailing; and excess plant capacity and excessive sales promotion expenditures in manufacturing.

The Canadian economy is not large enough to produce the number of lines and models of many secondary manufacturing industries that are required to satisfy the consumers' preference for variety, except at an excessive cost of short runs and too-small plants. The increased productivity that could be realized by the specialization of plants so that only one or a very few lines or models were produced could be attained only if the number of lines produced domestically were greatly reduced and the preference for variety met to a greater extent by imports. But the means to that end is not the removal of tariffs, as is usually recommended. Tariff removal, in the absence of special arrangements similar to the automobile agreement, would result in the disappearance of much Canadian secondary manufacturing altogether. And the parts of the Canadian industry which survived would become entirely integrated with their United States counterparts. There would be a continental intracompany specialization of plants and, excepting the products that are naturally protected by the cost of transportation, Canadian secondary manufacturing industries in which there were substantial scale economies would become branch plant operations. Such full economic integration with the United States would benefit the consumer because the productivity of labour and capital in Canadian manufacturing would increase substantially. But it is no more than a pious hope that output and employment in manufacturing in central Canada, and therefore total Canadian population, would not be very substantially less than they would be if sufficient tariff protection were maintained to prevent the wholesale migration of industry to the United States. The effects of the removal of tariffs upon the location of industry would depend crucially upon whether the only substantial advantage which Canadian secondary manufacturing would possess in its competition with American industry, lower real wage rates, would be maintained during the transition period when the continental, intracompany integration was proceeding. If Canadian wages remained lower, it would apparently be profitable for the international corporations in some industries to maintain or increase the capacity and output of their Canadian plants in the process of integrating operations in the two countries. But if, as seems more likely, the Canadian locals of international trade unions won even nominal parity of wage rates, the advantage of a Canadian location of a branch plant would be eroded and operations in Canada would be reduced. Even if the former, favourable outcome occurred, of course, the typical independent Canadian firm would have to increase in size at least fivefold and probably tenfold. And there is little ground for hoping that many Canadian companies could rise to that challenge; most would be taken over by large, nonresident corporatons.

There is an alternative to this continental, intracompany specialization and integration of operations that would result from the free trade with the United States which is advocated by many economists as the means to higher productivity and real income per capita and which would greatly circumscribe if not eliminate whatever vestiges of independence the Canadian economy still possesses. The alternative is the incorporation of tariff policy in and its subordination to the national competition policy. Every available inducement and threat would have to be used to impose specialization in fewer lines upon most companies in most tariff-sheltered secondary manufacturing industries. This would often require a considerable reduction in the number of companies. The least painful route to fewer companies would be by mergers. But the desired rationalization would not occur unless it were the only means to survival. And the goad to consolidation by merger and to specialization in a smaller number of lines would be the reduction of the Canadian tariff to the minimum level required for Canadian companies to survive and earn normal profits after they were fully rationalized. After the painful transition was completed by an industry, efficiency and high productivity could be maintained by the ever-present threat of potential competition from imports flowing over the much-reduced tariffs.

A substantial increase in the productivity of retailing and other service industries could also be realized only by equally bold measures. In 1952 the enforcement of resale price maintenance by manufacturers was made unlawful. But no dramatic increase in price competition among retailers resulted. Nor was this lack of impact occasion for surprise. The typical retailer, no less than the typical manufacturer, is an oligopolist who is acutely aware of the interdependence of the few firms selling in his particular market. And the typical retailer, not less than the typical manufacturer, has learned beyond forgetting that price cutting by one or a few, if it is successful in substantially increasing the price-cutters' share of the market at the expense of rivals, will eventually be challenged, and the ultimate outcome will be a detriment to most. Therefore, only the "professional price-cutter" engages in this risky tactic. Regrettably, the professional price-cutter is not ubiquitous in the Canadian economy. And most retailing is fairly easy of entry. Consequently, capacity in many lines of retailing is excessive by any reasonable judgement, and most retail dealers are dependent upon the maintenance of whatever average markup prevails. As the retailer becomes more vulnerable to price reductions that erode his margins, so also does his resistance to that catastrophe increase. There is therefore a voluntary adherence to manufacturers' suggested retail prices.

The excess of resources in these service industries could be reduced by the encouragement of the price-cutter. The only effective way to encourage price cutting is by removal of the manufacturers' right of refusal to sell not just to particular retailers but, more importantly, to distributors. Price competition among manufacturers of consumers goods is avoided by the integration of distribution and marketing with production. That integration confers upon the manufacturer control over the prices of his products at all levels up to the sale to the retail dealer, and either some form of franchise system or merely the use of suggested retail prices extends that control to the retail price. If the manufacturer were required to sell to all bona fide distributors without resort to price discrimination—even if the manufacturer were making all his sales directly to retailers through his own staff of sales agents— his control over prices charged to retailers of his products would be ended. Wholesalers who were professional price-cutters would enjoy a new lease on life and would set about breaking down the elaborate marketing systems built up by manufacturers. In the process, the wholesale/marketing margin would be much reduced and excess resources squeezed out of distribution. With price competition prevailing at the wholesale level, voluntary resale price maintenance would break down. A considerable reduction of retail markups would result, and much of the excess resources would be squeezed out of retailing, to the substantial benefit of the consumer.

Finally, with price competition prevalent at the wholesale and retail levels, it would be extremely difficult for manufacturers to avoid falling into price competition among themselves, at least occasionally, despite the strong recognition of mutual dependence. When wholesale and retail prices are unstable it becomes well-nigh impossible to discover whether a rival is breaking the unwritten convention not to cut prices to increase sales. It would also be more difficult for oligopolists to signal to one another that a price increase was desirable. Price leadership requires that there be stable, managed prices. As a consequence of the price competition at the wholesale and retail level, therefore, there would be intermittent outbreaks of price competition among manufacturers and a concomitant decrease in the dependence upon nonprice competition as the only outlet for rivalry. A considerable reduction in the resources devoted to protecting market shares and to sales promotion would result in some industries.

The complementary measures of the subordination of tariff policy to competition policy and the withdrawal of the firm's right of refusal to sell are the two most radical components of what I consider to be the indispensible constituents of an effective Canadian competition policy. But they do not exhaust the list of necessary conditions. Regulated industries should be exposed to competition as well as being subject to the much more effective regulation developed in the United States. The service industries should lose their exemption from combines law and should be subject, so far as possible, to the same inducements to price competition and efficiency as are the commodities-producing industries. Reform of the income taxes as prescribed by the Carter Royal Commission on Taxation for the improvement in resource allocation is overdue (excepting the integration of the corporation and personal income taxes which would result in a huge loss of revenue for slight tangible gain). Also, in circumstances where it is possible and beneficial to do so, price discrimination and predatory tactics should be banned and f.o.b. pricing made mandatory. Mergers that promise no gain in productivity, and especially those the main effect of which is to eliminate an aggressive, efficient smaller company or to further reduce the probability of price competition, should be disallowed.

Desirable as it is to have the simplicity and clarity of per se rules of conduct, it is apparent that they would not be feasible for many of the measures that constitute the suggested competition policy. For example, it would not be feasible to compel a manufacturer to sell at a uniform price to all persons who presented themselves as wholesalers; only bona fide wholesalers should qualify. Similarly, general rules cannot be framed that would segregate desirable from undesirable mergers. The only course is to establish a quasi-judicial agency that would apply general rules to particular instances. A set of rules should be formulated and should be binding upon the decisions of the agency. The task of the agency would be to discover the circumstance of the cases brought before them and, by doing so, identify the rules that apply. Sometimes the court would have to exercise considerable judgement, for example, to determine whether a merger was likely to increase productivity. At other times the rules would be more clear-cut. For example, the agency need only discover whether an instance of price discrimination brought before it was one of the banned types set out in the rules.

The policies advocated obviously call into question the conventional image of the free enterprise system as it operates in Canada. There are many members of the business community who realize that this image is a very poor facsimile of reality. I have witnessed a very few businessmen tacitly concede that the only justification for the fervent affirmation that the present operation of our market system is almost free of blemish is the conviction that any alternative to existing policies must be worse. It is taken for granted as an article of faith that government regulation is bad. If there are a few who are willing to make such a concession, surely there must be many more who are not, but who are equally aware of the actual state of affairs.

The great barrier—and indeed the only barrier of substance—to the adoption of an effective competition policy (or any other social change) is the rejection of realism and relevance. The barrier to change is the refusal to change a public stance, no matter how untenable it may be. Most people who have held executive positions with large corporations are acutely aware of the creed of the managerial class to which one must give at least lip service if one is to climb the ladder of promotion. Among other things, the creed prescribes that the freedom of the company is sacrosanct. As a consequence, the theorem has been developed that all markets that are free of government regulations operate well; the market system is the attainable optimum in this imperfect world.

This article of faith is applied not just to markets for commodities, services, and securities but also to markets for companies. Thus, the onus of proof of detriment to the public interest is thrown upon those who would interfere with the market for companies, that is, with mergers. Such a rule is not undesirable. What is undesirable is that the rules of evidence are asymmetrical. Almost any evidence supporting the conclusion that the market for companies operates to the benefit of the public interest is accepted, but proof positive beyond the peradventure of a doubt is required for evidence of public detriment to be accepted. Economists complain of this bias when they are trying to make a case supporting some orthodox prescription such as free trade or f.o.b. pricing. But the community of academic economists is itself by no means free of a similar ambivalence. For example, a leading critic of United States combines legislation at one time contended that the evidence of the prevalence of price competition lay all about us, but it was extraordinarily difficult to document because it was contained in confidential memoranda and papers of companies. The contention won a respectful hearing. But if anyone were to make an identical contention concerning the evidence of the lack of competition, he would be hooted out of court. The situation is so bad that there is not even a consensus among academic economists concerning the methodology appropriate for investigating the behaviour of the firm.

Perhaps one of the most striking instances of the divergence of a public image from reality is to be found in the promotion of new mining companies by the sale of penny mining stocks on the exchanges. It is almost incredible that recent findings of great waste should have done so little damage to the favourable public image of the industry that produces "paper mines."[4]

Possibly the second most formidable barrier to social change is the disposition to stay with the devil we know rather than the devil we don't know. The costs of change tend to be overestimated. For example, it may be feared that the creation of a competitive economy would reduce the pace of technological advance. It is argued in chapters 1 and 4 that, if anything, there would be a quickening of the pace of innovation, at least temporarily. In any event, such a fear would be strange indeed in a country that spends a lower proportion of its national income on research and development in the private sector than any other major industrial nation and that imports nearly all its innovations and exports most of its inventions at an early stage for development elsewhere.

1
The state of competition

It is self-evident that a person's view concerning the reform of Canadian competition policy is a reflection of his conception of how the economy now operates and how it would operate if conditions were changed. Some consider that, given human nature, the performance of companies is as good as can be expected, and little is to be gained by adding to government regulations. Others consider that there is considerable scope for improvement. The logical point at which to start an inquiry, therefore, is with a consideration of the nature and extent of competition in Canada in the 1960s.

The difficulty facing this logical procedure arises from our lack of knowledge. It is pointless to quarrel about questions of fact. The thing to do is to go out and confirm what the situation is. However, the mass of information required to determine the state of competition is not available. Ideally, we should like to have case studies of most of the industries of the country, conducted from the inside rather than interpreted from the outside. The few case studies available were made from the outside, and interpretations of the observed behaviour of industries differ crucially.

Given the lack of knowledge and the prevailing disagreements about how firms in different circumstances do and would behave, all that any economist can do is state his version. The connection between what he considers to be the existing state of affairs and his analysis and recommendations should be apparent. It is desirable that generalizations be documented so that they can be checked. However, it is not possible to do so when the information available is fragmentary and does not consist of studies that can be cited. As mentioned, very few in-depth case studies of the behaviour of Canadian industries have been conducted. Nevertheless, wherever possible, references are made to published works.

As a second best, I have attempted to cast the economist's analytical models—his classification system—into a form understandable by the

13

layman. I am confident that my descriptions of the world of business will be recognized by businessmen as the world which they inhabit; I am somewhat less confident that the version will win acceptance by my academic colleagues, since it departs in important respects from orthodox sets of models.

THE PURE-COMPETITION INDUSTRIES

The first of the boxes in the classification system consists of a slightly modified conception of the traditional pure-competition industry. This is possibly an unfortunate designation, because all industries are competitive in various ways and to greater or lesser degree. The terms used in the classification system are not intended to have honorific or pejorative connotations. Many economists do not regard pure-competition industries as exemplars, and some have written about its impossibility. The terms should be accepted simply as labels.

It is generally accepted that only a few industries resemble the abstract pure-competition model sufficiently closely that the behaviour of firms in the industry can be analysed and predicted by the model. The examples which come most readily to mind are sawmilling and the small, independent logging companies and, with respect to their decisions concerning output, farmers and fishermen. The distinguishing feature of these industries is that the firms in them cannot act upon the *recognition of mutual dependence*. The latter is a handy descriptive phrase which is used in this study sufficiently to justify the resort to jargon. The phrase simply means that each firm realizes that its sales and profits are affected by the actions of other firms in the industry. In the pure-competition industry there are so many firms selling in the market in question that the actions of a few have no discernible effect upon the sales of the others or upon the market price. There are too many firms for any understanding to be reached among them that the sensible course to follow is for all to reduce output when demand is low. Therefore, without government assistance, there is nothing the industry can do to reduce fluctuations in the prices of its products. There is no course which firms can collectively follow to achieve the security of a fairly stable and predictable price. In short, the large number of firms precludes them from acting upon the recognition of their mutual dependence. Consequently, the firm is "the plaything of market forces"; its fate hinges upon the changing conditions of supply in relation to demand.

In general, in the short run, pure-competition industries maintain output when market demand decreases in relation to supply; therefore prices decrease. The year-to-year percentage variations in prices are usually greater than the percentage variations in output. The industry always produces close to capacity and has to sell the output for whatever it will bring in the market. In agriculture, the inability to make accurate predictions of demand and supply before planting time also makes it difficult for the firm to adjust to changing market conditions by switching from one crop to another. The classic example of this flexibility is possessed by the farm which produces both hogs and corn. The obviously profitable thing to do is to feed the corn to the hogs when the price of pork is high in relation to the price of corn, but not when that price ratio is reversed. But to follow this course successfully, one must know some months in advance what the price ratio will be.

It is traditional for firms caught in these market conditions to view the instability of prices as the primary cause of the periodic inability of many of them to cover total costs and realize a moderate profit. Actually, the year-to-year price changes do not lie at the heart of their problems, although wide price fluctations in relation to costs certainly cause financial difficulties. The root cause of the low profits is always the persistence of excessive supply in relation to demand. If prices fluctuate between 75¢ and $1.50 per unit over a five-year period and average $1.25 while costs are steady at $1.00, the industry is not likely to be in poor financial shape; most firms would realize high profits over the period. This supposed set of prices should be preferred to a stable price over the period of, say, $1.15. The level of prices in relation to costs is more important than the variations of prices around their average. No doubt all firms would be willing to pay something for the guarantee of a stable price, but that premium has a limit.

At this point it is convenient to introduce another handy term which will be used extensively in this study. When the labour and capital employed in an industry are unable to earn as much as they could if they moved out to other industries, the industry is often said to be "sick." Thus, fishing in the Maritimes is chronically sick. The root cause of the sickness is an excessive quantity of capital and labour in the industry. There is overly great ease of entry and insufficient speed of exit. The mobility into the industry is not matched by an equally easy and rapid mobility out of it.

Sometimes the sickness appears in the form of low productivity. If the number of lobster fishermen in the Maritime provinces were halved and the minimum size of lobsters that government regulations allow fishermen to take were doubled, the lobster catch per man-hour of fishing could be increased by probably more than fourfold and the total output of lobsters more than doubled. And if the increased output were sold in markets not now served, it is quite possible that the average market price would be about the same. The more usual circumstance, however, is that there is no unserved market, so that any substantial increase in output would result in a large reduction in prices; demand is not very responsive to price changes. Thus, the sickness of the industry is directly attributable to excessive supply in relation to demand, perpetuated by the very easy entry into the industry not matched by a prompt exit from it. Then, low productivity often results from the low wages and profits, and the industry may sink from bad to worse.

These industries are usually composed mainly of companies which are absolutely small as well as small in relation to the size of the industry, although there may be a number of absolutely large companies, as there is in sawmilling, for example. It may be thought that the low productivity should be attributed to the small size of the firm. While this is often the case, the persistence of firms which are too small to realize most of the economies of scale is attributable to the low outward mobility. Hence the smallness of the firms is not the root cause of the trouble. Similarly, a persistence of the failure of the too-small firm to grow to an efficient size is attributable to the low wages and profits; they cannot put together the funds required for expansion. Sometimes, also, the low earnings are a barrier to the adoption of the most efficient production techniques and the acquisition of equipment which would raise productivity. Finally, the low earnings may result in below-average management and entrepreneurship in the industry. The last few sentences portray the prototype of a sick industry rather than the typical situation, of course. The point being made still stands. When the nature of an industry is such that the firm of moderate size can be as efficient as its larger competitor, capital requirements do not pose a barrier to entry. With great ease of entry and slow outward mobility, a quite rapid increase in total demand is required to prevent output from increasing more rapidly than demand with the result that prices are depressed and some considerable part of the industry becomes sick.

This picture of the pure-competition industry contrasts sharply with the standard textbook treatment and, to avoid misunderstanding, a reconciliation must be made. The reconciliation is most easily accomplished by picturing a pure-competition industry with just the right degree of ease of entry. The ideal requires that the minimum efficient size of the firm imposes capital costs just high enough to prevent an excessive entry of firms and yet still low enough so that any increase in price brought about by an increase in demand will promptly induce an increase in capacity. If the firms already in the industry do not expand capacity in step with demand, new firms will. Also, the ideal requires that the firm which is large enough to realize most of the economies of scale should yet be sufficiently small that there are a large number of firms selling in each market. It will be remembered that a large number of firms means whatever number is required to prevent them from acting upon the recognition of their mutual dependence, which nearly always takes the form of restricting output to the amount which can be sold at the prevailing price. Consequently, the industry is subject to the complete discipline of the market without showing any tendency for the capital and labour employed in it to receive lower returns than they could earn in other industries.

To complete the reconciliation it would be very convenient if we could cite a number of actual examples. Unfortunately for this purpose, no industry performs ideally, whether it has the characteristics of pure competition or pure monopoly or something in between. Since circumstances are constantly changing, all industries run into trouble or develop defects at one time or another. Perfect equilibrium would mean stagnation. For example, the grey cotton cloth part of the American textile industry conforms to the pure-competition classification very nicely. The smallest viable firm is quite large in absolute terms, yet the market is so large that none can affect the market price significantly. Nevertheless, the industry experienced very low profits during the 1950s—a symptom of sickness. However, a period of very high profits preceded the more recent, longer period of low profits. More important, during the period of low profits the industry had to make a very difficult adjustment. The consumption of cotton cloth increased slowly while synthetic fibres took over several of its markets. At the same time, productivity increased as much as in manufacturing in general. Hence the industry was plagued by excess capacity much of the time. (Whatever may be the case in other countries, in Canada the same situation has led to low profits in quite a number of industries which do not fit into the pure-competition classification; the manufacture of radios and petroleum refining are examples.) Finally, the decline of the New England branch of the industry continued. Decline is always a painful process, no matter what the structure of the industry. Altogether, the textile industry may fairly be said to have made a very large adjustment quite quickly and successfully, the speed of the adjustment being limited mainly by the rate of decline of the New England branch.

The aspects of the behaviour of the pure-competition model which have proved to be remarkably durable as elements of most economists' ideal normative model are as follows:

1. Since every firm is subject to the discipline of the market, it must be as efficient as the average firm in the industry, or eventually it will be driven out of business and the capital and labour it uses will be released to be more efficiently employed by other firms.

2. Not only output but also capacity of the industry is responsive to changes in demand. If demand increases in relation to the capacity of the industry, prices are bid up, which calls forth additional capacity and supply. Conversely, if capacity increases more rapidly than demand, prices are bid down, which discourages expansion. And the additional supply drives prices down to their initial level.

3. The consumer is supplied with the product at the least attainable cost. Thus the consumer's interest is protected by the discipline of the market. Whenever low-cost methods of production become available, every firm must adopt them as the condition of survival. Superior firms prosper and expand; inferior ones decline. Since entry is open, profits are driven down to whatever rates could be obtained by transferring capital to the most profitable alternative use. Consequently, capital tends to earn the same rate of return in all industries, which is a condition of its most profitable use.

4. The industry migrates to the least-cost locations. No firm has a choice; it must achieve the low cost achieved by its rivals. If this can be accomplished only at a new location, companies in the older, higher-cost locations must migrate or eventually go out of business.

5. Prices are flexible downward. If it could be obtained throughout the economy, it would be preferable to have prices vary up and down while output remained relatively stable rather than the alternative of prices remaining stable while output varies according to whatever can be sold at the stable price (where stable price refers to the price in relation to costs, especially wage costs). If the level of wages were fairly stable while prices varied up and down, it has been plausibly reasoned that there would be no short business cycle as we know it; there would be a very strong tendency for the economy to maintain full employment and full utilization of plant and equipment. Hence the need for government fiscal and monetary policy measures would be much reduced.

6. The economy is self-operating and self-regulating. There would be little need for government regulation. Since no firm would possess any market power, there would be no question of the abuse of such power.

As mentioned, these desiderata can be only imperfectly realized so long as the family-sized firm remains imperfectly mobile. When the firm of minimum economic size is larger than a family enterprise (that is, it hires labour outside the family), mobility of firms is greater and the constant adjustment to changing demand, costs, and methods of production more perfectly realized. In addition, the imperfect mobility of labour—and mobility of course imposes substantial costs—is an obstacle to the realization of all models of preferred behaviour.

It is apparent that much of the controversy whether an economy composed entirely of pure-competition industries would or would not perform ideally is pointless. Many markets are local and therefore too small to support a large number of firms of minimum size for efficiency; an economy of pure-competition industries is not an attainable alternative. Consideration of the desirability of the pure-competition type of behaviour may therefore be limited to two matters, which are actually two aspects of the same characteristic: whether all the capacity of a declining industry should be used, and whether prices should fluctuate with demand in relation to capacity.

Sometimes it is said that competition can be too severe. Would it not have been preferable for the output of the American grey cotton cloth industry to have been slightly curtailed during its difficult period of adjustment so that prices would have covered total costs, including a normal or average return to capital? From the point of view of owners, this certainly would have been desirable. And if nothing more were involved than the distribution of the gains and the losses, one would be at a loss for a rule by which to choose between the two patterns of behaviour. It is sometimes argued that a large loss to a small number of people outweighs a very small gain to each of a very large number of people, even when the dollar totals of the gains and the losses are equal. But this is a specious argument in the absence of information about the relative wealth of those who lost and those who gained. It would be difficult to make out a case, for example, that the heavy losses to a comparatively few shareholders outweighed the small gain to each of a multitude of consumers of textiles. A clear judgement can be confidently made only where there is severe hardship, as when the departure of an industry leaves a community without a means of earning a living. Even then the preferred solution is the creation of alternative employment; the perpetuation of an uneconomic industry is a poor second best. At any rate, with the single exception of severe hardship, the mitigation of losses caused by economic change is alien to the conception of free enterprise; this generalization applies with especial force to losses to equity ownership, since profits are the reward for risk-taking and there is no risk where there is no loss. It is a basic tenet of the free enterprise system that, in the main, the chips be allowed to fall where they may.

But we do not need to become "hung up" over the balancing of direct gains and losses, because something more than the distribution of the costs of economic change is at issue. If the prices of grey cotton cloth had been stabilized by a restriction of output, the capacity of the industry would have been greater than it actually was—a pure economic waste. The low profits caused the adjustment of capacity to demand, which is precisely the role which prices are supposed to play in a market economy. An efficient monopoly could have weathered the long period of slow growth of demand without suffering low prices and profits and without maintaining more excess capacity than the competitive industry did. But monopolies are not always that efficient.[1]

The other controversial aspect of the behaviour of the prototype pure-competition industry is none other than its most distinctive characteristic: the maintenance of output so that prices fluctuate up and down as demand varies in relation to the capacity of the industry. It may be argued that, so long as a long-run equilibrium is maintained between demand and capacity and so long as the average price over an appropriately long period is no greater than average cost including an average rate of profit, it is preferable that prices be kept stable while output varies to adjust to unpredictable variations of demand of short duration. And in some respects, it would be difficult to choose between the two pricing practices, provided that the equilibrium conditions mentioned were met. In contrast, when prices are maintained in the face of decreasing demand, what market force keeps prices from rising above the average, and what is there to prevent some firms from deciding that even though there is already considerable reserve capacity in the industry it would be a good idea to add to their capacity to be ready to increase their share of the market when the next upswing in demand occurs? When this happens, it is often a case of "what some do, all must"; to defend their shares of the market, all firms must maintain considerable reserve capacity. Clearly, a certain amount of reserve capacity is usually desirable from the public's point of view. The cost of absolute shortages can be extremely high, and even the cost of drawing supplies temporarily from an alternative source, such as imports, can be considerable. The undesirable outcome occurs when the reserve capacity grows to the point of being quite excessive. This does happen in imperfectly competitive industries, partly because the cost of carrying the reserve capacity becomes a component of the average price, and partly because the firm is freed from the strong discipline of suffering absolute losses as the penalty for mistaken forecasts.

THE NATURE OF OLIGOPOLY

Pure competition means there are "many" firms selling in the market in question—so many that none can affect the market price. This leaves all other industries to be peopled by a "few" firms, meaning that any one of them can affect the market price substantially. The single-firm industry, or monopoly, is the limiting case. Oligopoly literally means few sellers. Hence nearly all industries in Canada are oligopolies. Even when there are as many as a hundred independent dealers selling in a particular market (for example, gasoline stations in a large city) the industry is an aggregate of overlapping oligopolies. Each gasoline retailer has a few close competitors among the very many with whom he is in competition at the second remove. A strong competitive move by any of his close competitors is bound to have a noticeable effect upon his sales—sufficiently great that the competent dealer gives thought to what his most profitable reaction should be. And a strong competitive move by a less-close competitor will be felt by each firm eventually, through the defensive reaction taken by competitors closer and closer to it.

By definition, all oligopolies are mutually dependent: a change in the price or sales volume of any firm has a detectable effect upon all other firms in the particular industry and market. But this does not mean that their behaviour or their ability to act upon the recognition of their mutual dependence are the same. Their freedom of action is circumscribed most severely if it is fairly easy for new firms to enter the industry. So our first subcategory of industries composed of few firms is the oligopoly with ease of entry. A useful distinction can also be made between two groups within oligopolies which are protected to greater or lesser degree from the potential competition of new entrants by the existence of moderate or substantial barriers to entry. If the products can be successfully differentiated so that customers are not indifferent to which firm's products they use, companies can adopt nonprice forms of competition, notably sales promotion. These industries form a subcategory: oligopoly with barriers to entry and differentiated products. It has a companion subcategory: oligopoly with barriers to entry and homogeneous products. If the products are such that a firm cannot create a preference on the part of consumers for its brand, companies can compete among themselves in only three ways: by keeping costs lower than competitors do, by accepting a lower return on capital, and by developing superior products per dollar of cost (in the last instance, the product of the industry would cease to be homogeneous if the superior products could be patented). However, like ease of entry, product differentiation is a matter of degree. There is some scope for differentiation, even within industries which produce such relatively homogeneous products as newsprint and cement, in, for example, the development of close supplier-customer relations and security of supplies.

Typical types of competitive behaviour can be observed for these three classes of oligopolies and their effects analysed. The analysis is the justification for their classification. However, no matter how fine the classification of industries is made on the basis of typical behaviour, it is not possible to predict precisely the competitive strategies and tactics which an industry will follow at a given time. In particular, it is not possible to predict behaviour from information about the structure of the industry, that is, the number and relative size of the firms in the industry, the extent of vertical integration, the degree of ease of entry, and the extent of product differentiation. Behaviour and structure are closely related; if this were not so, the classification would be without point. But the correlation is not sufficiently invariant to enable precise predictions. Industries behave differently at different times even when their structure has not changed significantly, and different industries with similar structures often resort to different competitive tactics. Even the behaviour of the same firm in similar situations changes from time to time. The best that can be done is to identify recurring patterns of behaviour.

OLIGOPOLIES WITH EASE OF ENTRY

In the classification of models ranging from pure competition to pure monopoly, the model closest to pure competition is oligopoly with ease of entry. Two subclassifications of this model can be usefully made. The first is the industry composed of a few firms selling in an absolutely small market. Realtor and gardening firms, building contractors of certain types such as stone masonry, and certain branches of trucking are examples. The second subcategory is the industry composed of many firms, each of which has a few close competitors among the many with which it competes indirectly. Most branches of retailing and such service industries as laundries are examples.

In both subtypes of these oligopoly industries the economies of scale can be realized by a firm which is quite small in absolute terms, and often, the small firm has an advantage over the large one because the owner-entrepreneur-manager can closely supervise all operations. Because entry to the industry is not made difficult by a large capital requirement to build a plant of minimum size for efficiency, returns often tend to be relatively low, and sometimes parts of the industry are periodically sick, for example, corner grocery stores and gasoline stations.

Several different pricing practices and strategies are followed by these industries. Sometimes the firms periodically attempt to act upon the recognition of their mutual dependence, but their endeavours to avoid a reduction in the price level brought about by price cutting are usually unsuccessful due to the ease of entry into the industry. All firms already in the industry may realize that their competitors will follow suit if they cut prices, and therefore they refrain from doing so. But new entrants must get business somehow and usually endeavour to do so by low prices. Since the established firms cannot stand idly by and let new firms take over their markets, the low prices are met. Certain types of trucking are good examples of this type of behaviour. The classic example is to be found in the highway carrier industry in its early days. The established firms were not large enough to have achieved marked economies of large-scale operations, and entry to the industry was very easy. Consequently, even when the capacity of the industry was not excessive, prices were periodically driven below the level required to cover total costs and provide an average profit. It was an industry of price-cutters. The most successful, rapidly expanding companies achieved success by undercutting the rate schedule of the railways. But they in turn were undercut by more hungry rivals.

Similarly, the most active conceivable price competition is present from time to time in the tenders submitted by trucking companies to move earth for departments of highways. Indeed, from the outside it often appears that the price cutting is so great as to undermine the viability of the industry. However, the disparity in efficiencies among companies is apparently great enough to enable some to live with the great uncertainty. This must be so because some firms have survived, grown rapidly to substantial size, and earned substantial fortunes for their owners.

Another variant of the pricing behaviour of the ease-of-entry oligopolies appears when nearly all the companies are convinced that their most profitable strategy is to refrain from price cutting, but one or a few decide that their most profitable strategy is to maintain a significant margin between their prices and the average price of their more conservative rivals. The best-known examples of the use of this strategy are the durable consumer discount stores and the "private-brand" gasoline stations. A single maverick in a particular market may not endanger the general level of dealer margins, especially if the lower margin is accompanied by a decrease in service. For example, the occasional gasoline station selling private-brand gasoline at a discount may live peacefully among a number of major brand dealers who charge higher margins, provided that the discounter's sales volume does not increase so much that some of his closest competitors are caused serious financial difficulties. However, in these circumstances, the low-price strategy is not usually very profitable. To earn large profits by adopting the discount strategy of high volume and lower markup by maintaining a differential between his retail price and the prices of his competitors, a retailer must draw trade from a much wider area than his more conventional competitors do. The lower markup must be offset by a much higher sales volume. Precisely stated, the percentage increase in sales must exceed the change in the markup as a percentage of the new markup.[2] Thus, a 10 percent reduction in price cuts in half a markup of 20 percent, and more than a doubling of sales is required to make the price reduction profitable. Consequently, the strategy of the price discounter is a very risky one, and it is easy to understand why discounters are unpopular with their competitors. Thirty percent is a typical retailer's margin. A 10 percent reduction in price is then a reduction of one-half in the markup prevailing after the price reduction; sales must increase by one-half if retailers are to be as well off as before a reduction of the price level is forced upon them. But, patently, the sales of all dealers in the particular market do not increase by anything like that amount, and most suffer a decrease in profits.

If he is successful, the price discounter usually confers benefits upon the consumer by driving down retail markups and prices and driving excess capacity out of the industry. The consumer may gain less than is indicated by the reduction in prices, however. Retail services are also often curtailed. For example, self-service is now typical of the department store. It used to be that a surfeit of clerks stood and waited in the hope that a buyer might wander by; now it is the customers who do the standing and waiting even in off-peak hours. Moreover, sometimes the endeavour to make the consumer aware of the price differentials between retail outlets carries over into the endeavour to create the impression of a greater price differential than actually exists. The reputation for unethical practices earned by some parts of the used-car and secondhand-camera retailing industries, and even of some new automobile agencies, is the consequence of this mischannelling of the competitive urge into unethical practices.

Not all retailing has suffered the inroads of the price discounter. In many branches, the convention not to cut prices is observed even by new entrants, and the discounter is the rare exception. The convention is particularly strong in the retailing of books, drugs, jewellery, musical instruments, and furniture, among others. Most of the time, markups are fairly stable, although they are not always precisely uniform and price competition is not entirely absent. But price cutting stays on the safe side of precipitating a general reduction of margins. For the most part, competition takes the form of different mixes of price and service, more service and slightly higher prices competing with less service and somewhat lower prices. Consequently, there is an absence of the strong pressure upon markups which would be required to keep them to the minimum consistent with prices covering total costs including an average rate of profit when there is no undue reserve capacity in the industry.

The absence of price breaks and other forms of active price competition, however, does not protect most firms in these ease-of-entry industries from low profits. For example, although the multiunit grocery supermarket companies usually earn a considerably higher return on their capital than the average manufacturing company in Canada does, the small, single-unit family store is one of the most familiar examples of capital and labour receiving lower returns than they could earn in other uses. Some part of the industry is always sick on this definition. The process accounting for these chronic low returns is famous in the writings of economists as *monopolistic competition*. Since entry into the industry is so easy, small firms, many of which are quite inefficient, keep entering until the sales volume of most of the small stores is too small to support wages to members of the family at the prevailing market rates or to provide an average return to the small amount of capital employed. Thus, stable markups alone afford no protection to earnings.

From the social point of view, there is a waste of resources in these industries in the sense that much capital and labour could be employed more productivity elsewhere. However, the waste may not be so great as one might at first suppose. Many of the least profitable stores are staffed by low-skill workers who could command only low wages as employees. In fact, one might go so far as to say that the nature of the waste is elusive; one's measure of it depends in part upon his conception of the economic system. Free enterprise has been defined as "the right to be a failure." Freely interpreted, this phrase means that anyone who can get command of the required capital is free to make a try at being a success in the business of his choosing, no matter how obvious it may be to others that the prospects of success are almost nonexistent. If a person freely chooses to be self-employed at the cost of lower wages than he could obtain from working for someone else, productivity of the economy is lower than it might be, but the low productivity cannot unambiguously be termed economic waste. Presumably, the nonmonetary returns to the entrepreneur compensate in large part for his low money income.

Another prominent example of ease-of-entry oligopolies with stable prices is the realtors' industry. In many Canadian municipalities, by using their trade associations for the purpose, realtors have been able to take advantage of the exemption of service industries from the ban upon price agreements. The associations set rates of commission which are generally observed—an example of lawful, formal collusion resulting from the recognition of mutual dependence. This example, and others which will be cited below, indicate that a narrow range of numbers cannot be identified as the borderline between "many" firms which cannot act upon the recognition of their mutual dependence and avoid active price competition, on the one hand, and a "few" firms which are able to do so for long periods, on the other hand. Some writers consider ten to twelve to be the outside number for an oligopoly. But there are industries of more than a score of firms which behave like oligopolists and so must be classed as such. An active trade association can often stimulate the recognition of mutual dependence sufficiently for a convention not to cut prices to be observed by more than fifty firms. The large Canadian cities support scores of realtor firms which recognize the mutual advantage of price fixing, at least sufficiently to keep price cutting within safe bounds. There are also quite large numbers of motels which successfully observe a convention not to cut prices—sometimes, as in the case of realtors, with the active encouragement of an agency of a provincial government. The professional and trade association of lawyers, accountants, doctors, dentists, architects, consulting engineers, general plumbing and electrical contractors and the like often play a similar supporting role, so that these industries are additional examples of medium-to-large numbers of firms successfully acting upon the recognition of their mutual dependence.

The distinction between tacit collusion consisting of informal price fixing, which has a pejorative connotation, and each firm independently acting upon the recognition of mutual dependence, which so far has escaped pejorative connotation, is discussed in chapter 4. Until reading that chapter it is hoped that members of the industries just mentioned will defer concluding that they are inferentially being accused of anti-social behaviour. The intent of this study is not to prejudge, but rather to try to determine what behaviour, whether presently lawful, unlawful, or of doubtful legal standing, should be so regarded.

Price competition poses a dilemma for policy. When it is active, life can be very difficult indeed for companies and the persons they employ. When it is quiescent, either profit margins tend to become unduly high or the capacity of the industry tends to become excessive. And, paradoxically, the absence of price competition in ease-of-entry industries may often lead to more undesirable consequences than it does in industries with barriers to entry. The excessive capacity and the attendant low wages of most salesmen employed by realtor firms is a particularly marked example of economic waste resulting from the absence of price competition in an ease-of-entry industry. The gasoline retailing industry is another striking example.

OLIGOPOLY, BARRIERS TO ENTRY, HOMOGENEOUS PRODUCT

The next group of industries on our analytical spectrum consists of those in which the minimum economic size of plant is absolutely large. Capital requirements pose considerable barriers to new entrants, and few firms serve each segregated market. The third characteristic is that the products of the industry are *homogeneous*. Homogeneous product is often interpreted to mean physically identical articles. But this is not a useful meaning for the analysis of behaviour. To develop a useful meaning, we must first discuss the precise meaning of the *differentiated product*.

To the general public, automobile tires are differentiated. The producer is able to build up a preference for his trademarked product sufficient to induce some customers to pay slightly more than they will for competing brands. The differential is greater for some commodities than for others, of course. For example, most customers' loyalty to one nationally advertised brand of gasoline apparently does not often extend so far as one cent per gallon, provided that the buyer is aware of the differential. Comparisons among brands of tires are more difficult, and consumer attachment to particular makes may withstand a considerable price differential. Also, it usually requires a greater price differential to win customers away from nationally advertised brands to private brands which are little advertised than it does to cause them to switch from one nationally advertised brand to another, even though the products may be physically identical to all intents and purposes.

The extent to which makers can create preference for their products depends not only upon actual differences in quality, but also upon the information about the quality and performance available to consumers and the confidence with which the information is held. When one firm buys from another, information is usually quite complete, and successful differentiation depends almost solely upon differences in quality and performance. Therefore, tires, gasoline, and even trucks are to all intents and purposes homogeneous products in these "expert markets." Preferences cannot be created for trademarked products which do not serve the buyer's requirements better than do competing makes. And where there are actual differences in quality or performance, one expects to observe compensating price differences. Therefore, when buyers are expert, the line between homogeneous products, such as newsprint, and differentiated products, such as tires, disappears. One brand of tire becomes as perfect a substitute for another as, for example, Number One Northern Hard Wheat is for Number Two Northern Hard. Consequently, the homogeneous-product oligopoly classification includes almost all commodities purchased by one firm from another.

Where products are homogeneous in this sense, one would expect that competition could focus only upon price. It is true that the service component is not absent, particularly in the form of assured supplies of uniform quality at competitive prices. But all companies must qualify as reliable suppliers, and even so, it is customary for large buyers to spread their patronage over a number of suppliers to gain added security of supply. Quality is not completely absent as a competitive variable either, but a serious defect in quality can rarely be made good by a reduction in price; quality as good as one's competitors is usually a necessary condition for the survival of the firm.

It is not surprising that the interpretations of the behaviour of these industries should vary. To some, the price moves are evidence of competition; to others, the same price moves are interpreted as evidence of a strong recognition by the companies of their mutual dependence, which eliminates price competition among the established companies in any meaningful sense. An example of the former interpretation is found in *Report of the Director of Investigation and Research, Combines Investigation Act*, for the year 1965–66:

The basic price of newsprint had remained stable in Eastern Canada since 1957, although on occasion there were rumblings about unofficial price reductions during periods of oversupply. In Western Canada prices were also stable from 1957 until November 1964, when a large Canadian mill unilaterally reduced its price by $10 per ton. This decrease was followed by all the West Coast newsprint mills in both Canada and the United States, but the eastern mills did not follow suit generally, although those of them which competed in certain areas with western mills met the competition there. At this time, newsprint standard prices were $124 per ton in the West and $134 per ton in the East.

This situation remained unchanged for well over a year, when a leading western company with mills in both United States and Canada announced that it was within a squeeze between cost and prices, and increased its price by $10 per ton on February 28, 1966, effective April 1, thus cancelling the reduction of November 1964. The reaction of the industry to this change was for other western mills, over a period of some weeks, to adopt the new price and thus revert to the 1957 price of $134 per ton. In Eastern Canada several of the leading mills followed the western lead and announced a $10 increase effective April 1, 1966. This would have raised the eastern price to $144 per ton, $10 above the 1957 level. By March 11, 1966 some ten companies, the bulk of the industry, had made their announcement to this effect. However, on March 14, a leading eastern company operating mills in both United States and Canada announced that its price would go up only $7 per ton. Its competitors soon announced that they would have to reconsider their decisions in the light of this action. While they were doing so, on March 15, a leading U.S.

producer announced that its increase would only be $5 per ton. In the result, all companies had to revise their position and to restrict the price increase to $5 per ton. Later, most of them changed the effective date of the change to June 1, 1966. When it was all over, the current price in Eastern Canada settled at $139 per ton and in Western Canada it was $134.[3]

The circumstances . . . are inconsistent with the conclusion that a relatively simultaneous and uniform price rise took place as a result of collusive practices. Instead, we can observe a competitive testing of the market, consistent with what would be expected from independent and competitive behaviour in a market for such a commodity.[4]

Others interpret these events differently. The pricing manoeuvres could, of course, be claimed to be a screen to conceal formal or tacit collusion. But that would be an unproductive analysis. Like persons, companies are entitled to be considered innocent until proven guilty, and in any event intent is secondary to effects. It is not necessary to assume tacit collusion to be able to conclude that price competition is usually excluded from the competitive tactics of oligopolies. All firms are assumed to set their prices independently; each firm decides which price is the most profitable for it to charge *in the circumstances*. Each knows that it cannot for long charge a higher price than its competitors do, because it would lose most of its trade if it did. All know that if one or a few are allowed to charge lower prices for long, they will gradually take away the markets of the others. The lower-price firms would expand rapidly while the higher-price ones suffered stable or declining sales. Thus, one expects a uniform price in a given market. Every few years or so, however, especially if costs have increased while the uniform selling price has not, there are apt to be differing views concerning what the uniform prices ought to be. Even during quiet periods when there is no price manoeuvring, several of the companies may well favour a higher uniform price, but there is nothing they can do to realize their preference, because it is known that some large companies are committed to the existing price. When it is thought that a price increase is overdue, any company may try to nudge its rivals into action. It tries a flyer in the form of an announced price increase. On occasion, as in the American steel industry a few years back, if the venturesome nudger is a small firm it may state at the time of the announced increase that it will not be implemented if the other companies do not follow suit. But this is the exception. Usually, the company which tries to take the lead simply announces an increase. There is little risk attached to the move when a well-established pattern of close supplier-customer relations exists, as in the newsprint industry. Often these close relations take the form of long-term supply contracts which offer protection only to the customer. The contracts guarantee supply of stated quantities for a year or more in advance, but the quantity stated is, in fact, only a maximum guaranteed supply. There is no guarantee that the customer will always take the quantity stipulated; in fact, the supplier hopes that his customers will deal with their several suppliers equitably, cutting back orders from each by the same proportion if less than the estimated requirement is taken. Also, the price stipulated in the long-term contract is only a formal guarantee, without much substance. Often the contract price may not exceed the average of the prices charged by three or four large competing companies in the period in question. The guarantee is a formal one only because all large customers know that none of their suppliers would be foolish enough to actually charge more than its rivals. The risk of losing customers is too great. Therefore, when two or three companies try to nudge their rivals into adopting a higher price, they have the protection of being able to adjust their prices back to the old level retroactively if their endeavour is unsuccessful. The only risk they run is that of losing customers by gaining the reputation of being in favour of higher prices.

Sometimes, when such a price manoeuvre occurs, only one or two companies follow; the rest stand pat. The attempt to increase prices fails. At other times, most companies favour a price increase and they follow suit when one takes the lead. This causes the one or more which had not been in favour of a price change to reconsider their position. If they remain unconvinced of the wisdom of a price increase, they stand pat and the announced increases are rescinded by the other companies. More likely, the cautious companies may follow along, often by announcing a smaller price increase. Then all those which have announced higher prices scramble to get back in line. Accordingly, these pricing manoeuvres are concluded to be evidence of a very strong realization of mutual dependence, rather than of price competition. Price competition is absent because, when any firm acts alone, it is only in the endeavour to obtain a preferred price for the industry as a whole. Firms do not fight one another. The memories of what happened in the 1930s, when they did, are still strong enough to ensure that each carefully avoids the danger of open price warfare, which might result from any firm's attempt to benefit at the expense of his rivals by price cutting. Hence, the consequences to the consumer and to the operation of the economy of a strong realization of mutual dependence differ only in degree from those of formal, unlawful collusion.

In the circumstances being discussed, the effective *price leader* does not always lead. Indeed, it may never do so. Since it requires acquiescence on the part of all large companies for a price increase to be effective, while any large company can lead prices down, the leader is the large company which is least disposed to raise prices and most disposed to lower them. Thus, the leader does not lead prices up; it validates increases initiated by others. But it does take the lead in bringing prices down. Clearly, then, there can be more than one leader, although it is usual for only one to play the dominant role.

On this interpretation, the price leader is either the most prudent or the most cautious large company. It may also be the company which has accepted or taken upon itself the responsibility for maintaining the competitive strength of the industry, as the necessary condition for maintaining its own share of the market and protecting its profits over the long term. The leader may be the largest producer of the commodity, it may be the large company which has the lowest costs of production, or it may be one of the absolutely largest of the companies in the industry although its share of the market of the product in question may be less than that of several competitors. In the last case, the leader is in the strongest position to withstand any challenge to its management of the affairs of the industry because, being absolutely large in other industries and of only moderate size in the industry in question, it is in the best position to withstand periods of low prices.

In the circumstances described, why should a company decide to lead prices down, and why should it not acquiesce to a signal from others that the time is ripe for a price increase? So long as all companies act together in the knowledge of their mutual dependence, they possess considerable monopoly power because there are substantial barriers to entry into the industry. The invariant barrier consists of the large amount of capital required to build a plant of minimum economical size, establish a marketing organization, and withstand some years of losses; the variable barriers take the form of the likelihood of harassing tactics by the established companies. Since the established companies collectively possess considerable monopoly power, their primary concern must be the protection of that monopoly power. This provides the clue to why some companies prefer lower prices and profits than could be obtained in the short run. The limited monopoly power created by barriers to entry and a strong recognition of mutual dependence places oligopolies which are protected by considerable barriers to entry in the same general position as monopoly itself. The primary concern of all firms and industries which possess any degree of monopoly power (defined as the power, by controlling supply, to earn more than the average rate of profits) must be to maintain that monopoly position. The reason that a company sometimes refuses to increase its prices when its rivals raise theirs is that it is concerned to preserve its market position.

The threats to that position take various forms, hence the constraints upon charging the most profitable price are also varied:

1. The desire to avoid encouraging new entrants
2. The necessity of disciplining companies which try to expand rapidly under the umbrella of the established price or by similar tactics
3. The fear of alienating customers with whom there has been a long close relationship and long-term contracts and who might establish their own sources of supply or foster new suppliers
4. The necessity of discouraging established companies from making excessive additions to their capacity, which might lead to uncontrollable price breaks
5. The fear that larger profits may result in successful wage demands which would be irreversible and would reduce the industry's capacity to meet the competition of foreign companies and of competitive products
6. Sensitivity to government enquiries and public disapproval
7. Management's notions of fair pricing and of the company's responsibilities in serving the public interest

It will be noticed that the last constraint, unlike the first six, is not necessarily compatible with the objective of maximum long-term profits.

The last three constraints are self-explanatory, but the first four require some amplification.

Constraint 1. If the leader permits a relatively high rate of profits to be realized, the industry will certainly, other things being the same, be more attractive to new entrants even if entry is obstructed by harassing tactics. It is the prospective rate of profits after its initial period of losses, and after it has won admission to the club, which is the concern of the wise new entrant. Accordingly, barriers to entry must be exceedingly high to enable the price leader to realize unusually high rates of profits over long periods, as in the case of General Motors and General Electric in the United States.[5] However, to some extent, it is possible for the industry to have its cake and eat it too, if the structure of the market is such that new entrants can be made to suffer considerable financial losses, prevented from ever becoming profitable, or confined to a very small share of the market. The tactics by which these objectives can be achieved are fairly familiar, but price discrimination based upon basing-point pricing deserves special mention. If a new entrant builds a plant which is in a town where there is no plant belonging to any established company and which is some distance from all other plants, it is open to the price leader to make the new entrant's location a basing point and lower the price at that point. Usually, prices under a basing-point system are approximately equal to the price at the basing point plus freight to various points within the particular basing-point zone. Thus, the mill net to any plant is greatest from sales within its own basing-point zone. Therefore, by drawing a line around the location of the new entrant, making the area within it a new basing-point zone and setting a low price as the basing-point price for that zone, the price leader, with the acquiescence of the other established firms, can ensure that the new entrant never recovers his investment. Following his example is thereby discouraged. This tactic will not be costly to the established companies so long as the sales they make in the newly established basing-point zone are not a substantial percentage of their total sales.

The use of customary price discrimination among various lines or products to bleed and thereby discourage new entrants is perhaps more familiar. Thus, one of the charges against the Aluminum Company of America when it was the sole producer of aluminium ingot in the United States was that it kept the price of ingots to fabricators high in relation to the mill net it realized from sales in other markets. The difference between the prices which the fabricators paid for their aluminium and the prices which Alcoa charged for its fabricated products which it sold in competition with them was too low to allow the competing fabricators to realize a normal profit.

Constraint 2. There is an old saying that what all cannot do, one can. When there is a uniform price for a homogeneous product, it must be very tempting for a relatively small company to gamble that it will be able to expand rapidly by undercutting the standard price by a chosen margin. A relatively large company cannot adopt this strategy because its expansion would reduce its large competitors' share of the market sufficiently to make it almost a certainty that they would meet the lower price. The result would be a lower uniform price in the particular market, with the second situation worse than the first for all companies. But the relatively small company may calculate that its effect upon the market shares of its large competitors, while detectable, would be too small to cause them to bear the cost of meeting his lower price. However, there must always come a point when the inroads of the smaller companies which are allowed to follow this strategy, into the large companies' market shares, cause one of them—usually the leader—to retaliate. The forms which the retaliation can take depend upon the structure of the market. If there is no segregation of markets, so that there is a single price throughout the national market exclusive of freight, retaliation as such is not possible. The only course is to meet the lower price of a company which was once too small to bother about but has become large enough to be a threat. But if there are segregated markets, and the aggressive small company sells in only a few of them, prices can be lowered in these markets while being maintained in others. The revenue losses to the large companies are thereby minimized.

Contsraint 3. One of the characteristics of the pricing behaviour of the industries under discussion which has puzzled many economists is the use of waiting lists to ration supply when the commodity is in very tight supply, as several materials were in 1946–49, 1951–52, and 1956–57. For example, why did the Canadian mills not raise the contract prices for newsprint much more than they did in 1956–57 when newspaper companies were paying a premium of as much as $50 per ton for newsprint imported from Scandinavia? A comprehensive explanation would require a considerable recounting of the history of the industry and a lengthy analysis of the strategy of the price leader. The close customer-supplier relationships which characterize many industries in which both suppliers and their customers are absolutely and relatively large would figure prominently in this explanation. The best guess as to why the North American newsprint companies were willing to forego the additional profits available during these periods of short supply is that it was the strategy most likely to exclude overseas competitors in the longer term. If prices close to what the market would bear were charged during periods of tight supply, the newspaper companies would doubtless retaliate in later periods of easy supply by switching part of their purchases to overseas suppliers. The newspapers would also be encouraged to establish their own mills, as some large papers did in the 1920s. Finally, account must be taken of item 7 of the list of constraints upon pricing faced by oligopolies of the type under discussion. Economists like to reason from the assumption that all companies behave as if their objective were to maximize long-term profits. But, like all other persons, company managements possess diverse loyalties, and one of the strong constraints upon profit maximizing takes the form of their conceptions of fair pricing.

Constraint 4. The fourth of the concerns of the prudent price leader is that its less prudent rivals may act unwisely. If high operating rates are accompanied by very high profits, even its large rivals may be encouraged to add so substantially to their capacity that excessively large unused capacity will overhang the market for a substantial period and prevent a price increase. And worse, if the reserve capacity becomes very great the recognition of mutual dependence may break down. Some company may break ranks and cut prices in a peripheral market in the hope that the price cut will not spread through its own major markets. But concealed price reductions never stay secret for long in an industry characterized by close customer-supplier relations; therefore, if price cutting does occur, a long lean period of low operating rates becomes even leaner as a period of low operating rates and low prices.

As an interjection, the price leader is often pictured in unflattering terms in some of the writing about oligopoly. Sometimes this is deserved; but at other times one might better say, "Pity the plight of the poor price leader."

The pricing behaviour just described is that of oligopolies which are sometimes termed *mature*, meaning that all of the companies in the industry act on the recognition of their mutual dependence most of the time. Consequently, prices are fairly stable. The main occasions for price increases occur when costs have increased generally throughout the industry. Then, all companies are likely to favour a price "adjustment," and it is up to the price leader (possibly nudged by one of his rivals) to choose the appropriate moment and the appropriate public relations statements. The reason usually given is an increase in costs. Similarly, prices are likely to be led down by the price leader when there is a substantial decrease in costs or when this is deemed necessary to head off new competitors. However, in the mature oligopoly, prices do not rise and fall as output increases and decreases in relation to capacity. An unusually large amount of unused capacity may precipitate a price break, but this is quite rare; otherwise the industry is not classed as mature.

Some of the industries which fall into this category of mature oligopoly with homogeneous products and barriers to entry have been the object of repeated enquiries in the United States, for example, newsprint, steel, and cement. And in Canada some have been prosecuted for formal collusion, for example, fine papers. The reason for these enquiries may be taken to be the apparent monopoly power evidenced by the ability to maintain prices in the face of excess supply.

Differences between industries are always matters of degree rather than of kind. Thus, mature oligopoly shades into immature oligopoly according to the frequency with which price breaks occur in response to the emergence of excess capacity. And, of course, one encounters industries which do not fall neatly into any of the broad categories. Some of the ease-of-entry oligopolies discussed in the preceding section, such as certain branches of the trucking industry, are clearly immature, because price cuts are always being initiated by new or small companies. But even when there are substantial barriers to entry in the form of capital costs, prices may show variations, from the considerable to the extreme; for example, chemical woodpulp and refined copper, respectively. It is usually considered likely that the greater the number of firms selling in the particular market, the greater the price variation, because the more difficult it is for the established companies to act upon the recognition of their mutual dependence. Also, the larger the market, the smaller the barrier of a given capital cost, because the risk of not recovering an investment decreases with the size of the market. However, it will be remembered from the discussion of the ease-of-entry oligopolies that the correspondence between the number of firms and action upon the recognition of mutual dependence is far from complete. Consequently, the correspondence between the number of firms and the frequency of price changes is a loose one. About twenty independent companies sell newsprint in the eastern United States, yet the industry's behaviour is a classic example of maturity. Considerably more firms, including most of the newsprint companies, sell chemical pulp in the United States markets, and yet their prices do not change very frequently; the behaviour of the industry falls on the borderline between mature and immature, although the larger number of firms might lead one to expect that pricing would be quite immature.

When prices are very volatile, as in the case of refined copper, lead, and zinc, the explanation of the behaviour is straightforward: firms are unable to achieve a convention to vary output to stabilize prices. The several attempts to form a copper cartel in the United States before the 1920s broke down because of this inability. At the opposite extreme, as in the case of newsprint sold in North America, a very strong and persistent recognition of mutual dependence coupled with the success of the price leader in keeping prices down to the level which has earned only moderate returns on capital for a large part of the industry explains the marked price stability of that industry. It is the in-between cases which pose the puzzles. The fine-paper industry in the United States seems to be an in-between case. During the latter part of 1967, prices were at a discount of about 10 percent from list. The discount was attributed to the large amount of reserve capacity which emerged from the large investments of the previous two years.[6] It is safe enough to accept the excess capacity as the underlying cause, because it is usually a necessary condition. What is lacking in the explanation is the immediate cause. Prices do not rise and fall as capacity falls behind and catches up with demand; the emergence of reserve capacity does not invariably cause prices to decrease. Therefore, one would like to know what led to the first price cut and how it was that the discount did not exceed the moderate 10 percent off list. In the absence of detailed information concerning the competitive manoeuvring in the industry, one hypothesis is as plausible as another. It is even possible that the American fine-paper industry is a mature oligopoly showing a fairly stable margin between the cost of raw materials and the prices of finished products. The prices of chemical pulps were decreasing during 1967, and the decreases might be taken to be a sufficient explanation of the discount of fine-paper prices from list. There could be added the explanation that much of the paper selling at a discount was produced by new machines during their breaking-in period and was of inferior quality; hence the discount was only apparent and not real. It is apparent that one must have considerable information before venturing a firm hypothesis.

Chemical pulp is possibly a better example of an oligopoly on the borderline between mature and immature than is the fine-paper industry, and it is one which is replete with interesting price fluctuations. That the North American pulp industry is capable of acting maturely on occasion is fairly conclusively demonstrated by an episode which occurred during 1957–59. For a number of months during this period, pulp prices in North American markets were firm, despite the recent emergence of some excess capacity and a relatively easy supply situation. In contrast, although pulp was in short supply in Western Europe, prices were falling. The fact that United States companies were increasing their share of the European market at the time invites the speculation that it was they who were initiating the price softness in Europe. In the American markets, on the other hand, presumably no firm was taking a similar initiative, and freed of the threat of invasion from Scandinavian producers, the American producers were able to act upon the recognition of their mutual dependence.

However, the episode cited was apparently fairly short-lived. Since 1959, chemical pulp prices have shown considerable variability within a safe range, that is, price reductions have not been so great as to eliminate the profits of a fairly large proportion of the firms in the industry. So we are left with the classic puzzles of these borderline industries: Why do the prices vary immaturely? Why do they stay within a safe range, not dropping below average cost, let alone average variable cost?[7]

As mentioned at the outset, there surely can be no single comprehensive theory of oligopoly pricing behaviour. The immediate causes of the emergence of discounts from list prices take numerous forms. It may be that some firms are under financial pressure and must increase sales by price cuts even at the risk of precipitating an extremely unprofitable break in the level of prices. It may be that some firms are forcing their way into new markets by price reductions. Or it may be the accidental circumstance that some firm has decided to correct an anomaly in the relative prices of different grades or lines of a multigrade or multiline industry, and the correction is misread as a competitive manoeuvre and so leads to a reduction in the prices of most lines or grades. Or it may be that limited price variation is the customary practice of the industry. This last explanation is, of course, not an explanation at all, but only an observation. Without more information, however, one has at times to fall back upon it. For example, the North American steel industry shows most of the characteristics of the prototype of a mature oligopoly: action on the recognition of mutual dependence is very strong, and competitive price manoeuvring fairly rare. So prices vary mainly with variations in costs and therefore rarely decrease. In sharp contrast, the prices of the Belgian and other West European export steel companies fluctuate widely as output varies in relation to capacity. There is a similar contrast between the pricing behaviour of the Scandinavian newsprint and pulp industries and their North American counterparts. The former vary prices widely according to the state of demand; as we have seen, the latter do not. I do not pretend to know what accounts for these differences in behaviour, and therefore must list the behaviour of the European industries as customary practices.

To illustrate further the rich and unexplained diversity of the behaviour of oligopoly industries, the experience of the Scandinavian pulp industries in the 1930s may be cited. In 1929 Canadian chemical pulp companies possessed about 15 percent of the United States market. By 1937 they had almost no share at all; they had been backed out of it by the Scandinavian exporters. And the most interesting aspects of the behaviour of the Scandinavian companies were that their reactions to changes in prices and costs were "perverse." When prices dropped, their output increased. When their wage costs and again when the costs of wood increased, their output increased (prices constant). This would hardly seem to serve the goal of profit maximization. However, the first form of perversity can easily be explained away: prices were lowered deliberately as a competitive move, which succeeded. Their share of the market, and hence their output, rose. The maintenance and increase of sales at constant prices in the face of rising wood and wage costs may be explained in a similar way. The overall tactic was to maintain output, accepting whatever price and margin over direct costs resulted. But there was no necessity for the Scandinavian companies, acting in unison, to charge a price lower than that required to maintain sales in the American market; they needed only to charge whatever price was required in relation to the prices of the United States mills. That price was not affected by changes in their costs.

Finally, oligopolies composed of as few as three or four companies often find themselves in circumstances which make it impossible for them to act maturely without resort to formal collusion. That is, their recognition of their mutual dependence is not sufficient to screen them from actively engaging in price competition. One such set of circumstances obviously exists when contracts are let by bids at tender and installation or other nonstandard costs have to be estimated; that is, when the filling of contracts does not simply consist of shipping a number of price-listed commodities. Surely, excepting collusion, there is no way for the companies to know what estimates of installation costs are made by competitors. Similarly, once a practice of the competitive calculation of bids has become firmly established for whatever reason, one is at a loss to imagine how it can be stopped without resort to collusion of some form. It seems reasonable that a customary practice or pattern of behaviour must become established somehow if the recognition of mutual dependence is to be sufficient by itself to frustrate the competitive urge.

It may be argued that it is not inevitable that competitive bidding should drive prices down to unprofitable levels. This is true enough, but the likelihood seems very great whenever there is considerable unused capacity. Once the competitive calculation of bids becomes the practice, calculations are likely to be based upon incremental rather than average costs, because any contribution to overhead costs is better than none. And bids based on incremental cost inevitably lead to unprofitable price levels, if fixed costs are a large proportion of total costs. This reasoning may provide part of the explanation of the unhappy "great electrical conspiracy" in the United States a few years back, when several giant manufacturers of industrial electrical equipment were convicted for formal collusion to fix prices. Also, it has been contended that if all the sales by oil refineries were made by tender, which is the prevailing method of obtaining contracts from provincial and municipal governments and large commercial accounts, the oil companies would be simply "trading nickels." A substantial part of the tender sales covers little more than out-of-pocket costs, leaving fixed costs to be covered by sales of gasoline to service stations and sales of other products at list prices.

On the other hand, one can think of examples of industries which successfully live with competitive bidding at tender on all of their business, year in and year out. A prominent example is the commercial and industrial contracting construction industry. Perhaps the explanation lies in the small percentage of total costs accounted for by overhead and the fact that it is feasible for companies to expand and contract rapidly their volume of activity.

THE MANY FORMS OF PRICE DISCRIMINATION

Analysis of the competitive behaviour of oligopolies is frustrating to the economist because it can be precisely predicted only occasionally. The observable persisting patterns of uniformity of behaviour are not sufficiently persistent. Nevertheless, some of these recurring patterns are stable enough for policy purposes. Among these is the strong tendency to engage in price discrimination of several forms. In most economics textbooks, price discrimination is discussed with reference to monopoly. But if it were practised only by monopolies, it would not be a major concern, because there are so few single-firm industries. In fact, however, most price discrimination is practised by oligopolists. And the resort to discrimination is prima facie evidence of the realization of mutual dependence; it requires the observance of a convention for price discrimination to persist.

To pursue the analysis, it is desirable to have a clearly understood agreement of the matter under discussion. So we begin with the definition of price discrimination, which, at this point in this study, is assumed not to have a pejorative connotation. By *price discrimination* is meant simply the charging of different prices to different classes of customers for a particular time, for example, a day or a week. Thus, the charging of lower prices during a sale is not discrimination. And to give the concept sensible and general application, it is extended to include the charging of prices which differ by more than the transport cost when a commodity is sold at different geographic locations, and the maintenance of price differentials for different commodities which exceed or fall short of the differences in costs.

An example of the first type is the much-used practice of partial or full freight absorption. Any method of quoting prices other than f.o.b. the point of shipment contains some element of price discrimination. Accordingly, when a company has several factories producing an identical product, it is difficult and perhaps impossible for it to avoid discrimination altogether. Freight cost of total shipments from all the factories combined is not always minimized by serving each customer from the factory closest to him; sometimes a quite complex calculation is required to achieve minimum cost.

The second kind of discrimination is yet more complex. For example, if a factory produces two slightly different grades of a commodity, the average total unit cost of each can be precisely calculated according to standard cost accounting conventions, provided they are not joint products. If the price differential between the two commodities differs by more than the differential in costs, including a uniform return to capital, there is discrimination. Put another way, if more than a pro rata amount of overhead cost is allocated to either article, there is discrimination.

The reason why certain types of price discrimination practised by an oligopoly are prima facie evidence of acting upon the recognition of mutual dependence should now be apparent. If the price of an article at location A exceeds the price at location B by more than transport cost, for example, it is profitable for a company to sell more in market

A and less in B if no other consideration interferes. But other considerations always do interfere. An endeavour to increase sales in the more profitable market, other than by increased sales promotion expenditures, would drive down the price in A. And the second situation would be worse than the first. It requires only one large firm to cut prices to drive down the price level in the higher-priced market. The fact that the price differential in excess of transportation costs persists for a long period is therefore clear evidence that every firm in the industry calculates that continuation of the price discrimination is profitable for it because it cannot increase its sales in the more profitable market without retaliation from the other firms.

This example illustrates the point, but it is somewhat unrealistic because reference was made to the switching of sales from market A to market B. Obviously, the switching of sales from one market to another is necessary only if the company in question is operating at capacity. However, even a cursory reading of the financial pages of newspapers provides ample evidence that capacity operation of plants is more the exception than the rule. The relevant point is that a price which is the most profitable in one market is not the most profitable price in another market unless the price sensitivity of sales of the industry is the same in both markets, which is not often the case. Sales of carbon dioxide gas to hospitals are less sensitive to price than are sales of carbon dioxide to breweries, for example. Therefore, if hospitals pay a higher price than do breweries, profit considerations dictate that each firm allow the differential to persist.

Resort to price discrimination to maximize revenues seems to be the rule rather than the exception. The railways have practised it throughout their existence; it is the basis of the standard rate schedule. Much of the most profitable traffic moves at the standard schedular rates (which correspond to the list prices of the manufacturing company), while most of the bulky traffic, which has a low value per ton, moves at negotiated prices—which is a classic form of approved discrimination. There is active price competition, both between railway companies themselves and between the railways and trucking and air transport, in the setting of the negotiated charges. But there is no price competition, in any sensible meaning of the term, between railway companies with respect to the schedular rates, and they are now fairly well screened from sniping by trucking companies. The schedular rate traffic defrays most of the overhead costs, and it is quite evident that the deficit of the Canadian National Railway would be much larger if the standard rates were subject to the same kind of price competition that the negotiated charges are.

The combination of sales at list prices and at negotiated prices is an extremely prevalent form of price discrimination. For example, the company which buys a fairly large number of trucks can obtain a better price by buying directly from the manufacturer at a negotiated price than any other customer can obtain when buying through dealers. And there is almost certain to be price discrimination when the same commodity is sold directly to the public and also to other manufacturers who use it as a component part. The prices paid by automobile companies for tires are very much lower than the prices paid by retail dealers who sell to the general public. The prices paid for gasoline and diesel and fuel oil by municipalities, who enjoy the advantage of the oil companies' being willing to bid for their custom at tender, are lower than prices charged by the oil companies to service stations, even though the amount of gasoline bought by a large service station may be several times as great as the purchase made by a municipality. And, again, the sales in the higher-priced markets bear a disproportionate share of the overhead costs.

Often, the persistence of price discrimination can be attributed only to a customary practice which all companies observe. Thus, if a buyer can gain recognition as a jobber, he can buy at a discount. The securing of this classification confers a decisive competitive advantage over those who cannot secure it. The company which operates one or two large service stations, selling gasoline under its own private-brand name, is rarely able to secure jobber status even though the volume of its purchase may be quite large. But the department stores which follow the same practice are usually able to obtain recognition as jobbers, even though they perform no jobbing function. Similarly, painters, electricians, and automobile repair garages can buy their supplies at wholesale prices, even when buying single items, while other buyers who do not have that trade status cannot. The discounts from retail list prices which the former obtain are a substantial component of their net profits.

Price discrimination often figures prominently in the competitive manoeuvring within oligopolies. When the costs of transporting a commodity any considerable distance, say 100 miles, are large in relation to manufactured cost, as in cement, steel, and even partially manufactured products such as wire rope, prices are usually quoted on a zone basis, with the prices in each zone approximately reflecting the costs of transport from the nearest production centre. So long as the transport cost between two producing centres is substantial, the stage is set for intermittent raiding in each other's home market. Sometimes the competitor's price is undercut, but the more prevalent practice is to try to obtain sales at the competitor's price. In either case, since little profit is to be made by absorbing freight to make regular sales of a substantial proportion of a plant's output in the distant market, there is little danger that periodic poaching in the other's territory will precipitate outright warfare. However, whenever sales are slack and there is excess capacity, it is profitable to make an occasional sale in a distant market so long as the mill net exceeds incremental cost. It therefore may appear that the two producing centres are actively competing against each other, and in a sense, they are. But this type of competition offers no guarantee that prices will be driven down to lowest attainable cost.

Finally, price discrimination when coupled with basing-point pricing can isolate and confine price competition when it does break out. The most dramatic examples of this behaviour of recent years have occurred in the gasoline industry. When jobbers of private-brand gasoline were able to obtain supplies at discounts of several cents from the posted tank wagon price (the price at which the major oil companies sell to the service station dealers who sell their brand-name gasoline), their endeavours to obtain a substantial share of the market drove pump prices of gasoline below their "normal" level. The strategy adopted by the major oil companies to meet this competition was to convert all their dealers to consignment agents, so that the oil companies could lawfully set the pump prices. The posted wholesale prices then lost their significance in the price war areas; they were prices at which no transaction was made. The price corresponding to the wholesale price was the pump price minus the dealer's commission. This so-called net price was, in the well-documented British Columbia case, almost four cents per gallon lower than the Vancouver posted price, which was used for calculating prices at points within the Vancouver basing-point zone which were outside the price war area. The parts of the province inside other basing-point zones also reflected the posted Vancouver prices. Thus, during the period of consignment selling, there was a differential of almost four cents between the prices in various parts of the province and the actual Vancouver price plus freight to those points. The effects of the price competition from the private-brand jobbers and dealers were successfully restricted to the Lower Mainland and Vancouver Island. The cost to the major oil companies of confining the new entrants to small shares of the market was therefore less than it would have been if they had been able to meet the new competition only by lowering the posted Vancouver tank wagon price.

In the well-known Eddy match case, the dominant firm successfully coupled price discrimination with other tactics to retain its monopoly position by forcing new entrants out of business.[8] When the new entrants were about to place their products on the market, the Eddy company stocked up many of its retail customers with "fighting brands" adopted for the purpose. It was able to do so by offering the fighting brands at attractive prices which were lower than the price of its regular brand. The new entrants therefore had great difficulty in marketing their product. To gain entry to the market they would have had to have very long purses in order to survive the period during which the Eddy company kept the price of its fighting brands below total cost, including a pro rata share of fixed costs and an average return to capital. Obviously, if the law required that articles which are identical except for a trademark be sold at a uniform price, the cost of predatory pricing undertaken to exclude competitors would be much increased. But such a law would be exceedingly difficult to administer; the difficulties are discussed at some length in chapter 4.

DIFFERENTIATED PRODUCT OLIGOPOLIES WITH BARRIERS TO ENTRY

As mentioned above, to all intents and purposes differentiated products consist of commodities sold to the general public. When such articles as trucks and machinery are sold by one company to another, it may be assumed that the buyer usually knows enough about the performance of competing makes that any difference in performance must be compensated by a difference in price. The existence of these compensating price differences is the correct meaning of a uniform price in a particular market. And since the buyers are expert, competition focuses upon price.

Sales to the general public present an entirely different picture. Since the average buyer simply could not become knowledgeable about the great variety of products he consumes in a lifetime even if he spent all his spare time pursuing that objective, he must do the best he can with the information available to him. It is to be expected, therefore, that the average consumer develops preferences for trade names which he has found to be reliable and satisfactory. And it is understandable that, when he has little else to go by, he should judge quality partly by price. It is not surprising, then, that the creation and preservation of consumer preferences should have become the main form of competition within industries which produce consumer products. It is also to be expected that companies will endeavour to create a reputation for superior quality for their products even when no superiority exists. If there is occasion for surprise, it is not that so much sales effort is put into the promotion and marketing of consumer products; it is rather that, despite the fact that most competition is nonprice competition, the prices of rival products are so often identical.

The explanation of these identical prices in a given market is, of course, to be found in the realization of mutual dependence and the inability of any of the companies to convince a sufficient number of consumers that its trademarked product is sufficiently superior to the trademarked products of its rivals that they would be well advised to pay a higher price for it. When the consumer is not convinced that any of the brands are substantially superior, the only difference between products which he can readily recognize is a difference in price. Then, sales of a particular trademarked product are very sensitive to price differences between it and competing brands which are equally advertised and promoted. Consequently, the prices of close substitutes are kept identical, or almost so, because no company dares run the risk of pricing above its competitors. Like all generalizations, this one must be qualified. When the consumer is quite in the dark concerning the qualities of competing brands, stable price differentials may be maintained for long periods, as in the case of some patent medicines.[9]

Much of the effort which goes into creating preferences for particular brands eventually becomes defensive. Every sales promotion is bound to be matched by a counter. The net result is a considerable immunity of the consumer to the blandishments of the marketer and, where quality is comparable as far as he can judge, a readiness of many to switch brands on the basis of price. Accordingly, no competitor dares risk a price differential for long. If his rival is allowed to underprice him, he will gradually lose much of his share of the market.

Once this form of competition has become prevalent, there is nothing that any of the companies, acting singly, can do to change it. All are locked into the sales promotion race and all must act defensively. There are exceptions to this generalization, of course, as when one rival produces a product which is so clearly superior to the older products that it sweeps the market, until competitors match the superior design or performance. And most of us can recall several instances of new products which were placed on the market without expensive sales promotion and which so suited the preference of many consumers that their sales soared spectacularly. There are also exceptions in the form of little-advertised brands of quality products, for example, department store brands of automobile tires, which win a substantial share of the market on the basis of price alone. Very often, however, the unadvertised brand, even though physically identical to the highly advertised brand of the same company, goes unnoticed and unbought even if offered at a considerably lower price. The explanation must be that the consumer is not aware that it is of equal quality.

It has just been said that there is usually nothing that a company can do to break out of the mad race of sales promotion, which is cost- and price-increasing and which is of no value to the consumer, since one effort at persuasion is simply, in the main, cancelled by another. But neither is there any reason for an established company to want to substitute price competition for competition by sales promotion. The latter is comparatively safe. If any company tries to get one step ahead by cutting the price of its highly advertised brand, the others must match him, and all are worse off. But if the costs of sales promotion are pushed higher and higher, they can be recouped by higher prices so long as mutual dependence is sufficiently firmly recognized that rivals will follow a signal for a price increase. Moreover, it is possible for a company to outperform its rivals in nonprice competition; its marketing staff may be more imaginative than the others, or it may simply be lucky in hitting upon a sales promotion scheme which catches on. But when price competition breaks out within an oligopoly, it is certain that most of the rivals will lose and fairly certain that all will.

It is on this point that my interpretation of the nature of competition in Canada differs from that of most economists. I shall argue later that most Canadian industries are oligopolies—so much so that the major exceptions comprise a short list. The primary concern of oligopolies must be to prevent active price competition from breaking out among them. (It will be recalled that I use *active price competition* to mean the deliberate lowering of price to win a larger share of the market; all companies are subject to price competition in some form, but only the use of lower prices as a primary competitive device drives price levels down.) And more, firms have very good reason for this overriding concern to keep price competition within safe bounds: at least in the short run, success in confining price competition spells the difference between profits and losses. The dilemma of the private-enterprise market economy lies in securing just the right amount of price competition. We cannot live without price competition, but it must be admitted that it is often difficult to live with it.

It may appear that my great emphasis upon the avoidance of active price competition by oligopolists is misplaced, because they very often give the appearance of the contrary. The consumer is steadily bombarded with notices of special offers, trading stamps, and bonus packages. However, all these forms of temporarily reducing prices are safe forms of price competition. They do not lead to a long-term decrease in the price level. They are primarily means of inducing new customers to try a particular brand product on the expectation that a certain percentage of those who do will remain as steady customers. As such, they are well within the limits of the rules of the cooperative game worked out by oligopolists. Similarly, the annual and semiannual sales of department and clothing stores have become part of standard practice which does not rock the boat. Each rival takes his turn. It is not unusual, for example, to observe a large department store advertise a particular article such as a hot water tank at a much reduced price, during a sale, which is identical with the reduced price advertised by its competitor a week earlier during its sale. Similarly, the prices of most articles advertised by grocery supermarkets as their weekly special are identical. One has the impression that prices are constantly being reduced, but the average percentage markup remains stable, the lower margins charged on some items being compensated by the maintenance of the margin on most others. Also, when a special low price is made for a brand-name product, such as record players, it is often by special arrangement with the manufacturer and occurs most often when a particular style or line is being discontinued. In short, all the frenzy of special low prices and special deals are simply sales promotion tactics which are taken account of in advance when the average price of an article is planned for the year ahead; it has the appearance rather than the reality of active price competition. And sometimes the appearance is deliberately and unlawfully calculated to mislead, as when the regular selling price is stated to be higher than it actually is. It is unfortunate that yielding to the temptation to engage in such unethical practices seems to be more prevalent among the "professional price-cutters" than it is among large, established companies (which perhaps have more to lose), since in other respects, the professional price-cutter is often the consumer's best friend.

The preference for safe, nonprice competition is the most plausible explanation of the preference of manufacturers for resale price maintenance, which has puzzled many analysts of business behaviour. The reason retail stores should be in favour is no mystery. If a competitor cuts the usual markup, the average level of markups will eventually be driven down, and the resulting increase in sales will not compensate the retailer. In fact, the increase in total sales of a product in a given market consequent to a small decrease in the retail price of, say, 5 percent is usually sufficiently small that the trade discounts it altogether.[10] But what concern is this to the manufacturer? He surely does not have the retailers' welfare foremost in mind. Neither is the argument convincing that an end of resale price maintenance would result in loss-leader selling which would damage the product image. Loss-leader selling, however defined, is more likely to occur when a substantial margin is maintained by most retailers than when that margin is the lowest possible consistent with covering total costs when there is no excess capacity. No—the great desire of manufacturers to preserve resale price maintenance can be plausibly explained only on the reasoning that price competition at the retail level might lead to price competition among manufacturers. The argument that an attractive margin must be assured to the retailer to induce him to handle a manufacturer's product is valid only in the analysis of the position in which a particular manufacturer usually finds himself. He must do as his competitors do. But this reasoning has no relevance for an explanation of why manufacturers generally favour resale price maintenance as a system.

Reference has been made to the substantial amounts of capital which are often required to build a plant of the smallest size which can realize most of the economies of scale. These costs are sometimes the main barrier limiting entry to an industry and are, accordingly, the main explanation of the fact that an industry is an oligopoly composed of few firms, with each firm being large in relation to the market. In the case of many differentiated products, however, the economies of scale in sales promotion can be realized only by a firm which is much larger than a plant of minimum economic size. It is then the sales promotion economies of scale which pose the main barrier to successful entry. If only a local market is served, it is uneconomic to use nationwide advertising in magazines and on television.

The cost of service competition, such as credit card facilities, also diminishes rapidly as the number of customers and the volume of sales increase. For example, the credit card costs of the major oil companies amount to about one-half cent per gallon of gasoline sold to motorists, or one and one-half cents per gallon sold on credit. The latter cost runs as high as four cents per gallon for a small, new company which has relatively few retail outlets. It is no wonder, therefore, that the large established companies emphasize such services as a major competitive tactic.

The search for avenues of competition which avoid the danger of distress prices also accounts in large part for the demise of the independent wholesaler in many industries through the merging of distribution with production. In most industries the jobbing function is performed either by the manufacturer or by his franchised agents. This forward integration into distribution incidentally serves the objective of preventing an outbreak of price competition at the wholesale level. When the distributor is not a free agent he is not able to fall into the error of undercutting the prices of other distributors. The final step in the evolution of this "safe" competition takes the form of the buying-up of customers by the primary producer, for example, the purchase of paper box and paper board companies by large pulp companies. Such forward integration may be viewed as part of a sinister plot to eliminate all effective competition from an industry with the objective of higher profits. The more plausible explanation, however, is that it is the logical outcome of the competitive urge to retain or enlarge a company's share of the market. One does not have to hypothesize tacit collusion; it is simply the most profitable course for a company to follow, given the particular circumstance in which it finds itself. The move towards forward integration may be initiated by a company for any of a host of reasons peculiar to its circumstances. But once started, all rivals must follow, as a defensive strategy to forestall having their customers disappear.

In some circumstances, the integration of one stage of production with another reduces total costs of production. For example, the integration of chemical pulp with paperboard mills under one roof eliminates the cost of drying and bailing the pulp and its remixing. Similar economies are realized by the transfer of molten metals to adjacent fabrication mills. But few economies can be realized by the producer taking over the wholesaling function. On the contrary, as part of the strategy of stressing nonprice competition, the end result is usually an increase in the retail price because most forms of nonprice competition increase cost. Hence it is difficult to make out a case that the integration of production and distribution is in the consumers' interest. The amount of economic waste involved is discussed in chapter 2 and, since there is rarely anything which a company or even an industry could do to improve matters even with the best will in the world, it is argued in chapter 4 that the remedy can only take the form of changes in the rules of the competitive game.

OLIGOPOLY: THE CANADIAN VARIANT

The largest Canadian oligopolies that produce homogeneous products are export industries, and their competitive tactics reflect conditions prevailing in their major markets. This is precisely what one would expect. Nevertheless, the pricing behaviour of these industries has puzzled many observers. For example, many were at a loss to understand why the Canadian newsprint firms kept their price for delivery in New York unchanged from early 1957 to 1966, while the Canadian dollar varied between a high of about $1.06 U.S. to a low of $0.925.[11] Surely, it was reasoned, since the Canadian companies produced over three-quarters of the American supply, it would have been profitable for them to raise their prices when the mill net was reduced by the high value of the Canadian dollar. But this reasoning neglected the nature of competition in the industry. The year 1957 saw the appearance of considerable reserve capacity for the first time since World War II. Hence the Canadian mills did not dare raise their prices to compensate for the appreciation of the Canadian dollar. To do so would have been to lose permanently much of their American market; they could raise prices only if the American companies favoured the move. Similarly, when the Canadian dollar was devalued in 1962, thereby substantially increasing the Canadian dollar mill net from a constant U.S. dollar price, there was no mystery as to why the Canadian companies did not lower their United States prices. All favoured an increase in the Canadian mill net, and there was no move on the part of the American competitors to change price, since their situation was unchanged.

Not all Canadian oligopoly industries which produce homogeneous products are exporters, of course. Sugar and steel are examples of homogeneous product industries which serve the domestic market almost exclusively, behind tariff protection. Since the number of companies in these industries is very small (typically, three to five) it is almost impossible for them to avoid parallel pricing practices. So there are few puzzles in their behaviour.

It is the differentiated-product, tariff-sheltered industries which have attracted most attention and posed the greatest puzzles for the observer. Some of these industries are periodically suspected of practising tacit collusion to take greatest advantage of their tariff protection: for example, by pricing just a bit under the duty-paid cost of imports. On this hypothesis, all price changes should be explainable by changes in prices abroad and the necessity of occasionally decreasing prices to ward off the entrance of new import houses. One has reason, however, to doubt the universality of this hypothesis. There is evidence that many oligopolists which could exercise monopoly power when they tacitly act in concert choose prices considerably below the duty-paid cost of imports.[12] In the absence of any other plausible explanation, it is reasonable to accept the firms' public pronouncements and conclude that they practise fair pricing. Subject to the constraint of outside competition, they price to earn an average profit on their capital and so do not necessarily take full advantage of the tariff protection. I can recall being told of an industry, which may not be identified since the information is not documented, which was alleged to have followed fair pricing until it was prosecuted as an unlawful combine. Having been fined, as they saw it, for responsible behaviour, the companies thereafter adopted the practice of maximum prices to the full extent of their tariff protection, according to my informant. This is not to say that the behaviour subsequent to the conviction was unlawful; most forms of conscious parallel action are presumably not unlawful under Canadian combines law. I also remember being told informally about a tariff-sheltered industry composed of about a dozen companies which acted in concert in a manner that is presumably of doubtful legality. Each company mailed price lists to its competitors whenever prices were changed, and, it was alleged, all of the competitors immediately made price changes. The main reason given for reducing prices was "to head off fly-by-night import houses." It is unfortunate that much of the information one can obtain concerning the pricing behaviour of the Canadian protected oligopolies consists of such undocumented, inconclusive, anecdotal evidence. The fact that such information is hearsay is surely not sufficient reason for discounting it altogether, however, when trying to piece together a picture of the nature and state of competition. Such undocumented evidence rivals the reports of the Director of Investigation and Research, the Combines Investigation Act, and of the Restrictive Trade Practices Commission as a primary source of information about pricing behaviour. For example, during many informal discussions I have had with junior executives concerning the shifting of the corporation profits tax, I can recall no instance of a person in an industry which was effectively screened from foreign competition saying that his company did not pass on the tax to consumers. To the best of my recollection, there was universal insistence that the presence of a price leader or equally effective action upon the recognition of mutual dependence enabled the companies in the industry in question to avoid falling into price competition among themselves when selling to the general public in an effectively sheltered market. In contrast, the reports concerning intercompany sales and sales at tender presented a mixed picture. Sometimes price competition was described and sometimes conscious parallel action admitted.

The aspect of the behaviour of the tariff-sheltered industries which has been most puzzling to economists and which is most relevant to this enquiry, however, does not directly concern pricing. The industries enjoying fairly effective tariff protection are observed to market a full line of whatever commodities they produce. It is often wondered why the companies do not specialize in a selected number of lines and models in order to escape the high cost of short runs. To do so, of course, the company specializing in a few lines would have to under-price his rivals for a period sufficiently long to drive them out of the selected line and compel them to specialize in other lines, sizes, or models. Carried to its logical conclusion, such specialization would transform the typical import-competing oligopoly into an industry consisting of a small number of limited monopolists engaged in less direct competition with one another.

Surely the reasons why such specialization does not often emerge are obvious enough. First, the decision to specialize would be a very risky one. There would be no assurance that most of the domestic market for the selected lines, sizes, or models could be captured by cutting prices. At a minimum, the company should be prepared to face a series of loss years. And if the endeavour failed, the company could expect to go bankrupt unless it was a subsidiary of a very large corporation and was supported by its nonresident parent. The second reason is even more fundamental. The notion of capturing entire markets by price cutting is wholly alien to the customary modes of competition. The integration of marketing with production is so complete and the habit of competition in the form of sales promotion, packaging, and design is so entrenched that it is doubtful that the notion of specialization through price cutting would ever enter the thoughts of management. And, if suggested, it would not be seriously entertained. Also, if most of the companies involved are subsidiaries of American companies, the managers of the Canadian subsidiaries often follow in a small market the habits and strategies evolved in the very large market to which they are more appropriate. In any event, it would be the extreme of audacity for a company's management team to stake their careers upon the successful outcome of a price war.

If it is accepted that no deep mystery surrounds the reasons why protected industries do not specialize in the production of a few lines, some puzzling behaviour still remains to be explained. The reasons why all companies try to market a full line is clear enough. It is part and parcel of the marketing strategy which places almost exclusive emphasis upon nonprice competition. But why does each company consider that it must *produce* all the lines, models, and sizes it markets? It is known that most of the companies in some of the protected industries —electrical appliances, for example—produce lines which do not cover their costs. And it is a fair assumption that the same condition prevails in many of the protected industries. Why do companies continue to produce loss lines rather than buy from domestic competitors or from abroad? If companies called for tenders for the supply of their lines, sizes, or models which yielded negative or nominal profits, specialization within the sheltered oligopolies might evolve without the heavy financial losses which would result from price warfare.

LIMITED MONOPOLY

Limited monopoly is not a classification which is much used by economists, the objection being that all monopoly power is limited in some manner, and there is little point in treating a difference in degree as a difference in kind. However, all differences in the structure of industries are matters of degree, and I find limited monopoly a convenient category into which to tuck two quite common sets of circumstances that shape a firm's behaviour.

By *limited monopoly* I mean a company which produces a commodity or service that has no single close substitute, but faces several imperfect substitutes. For example, a gasoline service station which is several miles distant from its nearest competitor enjoys a limited, local monopoly. Consequently, there is usually a small range of prices which it is free to charge. And the operator is presumed to choose the particular price which is thought to produce the greatest profit. The most important fact which the limited monopolist must know when choosing his most profitable price is, obviously, the average of the prices charged by his nearest competitors. He must then decide how much business he would lose by keeping his price above the average by different amounts.

It is clear that such limited monopolies are subject to the usual constraints of changing conditions of market demand and supply. If the nearest competitors, which are usually subject to competitive pressures more directly than is the limited monopolist, reduce their prices, the limited monopolist's price would no longer be the most profitable and he should reduce it. The penalty for not doing so would be the gradual reduction of his sales volume. The freedom of action, then, consists solely of the freedom to choose the differential between his price and his competitors' prices within a narrow range. Such monopoly power by no means guarantees a monopoly profit. If a service station's location brings in little trade, it will not be able to cover total costs. Conversely, if the volume of sales is sufficiently large to generate much greater than average profits, a competitor is likely to locate sufficiently close to take much of his sales away. It is only when the volume of sales is fairly static that a retail outlet can enjoy a limited monopoly position for long. This is because, by our definition, this first category of limited monopolist cannot control entry into his market and therefore cannot control supply in the long run.

Other examples of this first category of limited monopoly are bowling lanes, lumber yards, hardware stores, and the like in small towns situated at some distance from the nearest other centre of population, or simply in any location within a large market such that the retail outlet is separated from its nearest competitors by significant costs of travel, including the costs of time loss and inconvenience.

This category of monopoly poses only one problem for government policy. If the existence of a single firm in a small market is the consequence of the size of the market, there is nothing which a government can do to improve matters. Usually, there is also little reason for wanting to make a change because, in this age of the automobile, the monopoly is likely to be tenuous. In the extreme instance, when a small town is so isolated that the single gasoline station, hardware store, or what have you, enjoys a profitable monopoly position for a long period, the case for regulation is more substantial. Then, the monopoly position will continue until the market grows to such a size that it can profitably support more than one firm or until some investor makes a mistake in thinking it can do so even when it cannot. The main constraint upon the monopolist's actions therefore is the fear that competitors may be attracted, and this may be an ineffective constraint. However, no other counter to the local monopoly power has been devised.

The policy problem posed by this first category of limited monopolist relates to mergers. If two or more firms are already sharing a local market, the consumer has an interest in a government rule which would prevent them from becoming a limited monopoly by merging, provided the market is large enough to support at least two firms. The benefit of competition between two firms may not appear impressive, but it is surely not negligible. There is not likely to be sufficient price competition to drive prices down to lowest attainable costs, including an average rate of profit on the capital employed and an average rent to entrepreneurial ability. However, at least the price level would be determined by whichever of the two firms was the more inclined to set modest profit goals or was more apprehensive of attracting another competitor. In addition, the consumer would have an alternative supply to turn to if for any reason he became annoyed with the one he was patronizing. Admittedly, the alternative might be no more attractive, but an unsatisfactory alternative is surely better than none. Much the same reasoning applies if the example is extended to three or four retail outlets.

On the other hand, if the local market is not large enough to support more than one firm, the alternative to the merging of the two firms is likely to be the bankruptcy of at least one of them. However, in these circumstances, one retail outlet would still have to be closed. So a merger is hardly likely to be attractive to both firms. In consequence, the desirability or undesirability of mergers from the public's point of view is not likely to arise.

The second category of limited monopoly is somewhat closer to pure monopoly than is the semi-isolated local market situation. It is created by the successful differentiation of a product by one producer so that his commodity or service ceases to have a close substitute but continues to face competition from a number of imperfect substitutes. Bayer aspirin is a good example of this situation. This brand is able to retain a major share of the market, although its price is considerably above the average of the competitors which produce an almost identical product—the reason, of course, being that many consumers are convinced that Bayer aspirin is superior. Since it has no close substitute, Bayer is able to earn monopoly profits. But since it faces many poor substitutes in the form of other brands, it enjoys only a limited monopoly position. If the average price of other brands is lowered, the most profitable price for Bayer aspirin is also a lower price, and Bayer's most profitable price is lower than it would be in the absence of all other brands. The Bayer company is also subject to another form of competition. Other companies, with greater or less success, have created similarly distinctive products, for example, Disprin, and market shares are fought over by sales promotion. So far, it does not appear that the competing distinctive brands are regarded as interchangeable by the public; if they were, Bayer would not be correctly classified as a limited monopolist.

Usually one would expect this second category of limited monopoly, like the first, to contribute nothing constructive to the forces of competition in the market, excepting that the search for truly distinctive products often produces superior ones, and this innovative process is a vital part of our economy. But creativity aside, the ability to persuade people that one brand is very much better than all others when, in fact, it is only slightly superior can scarcely be termed a constructive contribution.

Another good example of this second category of limited monopoly was Coca-Cola before Pepsi-Cola emerged as a successful close substitute. Then, Coca-Cola was closer to a pure monopoly than is Bayer aspirin today, because more than its brand name was patented, it possessed distinctive physical properties which gave it its unique flavour. Nevertheless, the demand for Coca-Cola was quite sensitive to the variations in the average price of all other soft drinks. One would not expect the limited monopolist to exert a strong restraint upon price increases. Indeed, one would expect the contrary. However this may be, in the immediate postwar years the price of Coca-Cola held firm for a longish period despite substantial increases in the cost of sugar. And the prices of other soft drinks were anchored with it. Whether this action was in the long-run interests of the consumer is not clear, since many competitors were placed in a difficult cost-price squeeze which could not be attributed to inefficiency. But the point remains that, on occasion, limited monopolists do engage in a form of price competition.

Since these limited monopolies usually fall into the complex market situation of "limited monopoly within an oligopoly industry," this brief discussion of their behaviour is incomplete. When a member of an oligopoly industry, the limited monopolist may engage in any of the competitive moves and tactics of the standard oligopolist producing a differentiated product.

In common with the first category of limited monopolist, the second category would not seem to require special mention in an analysis of competition policy. No device has been contrived by which a government could improve the performance of the limited monopolist other than certain general measures, such as requiring honesty in advertising, positive measures to increase consumer awareness of the qualities of competing products, the countering of artificial barriers to entry, and the banning of mergers which enhance monopoly power. And each of these measures should be considered in its own right.

PURE MONOPOLY

In my classification, pure monopoly is distinguished from limited monopoly by the absence of imperfect substitutes and by control over supply in the long run by controlling entry to the industry. Once again these characteristics are matters of degree.

Rayon and nylon tire cord are obviously close substitutes—so close that they may well be considered the same product. In contrast, in its day, cellophane was in a class by itself. In many uses, the demand for cellophane was little affected by the variations in the average price of all other wrapping material. Similarly, if one company possessed the sole legal right to manufacture glass, it would be entirely free of effective competition in many markets and uses; no normal variation in the prices of other materials would materially affect the demand for glass. In other uses, of course, glass faces several close substitutes.

It has been said that an oligopoly which acts in concert can exercise monopoly power provided that entry to the industry can be blocked. Therefore, when successfully making monopoly profits, the oligopoly's main concern must be to exclude new competitors. And so it is with the pure monopolist. The constraints upon the monopolist's inclination to charge all that the market will bear therefore take three forms: concern that imitators will be attracted; concern for public opinion and government regulation; and the management's notion of fair pricing.

Most monopolists' control over supply in the long run is derived from patent rights. The main threat to their monopoly positions therefore arises from successful imitation or worse from the monopolists' point of view, the arrival of a new product or process which is superior. It has often been reasoned that the able monopolist should try to calculate the effect which high profits would have upon the attraction of such competitors, but this does not seem very plausible. The incentives to develop an entirely new product or process are so great that the endeavours to do so are not likely to be much affected by a decision of the monopolist to price his product to yield, say, 25 percent on capital after taxes or only 20 percent. And in the case of imitation by a small modification, the competent imitator should be aware that it is not the price which a monopolist charges before an imitation appears on the market that is crucial; it is the price charged after the imitation appears. And there is no reason for supposing that successful imitation will not provoke a significant reaction.

Accordingly, the main reason why monopolists do not use their monopoly power to the full to earn maximum profits while their monopoly positions last must be management's notions of fair pricing and the fear of alienating public opinion and thereby attracting government regulation or loss of their monopoly position. Although impossible to document, it is my view that the former is the more powerful of the two. If so, it may be reasoned that such fair pricing reflects the effect of public opinion at one remove. Whether this speculation is correct or not, observation of the pricing of monopolists and the few well-documented case studies of monopoly leave little room for doubt that most monopolists take lower profits than are available to them. They practice fair pricing, although the rate of return to capital which seems fair to one may be double the rate which is obtained by another.

Moreover, observation indicates that, on the whole, monopolists set their prices very much as oligopolists do, hence there is no complete understanding of either behaviour. For example, during the deep depression of the 1930s, many oligopoly industries tried to prevent decreases in the prices of their products—some more successfully than others. In general, the price of oligopolies fell much less and were changed much less frequently than the prices of more competitive industries. One gains the impression that, if the oligopolists had had the power, they would have kept their nominal (dollars and cents) prices unchanged, which would have meant a very large increase in their real prices since costs fell sharply and the prices of many commodities dropped to less than one-half their 1929 level. And this was precisely the behaviour of the best-known monopolies; they kept their nominal prices unchanged when all else was changing around them. No satisfactory explanation of this unequalled price rigidity has ever been found.[13] If the prices of 1929 were either fair or most profitable, they certainly could not be so in the vastly changed circumstances of 1933.

The most plausible explanation seems to be that a large company's decision is a committee decision, made by the management team, and as so frequently asserted in anguish, the committee decision is biased toward inaction and ineffectiveness.

The fair pricing hypothesis fits observed behaviour in the 1920s and since World War II better than it does behaviour in deep depression. For example, when the Aluminum Company of America was a monopoly prior to the war, most of its price changes could be attributed to changing costs and to changes in the prices of imports from Europe. Also, models built on the postulate of long-term profit maximization cannot account for the use by Alcoa of a single-base basing-point pricing system, but it is possible to make a fair pricing model accommodate this "irrationality." Profit maximizing faced the constraint of the duty-paid cost of imports landed mainly at points on the east coast. Consequently, profit maximizing dictated the use of a multiple-zone delivered pricing system so that prices need not be lowered in the zones most sheltered from imports by transport costs when less sheltered markets were threatened by increased imports.[14]

It appears, therefore, that little would be gained by the conversion of the few monopolies extant in Canada into oligopolies of two, three, or four companies. And much might be lost if the market were too small to support several plants of economic size. In the discussion in subsequent chapters, therefore, little will be said about monopolies which already exist. In any event, ample justification for this omission should be found in the fact that pure monopolists which are free of direct regulation are few and far between.

SUMMARY: THE STATE OF COMPETITION

Having stated something of the structure and behaviour of the several categories of industries, we are now in a position to hazard some general statements about the nature and state of competition in Canada in the 1960s. It is generally agreed that pure competition is quite rare and probably becoming even rarer, thanks in part to government intervention. Unfortunately, several of the remaining pure-competition industries are marked by so great an ease of entry that they are chronically sick; that is, a significant proportion of the firms in the industry earn less than the opportunity cost of the capital and labour they employ. The labour is usually that of the entrepreneur-owner and his family, and it, together with the little capital employed, could earn more if moved to other uses. The real loss of productivity is less than it might appear at first examination because some value must be put on the strong preference of, say, inshore fishermen for fishing as a way of life. Also, the labour employed is often deficient both in general skills and in the particular skills in demand in large-scale manufacturing and the service industries. Hence, if the labour were transferred to other employment, especially without retraining, it would command relatively low wages.

Nevertheless, the real loss of productivity is still substantial. Whatever may be thought about the desirability of the pure-competition type of price behaviour, it is surely evident that overly great ease of entry into an industry is not beneficial. It should be remembered, however, that excessive ease of entry is not restricted to the pure-competition industries; it also plagues oligopolies, notably many branches of retailing.

For the United States, the number of pure-competition industries might run to a score or more. It would include such manufacturing industries as certain branches of textiles, such as grey cotton cloth. But in Canada the number of pure-competition industries is extremely small. We may put down most branches of farming, even though government marketing schemes mark a departure from the pure model. Much fishing is also clearly pure competition. To these may be added sawmilling and some parts of logging. There are doubtless other industries or portions of them which fit into the classification, but none comes to mind. Some analysts would add much base metal mining to the list, especially copper, lead, and zinc. Since much of the world output of these minerals comes from a few large companies, however, the classification stands in some doubt even though the few large firms must face the keen competition of quite a few smaller companies.

The other end of the spectrum, monopoly, is also the exception. But limited monopoly is quite prevalent. However, many enjoy a limited monopoly position within an oligopoly industry, hence the most important aspects of their behaviour fall within the oligopoly classification.

It may be concluded that at least 80 percent of Canadian commerce and industry, excluding agriculture, forestry, and fishing, is comprised of one or other of the several variants of oligopoly. Competition in the modern economy is competition among the few. And such it will remain in Canada no less than elsewhere. Even if all Canadian and United States tariffs were reciprocally removed, oligopoly would remain almost as prevalent in Canadian industry as it is now. Instead of being a member of a small, tariff-sheltered oligopoly with its activities mainly confined to the domestic market, the typical Canadian manufacturing company which survived without merging with a larger American company would become a full-fledged member of a North American oligopoly, and its behaviour would precisely parallel the behaviour of the American companies.

2
Economic wastes attributable to imperfect competition

The analytical model

CRITERIA OF WASTE

Economic waste is a relative term; it is the shortfall below some superior alternative. So, to begin, we need a model against which to compare performance of actual industries. Obviously, there would be little point in setting up a comparison model which was an unattainable ideal. In particular, one wants to be sure that the comparison behaviour of firms, industries, and the economy is viable. Having chosen a viable comparison behaviour, the next step is to identify the wastes in our economy in the form of departures from the comparison model. Even so, the economic wastes identified in this manner should not be assumed to be the measure of the gains which would result from making changes in the rules relating to business behaviour. There is bound to be a substantial shortfall of actual behaviour below that which is sought to be induced. The proper measure of the gains to be had from adopting a new competition policy requires an estimate of the changes in performance which would result and an estimate of the reduction in economic waste that would result from the changed performance.

This chapter deals only with the first stage of the procedure: setting up the comparison behaviour and identifying the economic wastes that exist in the form of departures of actual behaviour from the comparison behaviour. Discussions of the gains in income per capita which might result from changes in the rules regulating business behaviour are deferred to chapter 4, where specific rules are suggested.

Only a little reflection is needed to convince oneself that a comparison with a specific alternative is the correct procedure in discussions of economic waste, despite the fact that this procedure is rarely followed. For example, case studies of highly concentrated industries often end with the conclusion that the industry has been progressive and efficient: output may have trebled and costs have been cut in half in twenty years. But such a conclusion is only indirectly relevant. What one wants to know is whether the same, or more, or less, would have been accomplished in the same period if competition had taken a different form. The latter is the correct question because it is the only one useful for policy purposes.

The reference case which is still the most frequently used by economists is the pure-competition model, despite grave misgivings about both its performance and its attainability. But pure competition is used as a model only because it is assumed to satisfy most of the desiderata of performance. It seems preferable, therefore, to push past the model and seek out the criteria. And the criteria are to be found in the objectives; that is, a particular behaviour of an economy is chosen as ideal because it is thought to provide the greatest attainable efficiency and stability and is consistent with prevailing notions of fair income distribution. A fourth goal should be added, namely, that business should be conducted in keeping with the generally accepted ideas of fair dealing. Economic growth is not listed separately, since it can be divided into its two components of increases in average productivity per worker and the increase in the labour force. Productivity is part of our concept of efficiency, except when it is attributable to increases in the amount of capital per worker due to an increase in investment and saving out of a given national income. And the latter need be considered only if changes being contemplated would have a measurable effect upon the flow of investment. Consequently, changes in capital per worker are only indirectly related to the main focus of this enquiry.

I also consider it expedient to forego a discussion of the changes in overall income distribution and the stability of the economy which might result from changes in the prevailing mode of competition. To be of any use whatever, a discussion of income distribution would have to be quite comprehensive. Having gone through the exercise and concluded that a very substantial increase in price competition would have only minor effects upon overall income distribution, I feel justified in omitting a lengthy digression.

In any event, the economist's view of the effects of monopoly pricing upon the distribution of income leaves out what the consumer considers to be the most important aspect. The economist reasons that an increase in price competition would decrease the prices of some products at the expense of profits; therefore, profits would decrease as a proportion of national income, and the distribution of income would be somewhat less unequal if the share of profits in the national income were less. This reasoning is of scant interest to the general public. Quite rightly, the consumer who discovers that the price charged by a manufacturer is several times total average cost, including an average profit, is not interested in the small overall effect such actions have upon the overall inequality of the distribution of income. Rather, the consumer considers that he is entitled to buy goods at their lowest attainable cost and that the manufacturer is entitled to only a normal profit. On this reasoning the consumer's loss from monopoly pricing is the full amount of the excess of the monopoly price over the competitive price. It is of secondary interest to the consumer whether all of his loss is accounted for in the profits of the monopolist (or, more usually, the colluding oligopoly) or most of it represents avoidable costs.

Similarly, the economist reasons that the consumer suffers an excess burden from collusive oligopoly pricing because a monopoly price is higher than its *opportunity cost*, and consequently the consumer buys less of it and more of other goods than he would if the prices of all goods were equal to their opportunity costs. For our purposes opportunity cost may be taken to be the average cost of producing a commodity, including only normal profit. Obviously, such an excess burden is of little concern to the consumer as compared to the full loss of income just described (actual monopoly price minus competitive price).

The reasons for omitting a discussion of the effects of price competition upon the stability of the economy are somewhat different. A persuasive case can be argued that our economy would evidence a much stronger tendency to maintain a full-employment level of output if the prices of all commodities and services varied freely up and down in comparison to the level of wages.[1] Whether there would be less inflation in the absence of additional restraints upon the rate of increase in wages is an open question. However, the increase in stability envisaged requires that the prices of commodities and services increase promptly and substantially whenever output presses against physical capacity and decrease promptly and substantially whenever output drops below capacity. In the actual conditions faced by many Canadian industries, it is not certain that the positive profits earned in periods of short supply would exceed the losses of periods of easy supply sufficiently to ensure a normal return to capital. Normal profits could be earned only if output were close to capacity most of the time. However, there is reason to believe that the least-size economical addition to plant capacity in many industries is large in relation to the total output of the industry in the particular market. When this is so, it would not be economical for an industry to match increases in capacity with increases in demand precisely from year to year. Yet, the industry would earn negative profits if it did not do so and if price competition drove prices below average cost whenever capacity exceeded output by more than a small margin. In consequence, it is debatable whether the degree of price variability which would be required to impart stability to the operations of the economy would be viable. I happen to be sanguine in this matter, but others are not. What is clear is that it is most improbable that the required price variability could be induced by regulatory measures.

Finally, a consideration of the fairness of business practices is best deferred to the discussion of specific changes in government regulations which might be made to serve this objective.

All these provisos allow us to focus the discussion of economic waste upon the efficiency criterion in all its several aspects.

THE CONSUMERS' SOVEREIGNTY RULE

A productive discussion of either the actual performance of an economy or the expected performance of a reference model requires that the efficiency criterion be given precise formulation. This is most conveniently done by postulating a strong consumers' sovereignty rule. The rule proposed and discussed in this section has three parts: the consumer is entitled to be provided with the commodities and services he most prefers, at least attainable cost (provided that total demand is sufficient to enable total costs to be covered); the consumer is entitled to be provided with commodities accompanied by as much or as little convenience, service, and variety as he most prefers and is willing to pay for at prices equal to lowest attainable cost; the consumer is entitled to be informed concerning the variety, qualities, and prices of commodities and services available, and the information should be available to him at the least attainable cost of providing it. The three parts will be discussed in turn.

The first part of the consumers' sovereignty rule—that the consumer is entitled to be provided with any commodity or service he desires, at a price equal to the lowest attainable cost—implies, of course, that the demand be sufficiently large that the commodity can be sold at a price which covers total costs. The success of the free enterprise system in achieving this objective is a principal justification of the system. Provided only that there is sufficient price competition of the prescribed type, the market system provides the goods and services which consumers want, and it provides them at the lowest attainable costs. Achievement of the lowest cost depends mainly upon using the best available methods of production, the competence and vigour of management, and the mores of employees (the last lying outside our purview). The rate of profit earned on capital within a range of, say, 6 to 12 percent is much less crucial.

That the use of the least-cost method of production is critically important constitutes the strong point of the so-called new competition argument (though it is still termed new, the concept is actually of voting age). The development and adoption of new methods of production, new processes, new materials, and new products account for the greater part of the increase in productivity. Innovation is the dynamic means to obtaining greater outputs per unit of input. And some economists, in company with *Fortune* magazine, have argued that any major change in the structure of American industry, particularly the breaking up of large companies, would substantially reduce the pace of this process of "creative destruction" by which old processes and products are destroyed and replaced by superior ones. The essentials of the argument are that the American economy has achieved greater productivity than any other, that this high productivity is due mainly to innovation, that the high rate of innovation has occurred because it is the main form of competition among absolutely large companies, and that therefore the prevailing modes of competition should be preserved, not tampered with in endeavours to infuse more price competition into the economy. The argument now focusses on two points: whether innovation is in fact the main form of competition among large companies, and the actual contribution of large companies to inventions and their development and application.

The first part of the contention has not been sustained. While it is a simple matter to point to a number of oligopoly industries in which survival, market shares, and profits depend mainly upon the success of the firm's research and development programmes, whether this condition is present or not apparently depends mainly on the stage in the life cycle of industries that an industry happens to be in.[2] The rapid growth of new industries frequently results from the exploitation of an important invention or a new body of scientific knowledge. Older industries usually grow less rapidly because no major new technological advance is available to be developed. Typically, the number of firms entering an industry at its inception, when a technological advance is being exploited, is much larger than the number that survive into the mature stage, when the pace of innovation slackens. The size of the surviving companies depends partly upon the economies of scale in research and development. But the largeness of the firms surviving the period of rapid development of an important invention (the innovative stage of the industry's life cycle) is no guarantee that the industry will remain highly innovative. Consequently it can be concluded only that innovation is the main form of competition in industries that are engaged in developing important inventions. The incidence of new inventions depends mainly upon basic scientific research, much of which is sponsored by governments and most of which is conducted by nonprofit institutions, upon accidental discovery, and upon the activities of the lone inventor in his small workshop. Narrowly focused applied research conducted by large corporations is not as major a source as these; the small company and single-person enterprise have outperformed the large corporation in the invention stage of innovation.

Also, since many of the most important recent innovations were begun by small companies, many of which have grown to substantial size as a consequence of their successful innovation, and because much of the innovation in the new technology-based industries is conducted by firms that were small when they entered the industry, it cannot be said that the higher profits resulting from the relative security of oligopolies consisting of a few large companies is a necessary condition for rapid technological advance.

On the other hand, some support for the contention that firm size and innovation go hand in hand is lent by the finding that, for all firms in manufacturing in the United States lumped together, there is a correlation between size of firm and research and development expenditure per dollar of sales revenue. In particular, firms with fewer than 5,000 employees spend proportionately much less on research and development than do firms with more than 5,000 employees. Consequently, there is a correlation between the average size of firms in an industry and the research and development expenditure per dollar of sales. However, within industries there is little correlation between the size of firms with more than 5,000 employees and research and development expenditure per dollar of sales. Moreover, the direction of causality is not clear. The overall correlation between firm size and research and development in all manufacturing could be due to factors not directly related to firm size. Many of the industries that are very innovative consist of large firms, but this fact does not indicate that it is the largeness of the firms that created the inventiveness. On the contrary, in the light of other information available, it is more plausible that the firms are large because they are in industries that are in the competitive development stage of important inventions and discoveries and because there are economies of scale in innovation in those industries.

The one firm conclusion that seems to have emerged is that there are frequently marked economies of scale in the development of new products and processes once the seminal invention has proven to be commercially feasible; hence a firm cannot remain competitive unless it grows large enough to realize those economies.

Most of the investigations of the innovation argument have been conducted in the United States and, to a much smaller extent, in Europe.[3] And much of the recent concern in Europe about the relationship between the size of the firm and inventiveness is a consequence of the concern about the so-called technological gap between the United States and the rest of the world. The most plausible explanation of whatever technological gap does exist appears to be that American firms possess the advantage of a huge home market, the high income elasticity of demand for new products, and the stimulus of high labour costs in relation to the cost of capital.

It is apparent that most of the debate has limited relevance for Canadian competition policy. The Canadian economy is singular in the degree to which technology and innovations are imported. In general, on an industry-by-industry comparison, Canadian companies that are large by Canadian standards and also larger than the threshold of 5,000 employees do not spend a significantly lower percentage of their sales revenue upon research and development than do their foreign counterparts. But it happens that few of the large Canadian industries are the industries that are currently in the forefront of innovation. There is the additional factor that most of the research and development work of international companies doing business in Canada is undertaken by the parent corporations outside Canada. The conclusion would therefore seem to be that Canadian competition policy should be compatible with, and if possible conducive to, the entry of Canadian firms into the highly innovative industries, and they should not be prevented from growing large enough to realize the economies of scale in innovation, and perhaps should be stimulated to do so. There is also an obvious case for facilitating the development in Canada by Canadian companies of inventions originating here. The competition policy discussed in chapter 4 is wholly consistent with these implications.

The second part of the consumers' sovereignty rule is that the consumer is entitled to be provided with any commodity accompanied by as much or as little convenience, service, and differentiation as he most prefers. He should be free to choose to buy a commodity accompanied by the minimum of service and convenience or by a great deal, whichever his preference may be. And to meet the first part of the rule, the difference in prices of different product/service packages should equal the lowest attainable costs of providing additional amounts of the three qualities. So expressed, the rule is a statement of an ideal condition. In practice, the rule requires that commodities accompanied by a minimum of these qualities be available in every market. The Canadian economy is not deficient in providing adequate service, convenience, and differentiation. It is deficient in the provision of commodities with the minimum of these. The deficient provision of "economy packages" results from the stress upon nonprice competition to the exclusion of price competition.

Unless this economy package is available, unless the consumer is informed that the bare commodity is, for all practical purposes, identical to differentiated close substitutes, and unless prices differences equal cost differences, the consumer is not in a position to choose as much or as little service, convenience, and differentiation as he is willing to pay for. Conversely, if the economy package is available and if sufficient demand for the three additional qualities exists, their supply will be forthcoming, because the sale of higher-cost packages is usually more profitable than the production and sale of low-cost packages.

This matter is sufficiently controversial to warrant some elaboration. The optimum amount of service and convenience is easier to define than is the optimum amount of product differentiation. The success of the self-serve supermarket has demonstrated that a substantial proportion of consumers do not wish to pay the cost of more than a minimum of service and convenience. Consequently, when a commodity is not freely available at retail accompanied by a minimum of service and convenience, the first choice of a substantial proportion of consumers is absent, and the consumers' sovereignty rule is not satisfied. For convenience, a commodity accompanied by the minimum of service and convenience may be called the economy package. Whenever the economy package is freely available and there is sufficient demand for more service and convenience than it contains, it will be profitable for some firms to market the more-service, higher-cost package. If one has confidence in the free enterprise system, he perforce must have confidence that demand, provided that it is sufficiently concentrated, will call forth supply.

In large markets, when one observes that the economy package is present, one also usually finds that one or more higher-cost packages are also present. And when this is so, the latter requires no defence. Clearly, those who buy them are exercising their preferences; they have decided that the extra service is worth its cost.[4]

A range of choices consisting of the economy package and one or more higher-service packages may often be the closest practicable approach that can be made to the rule that consumers should be offered commodities accompanied by as much or as little convenience as they are willing to pay for. And more, if the economy package alone is available, it must be concluded that the demand for additional service is not sufficient to cover its cost. Also, if the particular market is large enough to support only one retail outlet, no precise statement can be made about the optimal amount of service and convenience. But in larger markets, whenever artifical restraints such as resale price maintenance, other restrictive marketing strategies of manufacturers, or even the resort to nonprice marketing strategies to the exclusion of price competition prevent the economy package from being freely available, the consumers' sovereignty rule is broken, and there is economic waste in the form of consumers having no choice but to buy more service and convenience than they wish.

Discerning the practicable optimum amount of product differentiation—including physically different commodities, styling, models, sizes, packaging, and trade names—is somewhat more complex. Let us assume that the preference for variety in widgets would not be satiated until forty models are on the market. Assume also that the total demand for widgets of all varieties, at any price within the relevant range, could be supplied by three plants of a size large enough to realize all but negligible amounts of the economies of scale and that any increase in the number of models of widgets produced beyond three causes average cost to increase. For convenience, any model produced at lowest attainable cost, that is, by a plant large enough to realize all the economies of scale and length of run, may be termed an *economy model*. In these conditions, on the assumption that the introduction of an additional model decreases the sales of all other models by varying amounts, the deadweight cost to all consumers of increasing variety is the increase in the average cost of producing all other models. It is clear that all who buy the new model are willing to and do pay its cost, but there is no ground for assuming that they would be willing to pay an additional amount equal to the increase in the cost of producing all others. In any event, they are not required to bear that cost. It follows that it is impossible for the market to identify the true optimum amount of product differentiation. Those who continue to buy the noneconomy models already on the market bear the greater part of the cost of increased differentiation.

To identify the true optimum amount of product differentiation, all consumers of widgets would have to be presented with all possible combinations of models from one to forty, with each combination accompanied by a set of prices. And the greater the number of models, the higher would be the costs and prices of every model except the economy models. (The price of the latter would remain constant because, by assumption, an economy model is produced in sufficient volume to realize all the economies of scale.) Consumers would have to know and to reveal their true preferences. Even if they would do so, all of the problems of weighting choices by different groups would need to be solved. The classic impossibility theorem of Kenneth Arrow concerning public goods would apply. It follows that the true optimum product differentiation cannot be identified.

However, a practicable optimum is attainable provided only that the consumers whose first preference is for an economy model buy a volume of widgets equal to or greater than the quantity produced by one plant large enough to realize all the economies of scale. In the example, if the first choice of at least one-third of all consumers is for the economy model of widgets, and if at least one economy model is marketed (at a price equal to the least attainable cost including normal profit), it can be said that the amount of product differentiation is at the practicable optimum. When at least one economy model is freely available, whoever buys a model differentiated from the economy model(s) willingly pays the higher price equal to the higher cost. And if there is sufficient demand for noneconomy models, they will be produced. It would still be true that the greater the number of noneconomy models, the greater would be the average cost of each. Consequently, whenever an additional model was successfully marketed, the greater part of the cost of the increased differentiation would fall upon consumers who continued to buy noneconomy models already on the market. However, since there is no way of allocating the costs of differentiation optimally, the actual allocation of that cost must be accepted as the best attainable. If it is correct to assume that the first preference of a large proportion of consumers of most products is for the commodity produced at lowest attainable cost, there is considerable appeal in setting up as the test of a practicable optimum the rule that at least one economy model must be freely available.

In the huge markets of the United States, it is not to be expected that there is much economic waste occasioned by the multiplication of models or other forms of product differentiation to the exclusion of economy models. For example, it is not asserted by critics of the durable consumer goods industries that the plant and firm and the length of runs of none of the models marketed are sufficiently large to realize the economies of scale. In general, however, much Canadian secondary manufacturing lies at the polar extreme; there is considerable evidence that typically no economy model is available to consumers and the shortness of runs is a major cause of the high Canadian, in relation to American, costs. This point is considered further later in this chapter.

The third part of the consumers' sovereignty rule is that the consumer is entitled to be informed. Obviously, the consumer is not able to exercise his preference effectively if he is unable to obtain precise information concerning the qualities of rival products or the range of products and services available, or if the cost of obtaining information outweighs the benefit. Information concerning the choice open to him should be supplied to the consumer at the lowest attainable cost.

Unlike the complex problem of the optimal amount of product differentiation, the general principle of adequate information is self-evident. The difficulties arise in the selection of a practicable optimum.

THE REFERENCE MODEL

The purpose of this section is to suggest a *reference model* of performance of an economy. The reference model postulates an economy in which, in the distributive sector, a substantial share of every market is held by firms that pursue the strategy of high volume and low margin and, in the production sector, a substantial market share in every industry is held by firms that practise minimum product differentiation and other marketing expenditures, including the advertising of trade names. This reference model performance would satisfy to the greatest practicable degree all three parts of the consumers' sovereignty rule.

In this section the overall argument of the chapter is stated in a general, approximate way. The ground is thereby prepared for a precise summary statement of the argument in the following section and for its development in later sections of this chapter and in chapter 4. It should be kept in mind that it is not contended that the conditions of the reference model can be attained in all markets and industries. But it will be argued in chapter 4 that a vigorous competition policy could push many Canadian industries towards the behaviour stipulated in the reference model, thereby effecting a significant increase in the productivity of the Canadian economy.

According to the analysis of chapter 1, most firms in most oligopoly industries refrain from cutting prices as a competitive manoeuvre because they recognize their mutual dependence. But the competitive urge remains strong and finds its outlets in endeavours to improve product quality and to reduce costs and by marketing strategies which include sales promotion, the control of distribution, product differentiation, and stress upon the service part of product/service packages. Improving quality and lowering costs, which are forms of price competition, always satisfy the consumers' sovereignty rule; but marketing strategies may not. Even though both sets of actions—price competition and marketing strategies—are copied by competitors, a company's preference for the latter is nonetheless rational. No matter what form the lower price takes, whether it be by a price reduction or by offering more quality per dollar, competitors endeavour to follow suit, and the usual outcome is a lower margin between prices and costs, which reduces profits for all the established companies. But the results of marketing strategies are not uniform. Product differentiation and sales promotion enable the most competent, imaginative, and fortunate firms to improve their positions without the erosion of margins between prices and costs, and superior marketing can be the substitute for the development of superior products which competitors can match only imperfectly.

The full range of marketing techniques complement one another, and all are usually present in various degrees. Sales promotion by the maximum exposure of the product to the market accompanies the extensive entertainment advertising of brand-name products, and the firm in an oligopoly industry realizes that it can achieve maximum exposure only by practising de facto resale price maintenance, that is, by minimizing the supplies of its products which get into the hands of retailers who do not adhere to the retail price suggested by the manufacturer. It is unlawful in Canada for the manufacturer to enforce resale price maintenance. But it is not unlawful for the manufacturer to market his product himself by selling directly to retail stores, or to grant the customary wholesale discounts only to recognized distributors. When all its competitors offer an attractive margin between the suggested retail price and the price charged to the retailer, any firm must do the same. Otherwise, the retailer will not stock his products or, if he does, will not display them or otherwise advance their sales. It is scarcely a puzzle, therefore, why a manufacturer becomes distressed if a discounter obtains a supply of his trademarked products and sells them below the suggested retail price. It is unlikely that the increased sales of the products by discounters will equal the decrease in the sales by other retailers, because the discounters have a smaller share of the market. The greater the sales by discounters, the greater will be the disinclination of other retailers to handle or push the product. Accordingly, the manufacturer must do what he can to protect the established retailers' markup. In short, the manufacturer must try as best he can to reinforce de facto resale price maintenance by trying to keep his products out of the hands of dealers who do not adhere to the suggested prices.

With the state of the law as it has been since 1952, these endeavours have led to an intricate game of wits, with the discounter gaining the upper hand only on occasion. The typical manufacturer of brand-name products has remained the ally of the typical retailer who, in his own interest, favours the retention of de facto resale price maintenance as protection against the rationalization of his branch of retailing. In the long run, the elimination of excess resources in retailing would be in almost everyone's interest. But the period of transition during which the excess resources were being eliminated would unavoidably impose heavy losses on many retailers. Such losses are the price of achieving higher productivity in a free-enterprise market economy.

Such defensive behaviour would be made vastly more difficult in the circumstances of the reference model. When a substantial share of the market is held by firms that pursue the strategy of high volume, low margins in distribution, and minimum marketing expenditures and product differentiation in production, price competition within an industry is all but unavoidable.

Solely to put the matter in sharper focus, it is convenient to indulge in some unrealism and imagine extreme conditions which go beyond the reference model and are unattainable and perhaps undesirable. Let us imagine a world in which there is no integration whatever between the functions of production and marketing. Let us imagine a massive resurgence of the independent wholesaler who is not tied to his supplier in any way whatever. And let us go to the extreme and assume that producers/manufacturers do not "sell" their products. Although they may advertise them, they simply maintain offices at which orders are received from wholesalers entirely at the latters' initiative. The manufacturer would be indifferent regarding to whom he sold, and he would charge a single price to all comers in the precise sense that any price differences would exactly equal the cost differences of making the sales, for example, a poor credit risk would have to pay the opportunity cost of any credit extended to him, including any additional bookkeeping cost. If a bulk order actually reduced handling costs, the price discount would exactly equal that cost saving. But there would be no discount based on the cumulated total of purchases by wholesalers during a year, and there would be no contract, written or understood, concerning guarantees of supplies or of purchases.

In such a world, distribution costs would be driven to rock bottom provided only that there were always present some wholesalers who adopted the strategy of high volume, low margins, and minimum sales promotion. Also, the retailer would be provided with a variety of product/service packages, so that he would have considerable scope to choose as much or as little service as he demanded at prices equal to costs.

Retailing costs in turn would be driven to their rock bottom, also provided that there were always present a sufficient number of retailers who adopted the low-margin, high-volume strategy. In general, also, consumers would be faced with a variety of product/service packages at prices equal to their costs, and they would be free to choose the amount and nature of service they desired at price differentials equal to the cost differences. All these conditions could not emerge, of course, unless the particular geographic market were quite large.

In the world imagined, the costs of distribution would be a significantly smaller proportion of the national product than is actually the case. This is also to say that the proportion of the consumer's budget spent upon distribution services would be reduced. Not all of the reduction would be a net gain, of course. The maximum of convenience now available, which the consumer must buy whether he wants it or not, does have some value to him. In the imagined market conditions, the consumer would buy only so much service as he wanted at their opportunity cost prices.

In the assumed market conditions, there is little doubt that there would be substantially fewer retail outlets—notably jewellery, drug, musical instrument, furniture and hardware stores, bank branches, and gasoline stations—and real estate, automobile, and insurance salesmen.

In the later sections of this chapter it is reasoned that most of the avoidable economic waste in the production of commodities would also be at a minimum if conditions approximated those stipulated in the reference model. In Canadian conditions, it is a reasonable conclusion that the gains from increased productivity in the production of commodities would be greater than the gains from the reduction of waste in distribution and other service industries.

The productivity of the typical Canadian tariff-sheltered industry is considerably below that of the corresponding United States industry. For all manfacturing industries, the *Fourth Annual Review* of the Economic Council of Canada suggests that the volume of output per employee is perhaps one-third less in Canada than it is in the United States.[5] The existence of lower Canadian productivity should occasion no surprise, although the magnitude of the disparity may. A disparity of considerable magnitude should not be surprising because, as compared to a firm which could sell internationally in competition with American firms, the plant of the typical Canadian import-competing firm produces the wrong products, with the wrong equipment, at the wrong location. The location is wrong because the locations chosen are those which minimize costs when sales are confined to the domestic market. The products are wrong because a full line of sizes, models, and lines is produced. Consequently, the plant encounters the considerable costs of short runs. And the equipment is often wrong because it is multipurpose equipment, designed to achieve lowest costs when multiple lines are produced. It is considered by many that a larger proportion of the lower productivity of the Canadian plants is attributable to short runs than to any other cause.

In the previous chapter it was said that the adherence of the typical Canadian import-competing firm to the production of a full line of products, models, and sizes puzzles many economists, but that no mystery surrounds such behaviour. The alternative would be for one firm to confine its output to a few lines and take over the market for them by pricing at a level which its competitors could not meet so long as they continued to incur the costs of short runs. The reason why no firm attempts to specialize and take over most of the domestic market for particular lines is clear enough. Nonprice competition is an ingrained habit. The possibility of deliberately embarking upon a program of price cutting is never entertained because it is assumed, with considerable justification, that the ensuing price war would be disastrous to all. As compared to the dangerous manoeuvre of trying to take over a market by achieving lower costs, competition by sales promotion is safe, because if costs are thereby increased, profit rates can be protected by all firms following the lead of whichever firm inaugurates a price increase.

In any event, the prevailing forms of marketing freeze firms into the production of a wide range and the marketing of a full range of lines and grades. When each firm has its own distributors, who handle only its products, the firm must have a full line to market. Specialization in a few lines would require that this form of marketing be replaced by a wholly different one.

These wholly different conditions are assumed in the reference model (remembering that the extent to which the reference model conditions can be achieved is held over for later consideration). Whenever a substantial share of the market is held by firms that use the competitive strategy of producing and marketing commodities at the lowest attainable costs, the required discipline of price competition is present.

To bring the matter into sharp focus, it is convenient once again to go beyond even the reference model and imagine that all distributing and marketing are performed by independent wholesalers. The conditions imagined would be the same as those just postulated for a world in which distribution costs were driven down to the lowest attainable. In the extreme, if all distribution were effected through independent wholesalers who handled most brands of the products of their trade, the need to produce full lines would disappear. Specialization would be feasible. And, in the extreme, many of the tariff-sheltered oligopolies might be transformed into limited monopolists competing less directly with one another. In that event it would be feasible for the government to lower tariffs to the minimum required for the sheltered industries to earn a normal profit when they were as efficient as their circumstances permitted.

If manufacturers were forced to sell on the same terms to all who wished to distribute their products, it is possible that wholesalers would reemerge in a considerable number of industries. And they would not care whether their full lines were drawn from a number of different producers. By shopping for the lowest prices, they might induce considerable specialization. It is to be expected that manufacturers would, one by one, give up their loss lines and the lines which returned least profit. Specialization in these market conditions would be much more attractive to the producer than it could ever be under present market conditions.

To gain most of the attainable increases in productivity, it would not be necessary to go to the extreme contemplated in the unrealistic, illustrative case in which no manufacturer adopted a nonprice competitive marketing strategy or even "sold" his product, but was simply an order taker. Most of the increase in productivity to be achieved by a vigorous competition policy would be realized, and the three parts of the consumers' sovereignty rule would be satisfied, provided that sufficient specialization could be induced so that there were at least one firm which would realize most of the economies of scale, prices were bid down to be approximately equal to the resulting lowest attainable costs, and a substantial volume of sales in each large retail market, say one-fifth, were made by firms pursuing the strategy of high volume and low margin.

While a saving in the costs of distribution and retailing and an increase in the specialization of certain of the tariff-sheltered secondary manufacturing industries would produce the most dramatic increases in productivity to be induced by the new competition policy proposed in chapter 4, significant increases in productivity would also take several other forms, which are discussed in the later sections of this chapter.

RÉSUMÉ OF THE ARGUMENT

In stark outline, the reasoning of this study runs as follows:

1. Most Canadian industries are dominated by firms which pursue nonprice marketing strategies that enable them to avoid intraindustry price competition. These nonprice strategies include the stress upon product differentiation and the marketing of full lines.

2. The absence of price competition is a necessary condition for the emergence and persistence of avoidable economic waste.

3. In the production of commodities, these economic wastes include some part of costs of plants too small to realize most of the economies

of scale, costs of short runs of multiple lines and models, and costs of multiple designs and stylings. Firms that produce differentiated products make and market full lines. The result is that more lines and models are produced than could cover their costs if the firms in the industry engaged in price competition. Sometimes, the absence of price competition also results in excessive reserve plant capacity.

4. The prevalence of nonprice rivalry in marketing also results in avoidable economic wastes in sales promotion; these wastes include the greater amount of resources devoted by manufacturers to selling to other companies and retail dealers, and the larger quantity of resources devoted to sales promotion directed at the general public than would be the case if every differentiated model were subject to the competitive restraint imposed by a standard model (the economy model of the consumers' sovereignty rule).

5. The prevalence of nonprice rivalry in marketing also results in avoidable economic waste in distribution, namely, the greater amount of resources absorbed by retailing than would be the case if there were always price competition among retailers. The excessive resources would be freed for a more productive use if price competition were not bottled up by voluntary price maintenance practised by retail dealers with the legal encouragement and active cooperation of manufacturers.

In this chapter *waste* is assumed to be the shortfall of actual productivity below that which would prevail under conditions of the reference model. That is, it is assumed that there is no economic waste if at least one model of a differentiated product is sold at a price equal to the lowest attainable cost and if a substantial proportion of sales at wholesale and at retail is made by firms that use the high-volume, low-margin strategy. In chapter 4 waste is more realistically defined as the increase in productivity expected to result from the measures proposed.

Wastes attributable to short runs, plants that are too small, and the excessive resources absorbed by retailing are probably each of considerably greater magnitude than all others combined.

There would be additional forms of economic waste to discuss if waste were defined as the shortfall below an ideal performance. Low innovative performance and slowness to adopt innovations is of paramount importance. But it is not contended that one can predict with any degree of confidence that an effective national competition policy would make the Canadian economy substantially more innovative, although a priori reasoning supports the contention that price competition spurs innovation. Of secondary importance is the loss of "con-

sumers' surplus" (discussed in chapter 4) attributable to the few instances of chronic departures of profit rates from normal. The sustained
high rates of profit of the medical drug industry, for example, constitute much less economic waste than the waste of resources by the
very extensive use of samples and detail men to induce doctors to prescribe trademarked products. However, when a monopoly or oligopoly
that produces equipment or materials which are used by other industries charges prices that are substantially higher than competitive prices,
there may be economic waste additional to the loss of consumers' surplus. If the monopoly price induces firms to use inferior, substitute
equipment or materials, costs of production are higher than the lowest
attainable because the resources used are greater than they need be.

Neither of these two forms of economic waste is discussed in the
following part of this chapter.

Forms of economic waste

DISECONOMIES OF SCALE

The first form of avoidable economic waste to be discussed is the diseconomy in production attributable to an excessive number of firms,
plants, lines, and models. Although interrelated, three aspects can be
distinguished: diseconomies in production due to plants that are too
small, the high cost of short runs, and avoidable costs of multiple designs and styling.

Various recent studies have cited evidence that a substantial part of
Canadian secondary manufacturing suffers from high costs due to plant
size being too small to realize most of the economies of scale in the
twin dimensions of size and of specialization.[6] Of the two dimensions,
small size and lack of specialization, the latter seems to be by far the
greater cause of high costs. Frequently the manufacturing plant would
be large enough to be economic if it produced only one or a very few
lines, but the multiplicity of lines raises costs substantially. Eastman
and Stykolt cite the automobile tire industry as an example: "In this
industry, the ratio of market size to the smallest efficient size of plant
was 7 in 1960, the actual number of plants was nine and some plants
were up to or exceeded the smallest efficient size. And yet only a very
small portion of the industry's output was judged to be made at

minimum costs, because of the large number of lines of tires made in each plant."[7]

An example of an industry suffering from both a lack of specialization and uneconomically small plants and firms is to be found in the furniture industry:

> Manufacturers are of the opinion that available economies of scale can be achieved in case goods or upholstery by a firm with an output of $15–$20 million per year. (Such a firm would have a separate breakout and dimension plant, one plant for chairs, one for case goods, one for occasional pieces, and one for upholstered goods. It would be able to centralize bookkeeping and maintain its own sales force.)[*]
>
> It is evident that the Canadian market is sufficiently large[†] to support several case-goods firms of this optimum size. Instead, there are over two thousand establishments, with the output of the largest limited to the $6 million range. Expansion of firms in the Canadian market has been deterred for two reasons.
>
> First, competitive pressures have not been allowed to operate to squeeze out the inefficient. Special government programs (tax concession, loans, etc.) have helped not only the efficient but also the inefficient. Even more important is the Canadian tariff, which has provided a price cover for furniture firms. While there is no evidence that the higher Canadian price has allowed higher Canadian profits, it has allowed continuing higher costs. But the nagging question remains: why has one farsighted Canadian manager not seized the initiative and, by increasing volume, reduced cost and price?
>
> Once again, the answer is that furniture is a taste item. And consumers prefer variety to lower cost. This is the critical trade-off. Industry spokesmen recognize that a large Canadian firm ($6 million sales) could decrease its costs and prices by 15 to 20 per cent by increasing its output to three to five times its present level.[‡] This policy is not undertaken, because this price reduction would be insufficient to attract such a large increase in sales.[8]

[* Estimates of optimal bedding plants varied greatly but ranged around a figure of $1 million in sales per year. Such an operation would include coilers, graneters, etc.

† Canadian sales of domestic case goods in 1962 were $126 million.

‡ i.e., we were told that a fully integrated firm could achieve full economies of scale at $20–$30 million sales (see above). Industry spokesmen estimate that this would involve a cost reduction of 15–20 per cent; our estimate (U) is $17\frac{1}{2}$ per cent.]

A crucial difference in the analysis of this study and of the Bond and Wonnacott study quoted above is indicated by the last sentence of the quotation. On the Bond and Wonnacott analysis, no Canadian furniture firm has expanded to the minimum size required to realize the economies of scale because, given consumer preference for variety over price, the domestic market is too small to enable a price reduction of 15 to 20 percent to increase sales by three to five times. A total of case goods sales of $126 million is an insufficiently large market to induce the emergence of even one firm with sales of $20 to $30 million.

If this analysis is correct, and if it applies to most other secondary manufacturing industry producing differentiated products, much of the analysis of the present study falls to the ground. However, while Bond and Wonnacott might be correct if they stated that managers are convinced that a decrease in price of 15 to 20 percent would not, in the long run, increase sales three- to five-fold, they are on treacherous ground when they assert, without qualification, that "this price reduction would be insufficient to attract such a large increase in sales." In the circumstances in question an extremely high cross-elasticity of demand is very probable. The commodities under discussion are extraordinarily close substitutes, for example, bedroom suites which are almost physically identical (Italian Provincial or Colonial Maple) but are made by different companies. Despite this, Bond and Wonnacott assume that none of the Canadian companies could win one-fifth of the market by undercutting their competitors by 15 to 20 percent. In contrasts, these authors expect that if there were free trade in furniture between Canada and the United States, Canadian firms would have to rationalize their operations and expand their total output to realize economies of scale in order to meet the prices of the American companies which would penetrate the Canadian market.[9] So it appears that no Canadian company could take over a large share of the market by underpricing its competitors, but the American companies could take over the entire market by underpricing *by the same amount*! It may be objected that the assumptions are not uniform; the American companies offer both lower prices and greater variety. While this is correct, there would be no significant decrease in the variety available to Canadian consumers if one firm won one-fifth of the market. For example, if there were fifty models of bedroom suites on the market made by fifty firms, most of them very small, and five of the largest combined to form a company with one-fifth of the sales, the number of models might be reduced to forty-five. Is it to be contended that the new company would not be able to retain that share of the market if its management decided to reduce the number of models produced, achieved economies of scale from specialization, and undercut its rivals by 15 to 20 percent? Further, are we to believe that a company which achieved one-fifth of the market by merger would not reduce the number of models, which are only slightly differentiated, in order to achieve lower costs by rationalizing its production? The argument that such a company would and could do so has even greater force when applied to mattresses, which is the other main category of furniture most discussed by Bond and Wonnacott, because the scope for variety in mattresses is markedly less than that for bedroom suites and other case goods.

A distinction must be made between two questions: What is the elasticity of demand for one among many slightly differentiated products? Why has no Canadian furniture company attempted to take over one-fifth of the market for bedroom suites by cutting its prices by 15 to 20 percent, on the expectation that its costs would be lowered by an equivalent amount once it has increased its sales by three to five times?

If the prices of all close substitutes remained unchanged, the answer to the first question is that the elasticity must be very high. The answer to the second question is to be found in some combination of three reasons. First, most companies with sales of $6 million would have difficulty finding the capital required to expand their capacity by three to five times and sustain the losses suffered for the first few years. Second, the risk attendant upon such a bold venture would be great. And, third, the company would not expect all its competitors to maintain their prices while it increased its market share fivefold. Probably the smallest Canadian companies would have no course but to maintain their prices to cover costs, with some going out of business as their sales decreased. But it is doubtful that the subsidiary of a large nonresident corporation would fail to react.

The decisive difference between the Bond and Wonnacott study and the analysis of this study is that the former implicitly uses a large-numbers monopolistic competition model, while I see the furniture industry as a conglomeration of oligopolies. In the former model, there are too many firms for action on the recognition of mutual dependence to be possible, and the products of all the firms are equally poor substitutes for each other, that is, all companies are equally close competitors with each of the others, although no commodity is a close substitute for any other (the symmetry assumption). In other words, product differentiation is so successful that the sales of each of the articles produced by the industry are insensitive to the prices of any of the other articles; the cross-elasticity of demand between different makes of bedroom furniture is sufficiently low to confer a significant monopoly power upon each company. I find these assumptions highly implausible.

The solution urged by Bond and Wonnacott to the low productivity of the furniture industry is that the Canadian industry be exposed to competition from the United States furniture industry and be offered access to the huge United States market. In contrast, it is a necessary argument of this study that there is an alternative route to the goal of higher productivity. If furniture manufacturers could be induced to engage in price competition, they would be driven into specialization, and the smaller companies would have to combine to survive. Alternatively, a less painful path to a rationalization of the industry would be by government encouragement of mergers and production agreements among the inefficiently small companies. In the likely event that inducements to rationalize operations would not be sufficient, the stick of reduced tariff protection could be employed.

It is relevant, moreover, that Bond and Wonnacott realize that the path of free trade for the furniture industry would not be without its difficulties:

> Because of its proximity, the United States provides by far the most promising export market. Even a limited probe into this market would greatly increase Canadian output and provide scale economies. But Canadian firms have not been able to market there at an attractive enough price. Even if full economies of scale were to be achieved by an expanding Canadian firm, its potential cost reduction . . . would allow a reduction in its prices only to about the U.S. factory price level. Even assuming that it could overcome initial design and distribution difficulties, the Canadian industry would be barely competitive.[10]

> However, the complete elimination of case goods production in Canada seems vastly too pessimistic a prediction; on the other hand, continued Canadian employment at present levels in case goods seems an overly optimistic view.[11]

> The most mobile segment of the U.S. industry (case-goods) that might otherwise find low Canadian wages an attraction has already gone (or is in the process of going) to the equally low-wage U.S. South. . . . Continued existence of custom work in Canada and (to a lesser degree) of upholstery and bedding is to be expected because of the localized or semi-localized nature of the product. On the same grounds there are good

prospects for the assembly of relatively inexpensive lines of metal furniture in Canada.[12]

It appears, in short, that Canada would retain the portions of the
industry that possess natural transport cost protection (and hence do
not require much tariff protection), but that much of the portion of the
industry which would be most affected by the reciprocal removal of
tariffs would migrate to the south of the United States.

It is suggested in chapter 4 that few gains in the productivity of
industries that produce commodities possessing a high value per pound
would remain to be attained by an effective competition policy if there
were already free trade in manufactured products between Canada and
the United States, because these industries would become completely
integrated internationally; that is, the production as well as the sales
operations of companies would straddle the border, and there would be
complete specialization. Alternatively, if one region of either country
possessed a marked competitive advantage for a particular industry,
total production for the combined market would be concentrated in that
region. For the former class of industries, free trade and price competition are alternative routes to the common goal of higher productivity.
For industries that enjoy the natural protection of high transport cost
as a proportion of the value of the commodity produced, and for the
service industries, an effective competition policy is the only route to
higher productivity; free trade would have little impact upon them.

The consequence of such an enforced rationalization of the furniture industry would, of course, be a considerable reduction in the
number of independent firms. But there need be no concern that action
on the recognition of mutual dependence on the part of the few remaining firms might be even greater than it already is. If tariff protection
were reduced to the appropriate level, the rationalized firms would be
unable to earn more than average profits after they had achieved the
lowest attainable costs from realizing the economies of scale in the two
dimensions of plant size and specialization. Potential competition from
imports would impose the strongest practicable inducement to efficiency
and competitive pricing.

Neither need there be any fear that the number of lines and styles
would be so much reduced that the consumers' preference for variety
would not be satisfied. While it may be a rational national policy to
ensure the continuation of a chosen volume of secondary manufacturing by tariff protection, including a chosen volume of furniture manu-

facture, it is not a rational policy to reserve all or most of the Canadian market for domestic production. Imports are the least-cost means of providing variety in lines and styling. If a forced rationalization of the Canadian furniture industry substantially reduced the variety of styles and lines produced domestically, the deadweight resource costs of product differentiation discussed under "The Consumers' Sovereignty Rule" in the first part of this chapter could be avoided by drawing upon imports to provide additional variety, so that the Canadian consumer could have a greater range of choice than he now has. If most lines additional to the economy models (which, it may be remembered, are by definition produced in sufficient volume to realize most of the economies of scale in the two dimensions of plant size and length of runs) were imported, the higher production costs resulting from a decrease in the output of all other models that resulted from the introduction of an additional model would be avoided. It is true that the consumer who preferred variety and therefore purchased an imported line would bear the (much lower) tariff. However, the duty paid by the consumer would not be accompanied by increased production costs.

The final effects of the rationalization would be an increased productivity of the furniture industry, accompanied by a moderate decrease in the share of the domestic market supplied by Canadian firms, and therefore a small increase in total imports and exports of the economy as a whole. Even assuming no reduction of United States tariffs, it is also conceivable that the Canadian industry might win a very small share of the United States market for the more expensive style goods.

SMALLNESS OF PLANTS

A very few industries that produce homogeneous products are entirely free from the diseconomy of short runs but have high costs because most of the plants are less than optimum size. Perhaps the best-known example is petroleum refining. Although scale economies are fully realized only by a refinery with a capacity exceeding 500,000 barrels a day, most are realized by a refinery of a 100,000-barrel capacity. Even in the largest Canadian refinery centres, however, not all the refineries are sufficiently close to the optimum that, for practical purposes, they may be said to produce refined products at lowest attainable cost. Eastman and Stykolt found that, when measured against their absolute standard of minimum least-cost size, no part of the industry was of "efficient size."[13] However, there are a few very small refineries that are clearly economic because a single refinery serves an isolated market, and the savings of transport costs available from location exceed the higher costs of refining. The defect of the existing situation, therefore, is that there are too many refineries in all centres in which there is more than one refinery. The explanation of this diseconomy is to be found in the nature of competition in the industry. The main product sold to the general public, gasoline, is given the appearance of a differentiated product, when to all intents and purposes it is homogeneous.

If regional markets were monopolized from the outset, there would be only one refinery. The monopolist would doubtless form several subsidiaries to market a number of competing brands, with gasoline being delivered from the single refinery to all service stations in the region. It must also be presumed that the monopolist would vary the optional additives among brands if there were any gain from doing so. In short, product differentiation could be as great as it actually is. If refineries which were of optimal size for each marketing area had been built at the outset, the full cost of refining crude oil would be a significant percentage less than it is. The gains to be had from a move towards the optimal situation, given the existence of the small refineries, would be much less. While substantial, scale economies are not sufficiently large that total cost would be reduced by the scrapping of a few small refineries and their replacement by a single large one. The economies of scale could be realized only gradually, as the increase in demand was met by the expansion of the largest existing refinery or from a new larger one, while the smaller refineries became obsolete.

It is noteworthy that free trade with the United States would not bring about a rationalization of refining in Canada, except possibly in the coastal regions, because the high costs of transportation determine the optimal locations for refineries. For example, the removal of tariff and other trade restrictions would not affect the behaviour of the major oil companies which operate refineries in Calgary. All are subsidiaries of United States parent corporations, and Calgary is separated from the nearest American refinery centre by transport costs. Free trade would provide no inducement to the major oil companies to enter supply agreements with one another with the objective of expanding or replacing one of the existing refineries while depreciating the others so that, eventually, there would be only one refinery, which would be of optimal size.

The higher costs of refining that result from the existence of too many refineries must be counted as a waste when the criterion is the shortfall below the performance of our comparison model, which requires that at least one brand of gasoline be sold at a price equal to the average cost of production, including normal profit, by a refinery large enough to realize most of the economies of scale.[14] How the optimal behaviour could be induced, however, is likely to be controversial. The government of Canada is presumably powerless in this matter. But provincial governments could use persuasion, since they possess the constitutional power to require the oil companies to divest themselves of ownership of service stations (which is the restructuring of the industry that holds greatest promise of maximum efficiency). In preference to this unwelcome alternative, the oil companies might be willing to rationalize their refining operations while maintaining their rivalry in marketing. If such an arrangement were attempted, it would be essential that the single refinery in a regional market be required to sell on uniform terms to all distributors, including private-brand jobbers who operate chains of price-cutting service stations. (The complications involved in eliminating price discrimination in complex situations of this sort are discussed in chapter 4.)

COSTS OF MULTIPLE DESIGNS AND STYLES

For some highly differentiated commodities such as television sets, the costs of model and style changes spread over a small volume of sales can be substantial. Where they are, some part of the design and related costs must be counted as economic waste, when the criterion is the shortfall below our reference model performance. The marketing of the existing number of lines and models would be incompatible with the production of at least one economy model, which was produced in sufficient volume to realize most scale economies. And this reduction in the fixed costs of tooling would be additional to the reduction of variable costs achieved by longer runs. Again, full rationalization would require that the number of models produced in Canada be greatly reduced and variety be maintained by increased imports. In some industries it is possible that the reduction in costs would enable a significant increase in exports to overseas markets.

WASTE DUE TO EXCESS PLANT CAPACITY

Although difficult to document, there is considerable evidence that Canadian oligopolies periodically have substantial unused plant capacity. Not all of it, however, is excess. A considerable part is consistent with production at least attainable cost because the smallest economic addition to capacity is often large in relation to the output of the firm. Oligopoly companies usually add to capacity at the same time, and the bunching of investment plays a major role in the short business cycle. It would be more economical if the investment in plant and equipment were undertaken by the companies in sequence,[15] and that behaviour would also reduce the amplitude of the short cycle. However, no one has suggested an effective way to induce the desired behaviour, so it must be counted an unattainable ideal; the shortfall of actual performance below it does not constitute waste by our criterion. Even a rationalization of the industries in which there are too many plants, by specialization and an increase in the average plant size, would not reduce the average amount of reserve capacity. With specialization, the capacity of each plant would have to be increased whenever its operating rate approached the maximum. And, if more scale economies were realized by plants being larger, the least-size economic addition to capacity would be correspondingly larger.

The excess capacity that should be counted as waste, therefore, is that which is not due to the indivisibility of plant or the maintenance of prudent reserve capacity. Excess capacity in this sense sometimes results from the inefficiency bred of too much security. One form of this inefficiency occurs when a stable oligopoly price promises an acceptable rate of return at low operating rates. Then, the firm is tempted to add to its capacity until its overall profit rate decreases to the minimum qualifying rate. The correct calculation, of course, should have regard only to the incremental addition to profits attributable to added capital expenditures. Also, the competitive urge seeks an outlet, and if other avenues are blocked, rivalry sometimes leads to the expansion of capacity before it is needed. Security and comfortable profit rates allow management to be slipshod in its forecasts—for example, by a naive extrapolation of recent rates of increase in demand. Also, the desire to increase market shares sometimes leads to the use of qualifying rates of return which, when discounted for uncertainty, are less than the borrowing cost of capital. This inefficient rivalry is particularly likely to occur with respect to sales outlets. And if the endeavour of one company to increase its share of the market is met by the determination of competitors not to allow their market shares to be reduced, substantial excess capacity can result.

Sometimes the socially wasteful excess capacity is seen as a means of discouraging entry. If excess capacity overhangs the market, the uncertainty of attractive returns to a new entrant is increased. And sometimes excess capacity results from a race among oligopolists to be the first to be ready to serve increased demand, possibly in the hopes that rivals will be discouraged from doing the same. If the tactic succeeds, though it rarely does, the bold firm stands to win a larger market share. Irrational as this behaviour may seem, it is not unusual. Towards the end of every investment boom, one can expect newspapers to carry reports of speeches by presidents of companies that are completing their investment projects, calling upon the industry to be prudent and not add unduly to capacity! And one can be confident that, a few months later, the same presidents will be voicing alarm over the large reserve capacity of the industry and urging all companies to "exercise self-restraint" and "engage in acts of statesmanship," meaning that individual companies should not try to improve their situations by cutting prices.

Finally, excess capacity results from the desire of the oligopoly firm to stake out a claim to a regional market which will be large enough, in a few years' time, for a single plant or sales outlet located in it to be profitable. Besides building the plant before it can be profitable, the claim-staker builds a larger plant than would be justified by the volume of demand alone and its expected rate of increase.

It is a reasonable expectation that, if price competition were present to impose a penalty upon overinvestment, oligopolists would be less inclined to engage in these socially wasteful forms of rivalry.

Since operating rates are rarely published, it is not possible to guess how substantial the loss from truly excessive capacity might be. Occasionally, however, objective evidence covering particular industries is available. For example, the fact that no shortage resulted from the prolonged strike that closed down about half the capacity of the meat-packing industry a few years ago indicated that capacity was excessive by any reasonable standard.

WASTES IN SALES PROMOTION

Much sales expenditure is defensive. If the efforts of rivals are not matched, a firm's market share will diminish. And if action on the recognition of mutual dependence enables the costs of increased promotion expenditures to be passed on to the consumer, there is almost no limit to the level to which sales promotion can be pushed. In a market economy, price competition is the only constraint that can hold marketing expenditures in check.

The proportion of sales promotion expenditures that is properly considered wastefully excessive is, of course, impossible to ascertain and highly controversial. But that considerable social waste does exist is also beyond challenge; the sales function is not accomplished with the least attainable resource inputs. For example, in 1964 the forty-one member companies of the Pharmaceutical Manufacturers Association of Canada spent 23 percent of their gross sales revenue to promote sales and provide information to physicians through sales agents, literature, and samples.[16] The main function performed was the conveying of information verbally to doctors and hospital purchasing agents—a very expensive and inefficient procedure. The practice persists because the consumer's interest is not protected by any form of competition that operates to ensure that functions are performed at least cost. A parallel occurs in the college textbook business. Publishers' agents call upon professors to bring to their attention new books which the professors may decide to prescribe for their courses, and the professors are induced to spend time with the sales agents by the free provision of books of interest to them. It is ironic that many of the most ardent advocates of efficiency in resource use, professors of economics, tolerate this inefficiency.

In addition to their sales promotion aimed mainly at the physician, in 1964 members of the Pharmaceutical Manufacturers Association spent 6.6 percent of their revenue on marketing expenses primarily directed to the pharmacist. Such inefficiency will persist so long as the consumer cannot avoid paying for the cost of a service because products alone are not available; only the package of sales service plus commodity is available.

It is also inefficient for manufacturers' sales agents to act as deliverymen and order-takers for small stores; the grocery supermarkets put an end to the practice years ago. The small merchant accepts the practice, for many lines of merchandise, because he cannot obtain lower prices by dispensing with the services. It is significant that this inefficiency has had to be eliminated by the independent grocery stores, such as the I.G.A. chain, which have decided that their best competitive tactic is to meet the lower prices of the supermarkets.

With the exception of advertising, most of the sales promotion expenditures of manufacturers are not readily observed by the final consumer. Probably this is why most complaints about high sales costs have focused upon advertising. Since advertising has been the object of greatest criticism, it is somewhat surprising that its most pervasive inefficiency is rarely mentioned. The standard and valid defence of advertising rests upon the function it performs, and that function is the conveying of information. Any critique, therefore, should include an evaluation of the effectiveness with which the function is performed. It is obvious that, by this test, the volume of advertising is grossly excessive—to the point of not just zero but negative marginal returns. The consumer is inundated by such a welter of conflicting messages that it is difficult for useful information to be received. There is no mechanism whereby he can select the information he wants to receive while blanking out the rest. The old saw about the world beating a path to the door of the man who builds a better mousetrap no longer applies. It is not just that he would have to advertise or the world would never know about his superior product; the situation is much worse. The volume of messages beamed at consumers that contain no information is so great that the inventor of the better mousetrap would have to have a very long purse to be able to buy the volume of advertising that could get his message through.

These statements are surely not exaggerated. Most direct mail advertising goes directly into the wastebasket. The small amount of information that is of interest does not justify the time and effort involved in searching for it. Similarly, most TV and radio advertising has become such a nuisance that few rely upon it for more than superficial information, although considerable persuasion is doubtless effected. Any improvement in the efficiency with which advertising conveys information must include a diminution of its volume.

The other major defect of the dissemination of information by advertising is inherent. There is always a bias against full disclosure when interested parties are involved. Public regulation might insure that the truth and nothing but the truth is stated. But it is not possible to compel disclosure of the whole truth.

In addition, any endeavour to increase efficiency of advertising as the means of conveying information faces the inherent difficulty that advertising is nearly always part of a package. The consumer is induced to accept what is not wanted (the advertising) as part of the price of obtaining what is wanted (TV and radio programs and the nonadvertising content of magazines and newspapers). In the latter instance, advertising is not just provided for a zero price; the consumer is, in a sense, paid to accept it! The price paid by the subscriber to magazines and newspapers would be much higher if they carried no advertising. It is anomalous that a substantial proportion of economists who share their profession's conviction that the price system is the most efficient allocator of resources fail to apply to advertising the rule imposed on all other goods and services, that is, that the correct amount is supplied and consumed only when prices equal opportunity costs. There is over-consumption whenever prices are below costs. How much more over-consumption must there be at negative prices!

Moreover, it is not only the advertising messages themselves that are overconsumed. Since the greater part of the cost of magazines and newspapers is covered by revenue from advertising, the price to the reader is much less than the full cost of producing the nonadvertising content. It follows that there is an overproduction of magazines and newspapers. Presumably the reason that economists rarely cite these products as examples of resource misallocation is that they consider that any dissemination of information has a high social value. But in view of the present-day surfeit of news and views available from all com-munications media, this is a questionable defence.

That the information content is not provided as a service which can command a fee offends the consumers' sovereignty rule in an additional way. If a consumer enjoys sponsored television and radio programs, he may well be willing to pay the price charged for the product-plus-program package. But the customer who does not enjoy the sponsored program is disadvantaged. The inclusion of its cost in the price of the product is analogous to the imposition of a tax. It is impossible to buy soap without paying for soap opera. The product minus entertainment is not available at a price reduced by the amount of the costs avoided. Accordingly, if the customer wants the product, he must pay the cost of the program. The latter is no more avoidable than is a sales tax.

The financing of radio and television programs by advertising rev-enue has some singular aspects. These programs have the characteristics of public goods; that is, if a program is provided for one or a few per-sons, it is equally available to all others who possess a receiver. There is no feasible way to impose a charge based on the number of programs consumed. Since they are public goods, the optimal amount of resources to be devoted to the provision of television and radio programs cannot be determined by the price system. Consequently, no very substantial improvement in the efficiency with which the functions are performed can be realized by an improvement in the performance of the price system, notably by the introduction of more price competition. The only choice lies between public provision of these services and public regulation of private provision. A particular defect of private provision is that undue influence over these communications media may be gained by advertisers. However, we may justifiably set aside this important policy issue as not falling within the scope of our enquiry, because only the elimination of advertising as the main source of revenue for newspapers, magazines, radio, and television could meet the undue-influence criticism. And that change would require far more than a reduction of advertising expenditure induced by changes in Canadian competition policy.

The fourth strand of the criticism of present-day advertising is that it erects barriers to entry to industries and places small firms at a competitive disadvantage by conferring an advantage upon the large, established firms: the economies of scale of advertising often extend far beyond the economies of scale of production.[17] In the main, these barriers are part of the circumstances which result in the prevalence of nonprice competition. They should not therefore be counted as defects additional to the wastes which result from the non-price competition. However, there is one exception. It is possible for firms which are already established in the market, and which are extremely effective in their advertising, to benefit more from an innovation than does an innovator. If the innovation can be copied, the ability to promote sales effectively may be more crucial to success than is truly original innovation. To the extent that this is so, the innovator is deprived of much of his proper reward and the drive to innovation is thereby diminished.

In view of all these structural defects, it may be concluded that whatever the amount of reduction of sales promotion expenditures that might result from an increase in price competition, it could be counted as pure gain. Since, for the most part, these expenditures have run into nominal if not negative marginal returns, the value of the resources freed for other uses would be an appropriate measure of the reduction in economic waste.

CHRONIC EXCESS CAPACITY IN RETAILING

To gain some notion of the magnitude of the savings which might be effected in retailing and similar service industries if the price discounter were ubiquitous, we may consider the gasoline service station business, branch banking offices, realtors, and the life insurance industry.

The price discounter does enter the service station business from time to time, often with dramatic effects, but his activities have been sufficiently contained that a full rationalization of the retailing of gasoline has not been forced in any part of Canada. That the resources used in gasoline retailing are grossly excessive is conclusively indicated by the fact that the rents paid by the lessee-dealers of the major oil companies do not cover the costs of the stations leased (maintenance, taxes, and depreciation).[18] This is despite the absence of the degree of price competition among the dealers which would drive their margins down to average cost, including normal profits, when their sales volume was at capacity (where capacity is defined as the number of customers that could be served at the peak hour without keeping any waiting). When private-brand jobbers and dealers secure supplies of gasoline at prices which are sufficiently low to enable them to post pump prices that are as much as five cents below the average pump prices posted by the major-brand dealers, the former's sales expand rapidly. In these circumstances, the sales of gasoline by the private-brand station are often two to five times those of the average major-brand dealer. The consequences are that the major-brand stations which are close to the discounting private-brand outlet lose volume and are unable to cover their total costs without assistance, and the major brands' share of the market decreases quite sharply. For example, it may take as much as two decades for a major-brand company employing the usual nonprice competition to gain 15 percent of a market, even providing that they are successful; the private-brand dealers have on occasion won as large a share in three years.

If the major-brand companies' reaction to this erosion of their market shares consisted solely of lowering their prices of gasoline sold to service stations, a rationalization of the service station industry would occur. Since the private-brand stations cannot cover costs without a higher volume than that of the average major-brand dealer, because their income from other sales (tires, batteries, accessories, and repairs) is negligible, they would be constrained to continue their low-margin policy. The resulting price competition would push a substantial number of dealers (some of them private-brand) into insolvency. An equilibrium would not emerge until sales per station had risen close to the physical capacity of stations to serve customers at the peak hours of trade without keeping others waiting and the average dealer's margin had become just sufficient to provide a normal return on his capital. In this equilibrium situation, with the industry fully rationalized, the price and cost of retailing gasoline would be the lowest attainable, and consumers would have their free choice of whatever product/service package they were willing to pay for. In high-income districts, a maximum of convenience, appearance, and service might persist; in low-income districts, no doubt the reverse situation would emerge. And there would be differentials in pump prices reflecting the differences in services offered. Hence all requirements of the consumers' sovereignty rule would be met.

The rationalization described above does not take place, mainly because the competitive tactics of the major oil companies prevent it. During the last decade, a standard strategy has been followed to confine the private-brand jobbers and the stations they operate or supply to a minor share of the market. First, the major-brand dealers are made consignment sales agents, so that the oil company becomes the retailer and can lawfully set pump prices. This accomplished, the pump prices of all the major-brand stations in the market in which the private-brand discounters are active are lowered to within a chosen one cent or so of the latter's pump prices. If the private-brand stations lower their prices to restore the initial differential between private- and major-brand gasolines, the major-brand companies lower their pump prices by the same amount. A price war ensues. It continues, with each price decrease by the private-brand dealers being matched by the major oil companies, until the former realize that they are not free to choose the differential between their pump prices and those of their major-brand competitors. That is, the price discounter is made to realize that he will not be allowed to capture a substantial share of the market by the device of pricing under the umbrella of a stable price maintained by the major-brand stations.[19] If the private-brand companies concede defeat, the pump prices are raised by successive steps, the major-brand stations leading and the private-brand stations following, until a new level of pump prices prevails. In Toronto the major oil companies have apparently not been able to win out over the chains of private-brand stations. Elsewhere, price discounters have been confined to small shares of the market. Nowhere, however, has the market been fully rationalized.

The proliferation of branches of the Canadian chartered banks is also often cited as one of the most striking examples of economic waste in the sense that the cost of the service is not driven down to the lowest attainable. The general reasoning applied to service stations can be applied to branch banks, with the important exception that a price discounter has never entered the market (and is not likely to do so). Before the 1967 amendments to the Bank Act, to all intents and purposes competition among the Canadian banks was restricted to the staking of claims to new territory by the building of branch offices in advance of the development of local demand sufficient to enable the new branches to pay their way and to the active bidding for the deposits of large accounts. Since the amendments, new competitive activity has emerged in several forms. The banks have met the competition of the trust companies by extending the hours during which they are open for business—a gain to depositors. Second, banks have introduced a new form of credit card. Competition among the banks has also bid up the rate of interest paid on savings deposits, and as a device to protect reserves against drainage through the clearances, much more extensive use has been made of compensating balances. (A compensating balance is the proportion of a loan which a customer agrees to keep on deposit with his bank as a minimum balance; it is the part of the loan which the borrower agrees never to use.) It remains to be seen whether this somewhat surprising outbreak of new forms of competition that followed the amendments to the Bank Act will extend to any cost-reducing rivalry.

The third "horrible example" of waste at the retail level is the realtors' profession. Unless he wishes to dispense with the realtor's services altogether, the person who wants to sell his house must buy what often appears to him to be an unnecessarily large amount of ineffective sales effort in the form of salesmen being constantly available to try to make a sale in the event that a customer might wander into their offices. And people consume this service to satisfy their curiosity even when they have no intention whatever of making a purchase. Like the major oil companies, the realtor companies are caught in the snare of service competition. Entry is easy, and salesmen are paid mainly by commission, so the firms compete by adding to their sales staff. In consequence, the average earnings of real estate sales agents remain low in relation to comparable employment, and there is a very high staff turnover. When, to rectify the situation, commission rates are increased, the effect upon salesmen's earnings is soon dissipated by an increase in their numbers. So the situation is perpetuated. One (bad) solution would be to restrict entry, as some real estate boards attempt to do (on occasion with the assistance of provincial governments). The other solution is the competitive one. If some firms offered less service to buyers but equally effective results to vendors for a lower commission, the industry could be rationalized. The most important component of the service being sold is information. Purchasers want information about the properties available, and vendors want them to have it. In the extreme, one can imagine a central exchange board at which all properties offered for sale could be listed for a fee per month. If a purchaser wished to consult the board, he could gain access for a fee. If he wanted to receive advice from a real estate agent, this too could be available to him, at a price. And if he wanted to be taken round by a salesman to inspect various properties, this could be available to him, at a price. Surely the excessive commitment of resources to real estate selling stems from the offer of services without a charge, coupled with the legal power of real estate firms to agree upon the commissions to be charged. If such lawful collusion were proscribed, it is barely possible to imagine that the counterpart of price discounters would appear in the largest cities and force a rationalization of the market. Even as matters stand, at least one such attempt has been made. However, without positive government action to get cost-reducing competition started, the prospects of a rationalization of the realtor industry do not appear to be very encouraging.

The final example of much-criticized excessive sales promotion is the life insurance industry. Group insurance is low in cost because sales as well as administrative expense is minimized. But the person to whom group insurance is not available cannot walk into an insurance office and buy insurance alone. He must also buy a salesman's services and pay a pro rata part of a similar service rendered to other persons to whom the salesman's attentions are equally unwelcome. The only hopeful remedy lies in the provision of information and advice for which a separate charge is made, coupled with the availability of insurance at prices equal to costs that include no element of sales effort. Such a system would also considerably reduce the magnitude of the existing violation of consumers' sovereignty in the form of incomplete information. It is more profitable for a company to sell a whole life policy than it is to sell a policy for term insurance with the same premium payable. The consequence is that term insurance is emphasized by very few companies, and customers often buy less protection and more saving than is appropriate to their circumstances. As in the case of the realtor industry, it is difficult to imagine that a rationalization of the industry is likely to occur in the absence of positive measures taken by governments to push the industry into cost-reducing forms of competition.

If asked to cite the branch of retailing that was the most efficient, had the least excess capacity, and engaged in price competition to the greatest extent in the sense that the adoption of the low-margin, high-volume strategy had forced the average markup to the lowest attainable, many consumers would probably choose grocery stores. However, this favourable reputation has been challenged by the Royal Commission on Consumer Problems and Inflation (Batten Commission).[20] On first reading, the finding of this commission of a rate of capacity utilization of only 50 percent may seem incredible.[21] However, objective evidence of the existence of gross excess capacity even in this relatively efficient branch of retailing was provided by the long strike of meatcutters and clerks in Vancouver in 1969. Nearly all the supermarket stores were shut down for several weeks, but the expected queues at the small independent grocery stores and butcher shops did not materialize. The modest inconvenience experienced by shoppers occasioned considerable surprise.

From the 1920s until perhaps 1950 or so, the winning of larger shares of the market by the grocery supermarkets forced a rationalization of that portion of retailing by squeezing out excess resources. Now, however, the rationalizing force of the supermarket seems to be spent. The large chains act like mature oligopolists.[22] They appear to be content with their return on equity capital, which is well above the average in Canadian manufacturing.[23] They do not shave gross margins to win larger shares of the market. And the small neighbourhood grocery store has retained a place in the market by offering service, mainly in the form of convenience of location and shopping hours, that some consumers are willing to pay for. Moreover, in the main, it has been in the grocery lines that supermarkets have low margins. The supermarkets erode gross margins on other lines, such as gardeners' supplies, only by featuring special sales during which large quantities of a commodity are sold at low prices. It is particularly significant that the Canadian supermarkets do not depart from the voluntary resale price maintenance of magazines, paperback novels, toilet articles, and medical supplies.

In the largest Canadian cities, especially Toronto, discount houses selling consumers' "white goods"—refrigerators, washing machines, and the like—have forced a considerable rationalization in those lines. One consequence has been that not much more than a little floor space is now devoted to the selling of these bulky electrical appliances in some of the large Canadian cities. However, the rationalization is far from complete, and the discount houses appear to be less active than they were during the 1950s.

In the bulk of all other retailing in Canada, any rationalization whatever is conspicuous by its absence. In many lines, the average gross margin is considerably higher in Canada than it is in the United States. And it is a common observation that the adherence to manufacturers' suggested retail prices is far more pervasive in Canada than it is south of our border. It was more than a decade ago that the activities of discount houses in the United States brought about the demise of most of the fair-trade laws which were enacted in the 1930s to enforce resale price maintenance.

3
The effects of the present law

Presumed intent

Although it is the effects of the Combines Investigation Act that are of primary importance, the degree to which the presumed intent of the law has been realized is also of interest. If it were decided that the objectives of the legislation had not been attained, there would be a prima facie case for legislative amendment. However, ascertaining the degree to which the objectives of the legislation have been realized is difficult because the intent of the statute is by no means easy to discern. There are six different sources of evidence of intent, and they are not likely to yield a unique interpretation. In addition, intent surely differs in degree even among members of the cabinet, and over time; also, it would be mistaken to assume that Parliament could know in advance of the application of general provisions in various circumstances just how they would want them to be made to apply.

The sources of evidence of the intent of the statute are as follows:

The plain meaning of the statute. This source cannot be decisive unless the provision in question is free of all ambiguity and of qualitative elements. And only one major provision is unequivocal—the ban on resale price maintenance. Even in this instance ambiguity is present, because no positive steps have been taken to ensure that the presumed intent is realized, namely, that the consumer should enjoy the presumed benefits of competition among retail dealers.

Debates in Parliament. This obvious primary source of intent comprises the speeches in Parliament when the statutes were enacted and amended and the reports of committees of the House of Commons and of Royal Commissions. However, conflicting views are present in these, and ministerial statements are notorious for their ambivalence.

Judicial interpretation. The use of this source implicitly assumes

105

that Parliament accepts the courts' interpretation as its present intent, despite possible apparent departures from the plain meaning of the operative sections of the statutes. But such an assumption is unrealistic. It is unlikely that members of Parliament or of the cabinet are well acquainted with the judicial interpretation of the statutes. Even if they were, it would not be realistic to expect that they would be in a position to push for amendments if they were not satisfied with the courts' interpretations. There are many calls upon their energies, and those who desired change would have to create a consensus.

In any event, the 1966 Reference to the Economic Council to study combines, mergers, and monopolies implies some doubts that present intent and current operation of the legislation are completely congruent.

Reports of the director. A secondary source concerning intent, which is in its own class, is the reports of the Director of Investigation and Research, Combines Investigation Act, since he is the official primarily responsible for enforcement of the provisions.

Cases taken to the courts. A complementary source is the cases taken to court and those which are not taken, and the cases lost by the Crown and not appealed to the Supreme Court. However, one might be mistaken in assuming that those responsible for the operation of the statute are always content to accept all judicial decisions as conclusive. It is possible that they intend to seek a new precedent concerning an operative section of the act when the appropriate case comes to hand.

The effects of the statute. One might examine what effects the legislation has had and reason back to intent on the unrealistic assumption that the actual effects must be what is now intended, whatever the original intent may have been. This procedure is based on the assumption that the provisions of the statute would be amended if they were not having the desired effects. This approach would produce the curious conclusion that several of the provisions of the law were not intended to have any discernible effect at all, since it is a reasonable conclusion that they have not had any.

One would expect that these six sources would produce somewhat different conclusions concerning intent, and all would be ambiguous to various degrees. In view of the impossibility of discovering intent with any degree of accuracy, the most convenient procedure is to start with the paragraph repeated without change for a number of years in the reports of the Director of Investigation and Research, Combines Investigation Act. This statement appears on page 9 of the report for the year ended March 31, 1968:

The purpose of Canadian anti-combines legislation is to assist in maintaining free and open competition as a prime stimulus to the achievement of maximum production, distribution and employment in a system of private enterprise. To this end, the legislation seeks to eliminate certain practices in restraint of trade which serve to prevent the nation's economic resources from being most effectively used for the advantage of all citizens. Parliament's intention, as expressed in the legislation, has been *to create an atmosphere in which those who are willing to compete for economic gain are free to do so. The statute does not require competitors to compete but merely seeks to remove certain classes of restraints on the process of competition.* Parliament has therefore enacted legislation which will prohibit or discourage the regulation of industry by members of industry and which will encourage the regulation of industry by the forces of competition. (Italics added.)[1]

It is a reasonable interpretation of this statement that the intention of the legislation is that the market should be allowed to work. It is implied that most companies prefer to engage in the required forms of competition or are constrained by market forces to do so, and therefore the market works well, provided only that those who would profit from erecting barriers to competition are prevented from doing so. The latter are assumed to be a minority; there is no need to induce the preferred behaviour. The legislation is negative in the sense of attempting to prevent proscribed forms of behaviour rather than positive in the sense of seeking to induce the behaviour desired.

Prohibited practices

There is no better starting point for a discussion of the specific practices prohibited than the operative provisions of the Combines Investigation Act. In the remainder of this chapter, each major provision is paraphrased and, where appropriate, a statement is made concerning its accepted interpretation and operation. These statements are followed by an assumption concerning the prima facie intention, a discussion of the extent to which that assumed intent has been realized, and a commentary concerning the probable economic effects of the provision.

COMBINATIONS, NOTABLY PRICE AGREEMENTS

Section 32 of the act provides that it is an indictable offence for anyone to prevent or limit unduly the production of an article, to enhance its price unreasonably, or to prevent or unduly lessen competition in the production, purchase, sale, storage, rental, transportation, or supply of an article or in the price of insurance upon persons or property.

Section 32 has been interpreted to mean that a price agreement is unlawful if the parties to it constitute nearly all the competitors in the market in question. It is assumed that the public is entitled to the presumed benefits of competition, so that any almost complete elimination of price competition by an agreement is undue. The minimum share of the market that must be possessed by companies not party to an agreement (and presumed to engage in competition with the companies party to it) in order to assure the public of the presumed benefits of competition has not been decided.

It is still not clear what the intention of section 32 originally was; there are several possible meanings of the words "unduly" and "unreasonably" in the injunctions regarding limiting production of an article, enhancing its price, or lessening competition. A generous interpretation would be that a restriction is undue and an enhancement of prices is unreasonable whenever a net disadvantage to consumers results. This meaning would imply that a rebuttable presumption was intended and the courts should be prepared to hear argument that a price agreement resulted in a net benefit to the public. And if this reasoning were correct, it would be conceivable that the courts would rule some price agreements to be lawful which are now banned. And if this were so, it could be reasoned that formal collusion is less prevalent and informal collusive behaviour is more prevalent than was originally intended.

A more realistic interpretation can be constructed by imagining what was going on in the minds of the legislators when the wording of section 32 was first drafted. Such words as "unduly" and "unreasonably" used as they are in the act, imply that the legislators had some sort of fair price in mind, just as most people still have. It would be a mistake to assume that legislators realize that there is no workable definition of a fair price except the price which emerges in the market under certain competitive conditions. And it would obviously be one to assume that the legislators anticipated that the courts would have no alternative to ruling that any agreement in restraint of competition was undue if entered into by suppliers who accounted for most of the sales in the market in question. Also, it would be unrealistic to assume that the legislators realized that any price agreement which did not include nearly all the suppliers would not be effective and that therefore, in effect, their wording banned nearly all price agreements.

Prior to the Second World War the Crown did not win an impressive proportion of the relatively few combines cases taken to the courts. The performance was reversed after the war. And there is some evidence that it took the cases won by the Crown, up to and including the fine-papers case,[2] to convince the business community that there was no rebuttable presumption, that the word "unduly" was not to be applied to the reasonableness of an agreement, and that, in effect, all successful price agreements were subject to a general ban.

The number of prosecutions of combines to fix prices has decreased in the last few years. One may conclude, therefore, that behaviour has changed so that where there was easily detectable formal collusion before, there is now either more carefully concealed formal collusion or conscious parallel action amounting to tacit collusion, or the independent setting of prices on the recognition of mutual dependence. But one cannot conclude that Canadian oligopolies engage in price competition to a greater degree than they would in the absence of the ban on price agreements, because there is little evidence of effective price competition among Canadian oligopolists. Nor has an allegation of tacit collusion been taken before a Canadian court.

Moreover, even if one were to assume that price competition had increased, one could not conclude that consumers had benefited substantially from lower prices attributable to lower profit rates. With few exceptions, the companies party to price agreements found to be unlawful have not earned profit rates much above average. However, it can be argued that these companies would not have restricted their profits to the amounts actually taken if collusion had been lawful, because company executives would have felt less compunction to justify their actions. When acting in a way clearly or probably unlawful, management must justify its action to itself. However, this last line of reasoning is not supported by the observation that the decades of legal price-fixing agreements in Britain did not result in significantly high profit rates.

On the other hand, if the ban on price agreements had resulted in a substantial amount of price competition, it could be reasoned that there had been a gain in efficiency of greater than negligible magnitude. Price competition is a goad to efficiency. Since it cannot be concluded that price competition has been induced among oligopolists, however, the increase in per capita income resulting from the law must be very small—too small to be expressed as a fraction of 1 percent. This conclusion stands, even though there is reason to assume that the total effect of the Canadian combines law has been greater than one is likely to conclude from a consideration of the probable impact of each operative provision separately. There is a subtle, indeterminate influence of the law and of public opinion which moulds the ethics and mores of the business community and thereby influences its behaviour in many inconspicuous ways.

The main reasons for the retention of the general ban on formal collusion, therefore, are that it is a necessary part of any coherent and effective competition policy designed to induce improved performance and that the independent setting of prices by oligopolists on the recognition of their mutual dependence is superior to collusive price fixing for the reasons discussed in the next chapter.

THE EXCLUSION OF SALES IN FOREIGN MARKETS

Subsections (4) and (5) of section 32 of the act provide that arrangements relating only to export trade do not come within the prohibitions of the act, so long as they do not restrict the volume of exports, injure the export business of domestic competitors, limit entry to the export trade, or lessen competition unduly in the domestic market.

Clearly, this hedged exclusion of exports from the ban on combines is among the most ambiguous and puzzling of all the provisions of the act. One is tempted to conclude that the legislators did not know what they were talking about. It is difficult to conceive of effective collusion among a group of Canadian companies with respect to their exports to their principal market, the United States, that did not have one of the following, either as an effect or as an objective: maintaining or increasing prices in export markets and therefore necessarily decreasing the volume of exports; maintaining or increasing the companies' share of an export market, thereby decreasing the share enjoyed by domestic as well as foreign competitors; excluding new entrants to the export trade; or, as a consequence of entering price agreements with foreign as well as domestic competitors, increasing foreign and therefore also domestic prices.

A generous interpretation of intent would be that Canadian companies should be encouraged to band together to plot jointly their marketing strategies and competitive moves when engaged in the trade warfare which characterizes the competition among some international oligopolies. This interpretation would necessarily contain the assumption that such banding together would or could increase exports. However, it is likely to have the opposite effect because joint action discourages price cutting by individual companies and discourages the meeting of price cuts by foreign competitors. A lower price may at times be profitable for one company when it is not profitable for all. In any event, the difficulties of arriving at a joint decision usually impart a bias in favour of inaction and sap the vigour of the most aggressive firm. The efficiencies sometimes available from combined action are likely to be realized only by an outright merger, and probably even then only when the most aggressive and efficient managers take over the operation of the merged companies.

The effects of the exclusion of exports from the ban on combines are not clear. It may be that some companies have been more inclined to cooperate with respect to exports (provided that they are not subsidiaries of United States parents). If so, the effects of the greater inclination are not apparent. In any event, it has been a long-standing complaint of some export companies that the exclusion is insufficient protection against their being found to have acted unlawfully when cooperating with each other in good faith to increase exports. Unfortunately, they have couched their complaint in such general terms that the precise purport is elusive.

The information of the Director of Investigation and Research is that the provision was not used extensively in the first few years during which it was in force.[3] There has been no report that its popularity has increased since then.

MONOPOLY BY MERGER

Section 33 of the Combines Investigation Act makes it an offence to participate in a merger which has lessened or is likely to lessen competition to the detriment of the public.

This provision of the act is generally regarded as being without effect. Only three cases have been taken to the courts under the present act. The first two were lost by the Crown, and neither was appealed to an appellate court. On the courts' interpretation in these two cases, there is no public detriment unless mergers are carried to the point of eliminating almost all competitors and hence all effective competition. It is not an accident that this interpretation is consistent with the interpretation of section 32 concerning combines; precedents interpreting the latter section were consulted to aid in an interpretation of the former. The courts distinguish only between the presence of competitors and their absence. Especially in certain recent cases, they have refused to hold that more competitors, and hence presumably more competition, is preferable to less. They have rejected the view that a decrease in the number of competitors imposes detriment upon the public unless the dominant firm, or group of firms, has reduced its competitors to an insignificant share of the market. In fact, if the judgement in *Regina* v. *B.C. Sugar Refining Company Ltd. et al.* stands as a precedent, a merger that absorbs all companies competing in a market is not necessarily in violation of the law.[4] In this case, the trial judge ruled that it had not been proven that the merger had operated or was likely to operate to the detriment of the public interest because, while no competitor actually sold in the regional market in question (the four Western provinces), there existed substantial potential competition from companies outside the region (from the three sugar refineries in eastern Canada).

In the third prosecution on a merger charge under Section 33, the issue was less clear-cut than it was in the first two. A producer of agricultural and industrial phosphates headed off potential competition by acquiring a company that had announced plans to extend its operations from the production of only agricultural phosphates to both agricultural and industrial phosphates. By doing so, the acquiring company retained its position as the sole Canadian producer of many industrial phosphates. Easy access to foreign supplies deprived the company of monopoly power with respect to its large customers, who bought 80 percent of its output. But twenty small purchasers lacked that protection. Although the company was convicted of three charges of monopoly behaviour, discussed below, the charge of monopoly by merger was dismissed.

It appears therefore that only two qualifications are required to the conclusions that the merger part of section 33 is a dead letter and has no effect of any significance. The first is that the most recent judicial interpretations may not be *stare decisis* and a new interpretation may be sought when a suitable case is available. The second qualification is that the compliance program instituted by the Director of Investigation and Research a few years ago may have discouraged a number of mergers. Under the compliance program, the director has encouraged companies to consult with him concerning the probable lawfulness or unlawfulness of actions being considered.

MONOPOLY BEHAVIOUR

Section 33 also makes it an offence to participate in a monopoly which has operated or is likely to be operated to the detriment of the public interest; the exercise of patent rights is specifically excluded.

There have been only two judicial decisions relating to monopoly behaviour: the *Eddy Match* and the *Erco* cases.[5] In 1952 the Eddy Match Company was convicted of maintaining a monopoly by successfully pursuing a policy of acquiring new competitors after undermining their trade by cutthroat methods and discriminatory sales practices. But the mergers in which it engaged were not dissolved, on the ground that the amendment to the Combines Investigation Act providing for orders of prohibition of the continuation of offences and the dissolution of mergers had not come into force until after the offence. In 1970 the Electric Reduction Company of Canada was convicted on three counts of monopoly behaviour and prohibited from entering arrangements with actual and potential competitors relating to prices or the division of markets, limiting the supplies of raw materials to competitors, impeding the entry of potential competitors, and for a period of twelve years, entering contracts for a period greater than one year for the supply of an industrial chemical of which it was the sole Canadian producer. The order of prohibition also required that, for a period of ten years, the prices of certain industrial phosphates charged to purchasers of a minimum quantity of a carload lot should not exceed the lowest prices charged by more than stipulated percentages. This prohibition extended to small purchasers the protection that easy access to foreign supplies provides to large buyers.

In addition to these two cases, there has been at least one instance of the prompting of a monopoly to change its marketing practices without its being taken to court. In their report on certain types of ammunition, the Restrictive Trade Practices Commission was critical of the restriction of the number of authorized dealers of the monopolist.[6] Subsequently, following discussions with the Director of Investigation and Research, the company increased the number of its retail outlets.

PRICE DISCRIMINATION

Section 33A provides that it is unlawful to grant any price concession or other advantage to a purchaser which, at the time of the sale, is not made available to competitors who buy articles of like quality and quantity. There is no offence unless, to quote from the act, the price concession "was granted as part of a practice of discriminating," and the return of a surplus made from trading operations by a cooperative society to its members is specifically excluded.

The price discrimination ban was first enacted in 1935 as section 412 of the Criminal Code but, as yet, no prosecution of an alleged violation of the provision has been pressed before the courts. It is possible, however, that certain types of price discrimination may have been discouraged by the director's program of compliance and by the unfavourable comments made in a few reports of the Restrictive Trade Practices Commission.

Three reports of the commission released in 1961 dealt with the distribution and sale of gasoline in Toronto. In the Texaco case, one independent service station dealer (that is, one who owns his business premises) received a discount from the standard selling price to dealers under the provisions of a long-term agreement. But no finding of discrimination was made because the allegations made by the director related only to the granting of "temporary competitive allowances." These allowances were discounts from the list price that were granted by the major oil companies to their dealers who were most affected by price cuts made by competitors during price wars. In the Texaco case, temporary competitive allowances were granted to a competitor for short periods when they were not granted to the complainant. The commission ruled that there was no practice of discrimination because the failure of the complainant to be granted an allowance at the same time as his competitor "was not due to an unwillingness on the part of Texaco to grant such allowances . . . but to a decision on the part of [the complainant] not to modify his pricing policy so that he would receive them"—an indication that the interference by the oil company in the pricing practices of its dealers was tacitly condoned by the commission.[7]

In the Supertest case, the commission again ruled that a temporary competitive allowance did not constitute a practice of discriminating. However, a long-term discount (of two cents per gallon) from the list price granted to a competitor but not to the complainant was ruled to be in violation of the ban on discrimination, and the commission recommended that a court order be sought which would restrain the supplying oil company from granting to the named competitor any price advantage not offered to the complainant. Inter alia, the commission rejected the argument of the oil company that the total cost of selling gasoline to the complainant who leased his station from it was greater than the cost of selling to the competitor who received the discount. The main cost difference resulted from the provision of a station to the lessee dealer at a cost of three to four cents per gallon sold to him in excess of the rent received. The reason given for refusing to take account of all provisions of the package of contracts made between the oil companies and their dealers was that the loss on the leased station was "not related to the cost of making a sale of gasoline but, rather, to the provision of service station facilities."[8] This conclusion is surely a prime example of refusal to look through the form to the substance of a series of related transactions. The real estate transactions would not have been undertaken in the absence of a supply contract tying the dealer to the oil company from whom he rented his station at less than cost.

In the British American case,[9] the circumstances and findings of the commission were substantially the same as they were in the Supertest case. Both cases were referred by the Director of Investigation and Research to counsel, with instructions to institute proceedings unless he concluded that the evidence was insufficient. Apparently he so concluded, since neither case was taken to court.

More recently, in 1966, the Restrictive Trade Practices Commission criticized some of the pricing practices of a producer and distributor of knitting yarns.[10] The company divided its retail store customers into three categories. "Small stores" were charged the suggested retail prices less discounts of 36 to 38 percent. "Small department stores" were granted discounts of 40 percent and "large department store chains" 42 percent. One very large purchaser received additional discounts not received by other customers. It was alleged that the company discriminated against stores in the first two categories that were in competition with stores in the third category and also discriminated against stores in the first category that were in competition with stores in the second category. The commission found that the discounts were discriminatory because the classification of customers into the three groups was very rough and ready and the discounts were not closely related to the volume of purchases nor were they in such a form that uniform discounts could be made available to competing purchasers buying like quantities. No criticism was made of the extra discounts received by the single very large buyer because it was concluded that they would have been made available to other purchasers of like quantities if there had been any.

The Director of Investigation and Research obtained a prohibition order restraining some of the pricing practices criticized by the commission.

PREDATORY PRICING

One of the several types of predatory pricing is coupled with price discrimination as a banned activity. Subsection (b) of section 33A (1) provides that it is an offence to engage in a policy of selling articles in any area of Canada at prices lower than those charged elsewhere in Canada if the practice has the "effect or tendency of substantially lessening competition or eliminating a competitor in such part of Canada, or [is] designed to have such effect."

A few recent reports of the Restrictive Trade Practices Commission concern alleged predatory pricing, and the reports of the Director of Investigation and Research of the last several years refer to a number of complaints received.

The most intriguing case that involved flagrant price discrimination was strangely not taken to the courts. In the Zinc Oxide case a processing company was able to eliminate competitors by underpricing them because its supplier of the primary raw material favoured it with secret discounts from the prices charged to competitors.[11] Among the puzzles of this strange case is the apparent absence of any advantage accruing to the supplying company.

The only case taken to the courts on a charge of predatory price discrimination was lost by the Crown.[12] The case was heard in the Alberta Court of Appeal in 1969 and concerned competition among three evaporated milk companies (Carnation, Pacific, and Alpha), each endeavouring to increase its share of the market. At the start of the period investigated, Carnation held 10 percent of the British Columbia and 20 percent of the Alberta markets, respectively. Pacific held 80 percent of the British Columbia and less than 30 percent of the Alberta market. Alpha had withdrawn from the British Columbia and held about 50 percent of the Alberta market. Then, in 1959, Alpha began marketing in British Columbia again. To gain reentry, if offered a price discount of 50 cents per case (1.04 cents per can) on a small number of cases of evaporated milk sold to wholesalers and placed 15,000 cases (1.5 percent of total sales of canned milk in the province) on the shelves of retail stores, advertised and sold at 2 cents below the going retail price for all canned milk sold by the three companies. That is, there was a strongly entrenched practice of price leadership and voluntary resale price maintenance. Pacific agreed to regard the two price discounts as promotions undertaken by Alpha to reenter the British Columbia market. Carnation, however, informed Alpha that it regarded the discounts as competitive price cuts, reduced its wholesale price by the 2 cents per can (96 cents per case) allowed by Alpha on a small number of cases, and cut its wholesale price throughout British Columbia and Alberta by an additional $1.00 per case. Pacific responded to the Carnation price cuts by reducing its wholesale price by $1.00 per case in all its markets, that is, the four western provinces.

An explanation of why Carnation responded to Alpha's price reduction of 2 cents per can (96 cents per case), given directly to the public on a small number of cases, by cutting its price to distributors by $1.96 a case was given by Carnation's sales manager in conversation with Alpha's sales manager. The reason that the price was cut in Alberta, where Alpha had a large sales volume, was that Alpha would not be hurt enough if Carnation just met Alpha's lower price in British Columbia. An additional explanation, according to one of the three judges of the court of appeal, was that Carnation seized on Alpha's promotional price cut as a means of eliminating the use by Alpha and Pacific of successful marketing practices which Carnation could not counter. During the period of low prices, representatives of the three companies met to discuss which marketing practices should be regarded as unethical and should be discontinued (for example, a price discount of 10 cents a case was granted by Pacific to a large wholesaler in Vancouver). In due course, several of the practices to which Carnation objected were discontinued and the price cuts were withdrawn.

In the view of one of the three judges of the court of appeal, the price cuts posted by Carnation constituted a practice of price discrimination designed to substantially lessen competition (Carnation maintained its prices in its major Canadian markets while reducing them in British Columbia and Alberta). However, another of the appeal judges was of the view that there was evidence on which the trial judge could reach the decision that he did, and therefore that decision should not be reversed. The third appeal judge conceded that Carnation might have seized upon the price war as an occasion to eliminate competitive practices but that such action was an incident of the price war and not an intent. Hence, the price war did not constitute a policy of discrimination having the effect of substantially lessening competition.

It appears from this very recent case that it may be well nigh impossible for the Crown to win a conviction on a charge of predatory pricing that results in a reduction of competition, no matter what the intent may be. It also appears that there was evidence for a prosecution of all three companies on a charge of tacitly collusive behaviour equivalent to a conspiracy to fix prices prior to and subsequent to the price war. Indeed, the negotiations among the companies to determine which promotional practices would be regarded as permissible departures from a uniform price established by price leadership might well be regarded as formal collusion to fix prices. The effects are indistinguishable.

Subsection (c) of section 33A(1) provides that it is an offence to engage in a policy of selling articles at unreasonably low prices with the objective or effect of substantially lessening competition or eliminating a competitor.

In 1966 a case taken to magistrate's court under this section was dismissed and the dismissal was upheld by the Ontario Court of Appeal.[13] However, the case was not a strong test of the provision, although it did reveal a great deal about the nature of competition in the dairy industry in Ottawa in the early 1960s. It was customary for the supplier to sell a limited quantity of milk to a new outlet of a chain of grocery supermarkets at half price for the first few days that the new store was open. In 1961 one of the four major dairies doing business in Ottawa arranged such a special for the opening of a large new retail outlet. The special was to run for two days, with each customer being allowed to buy two quarts of milk for the price of one. On the same day that this special was advertised, the newspapers carried an advertisement of a similar half-price special by the four Ottawa stores of another chain of supermarkets. None of the four was a new store. The dairy sponsoring the giveaway was a local, independent company. In response to this extension of the accepted practice, a competing dairy cut its price to all its wholesale customers, including the chain stores, to the wholesale price of the giveaway. Another of the four major dairies followed suit, and for two days a great deal of their milk was bought at chain stores. The sales of the other dairies, including the one which sparked the price war, and all door-to-door sales decreased correspondingly. On the third day of the low prices, representatives of the dairies met to discuss calling off the price war, the two price-cutting companies, faced with the threat of a strike by the door-to-door delivery-men, withdrew their low wholesale prices, and competition returned to its customary course.

It may be concluded that section 33A(1)(c) remains to be appropriately tested in the courts.

MISLEADING ADVERTISING CONCERNING PRICES

The 1960 amendments to the act added the new offence of promoting sales by making materially misleading representations to the public concerning the price at which articles have been or are ordinarily sold (section 33C). This section has proven to be the most popular of all the provisions of the act, with over a score of cases being taken to the courts for summary conviction. Most of the charges have concerned patently false statements that articles regularly sold for prices higher than they did—higher even than the manufacturers' suggested or list prices. As well as providing evidence of the effectiveness of the new provision, within the narrow confines of its wording, these cases indicate the deplorable absence of ethical behaviour on the part of some sections of retailing. Moreover, the subtler forms of misleading price advertising, such as an alleged special price of a newly introduced brand in circumstances in which it is difficult to conceive how the price could be special, have escaped scrutiny almost completely. Nor is it surprising that a substantial proportion of the convictions of the first few years after enactment of the provision concerned misleading statements by discount houses and by retailers who sought to create the impression of being price discounters. The manufacturers of the articles and competing retailers had a particular interest in lodging complaints.

Doubtless the provision has decreased the number of instances of the most callous disregard for truth in advertising. That the provision has also had more than a nominal effect upon the extent of price competition is rather doubtful.

RESALE PRICE MAINTENANCE

The winner among all of the provisions of the Combines Investigation Act is the ban on resale price maintenance. Section 34 provides that no manufacturer or supplier shall attempt to require or induce any other person to resell an article at a specified price, or for not less than a specified price, or to refuse to supply a customer because he has refused to resell an article for not less than a specified price.

The ban was first enacted in 1951, on the recommendation of the Committee to Study Combines Legislation (McQuarrie Committee).[14] In 1960 four forms of defence against prosecution on a charge of refusal to sell were provided. These are, to quote the Combines Investigation Act, that the person charged "satisfies the court that he and anyone upon whose report he depended had reasonable cause to believe and did believe" that the dealer was using the article as a loss leader, that is, "not for the purpose of making a profit thereon but for purposes of advertising"; that the dealer was using the articles "not for the purpose of selling such articles at a profit but for the purpose of attracting customers to his store in the hope of selling them other articles"; that the dealer was "engaging in misleading advertising" in respect of the article; or, that the dealer "made a practice of not providing the level of servicing that purchasers . . . might reasonably expect."

There is some evidence that the initial enactment of the ban had some effect upon the retail margins of at least certain commodities.[15] In addition, the appreciable number of enquiries and prosecutions indicate that the provision decreased, at least for a time, the resort to refusal to supply to enforce resale price maintenance. But it is not clear how much further one can go in deducing the effect upon the prevalence of price competition among dealers and manufacturers.

On the negative side lies the hearsay evidence of the last few years that the 1960 amendments have encouraged a return to the policing of the adherence to suggested retail prices. It is a common complaint that retailers of well-known, trademarked articles have refused to bargain over prices, claiming that, at a maximum, manufacturers would stop their supply if they did so or that, at a minimum, failure to adhere to the manufacturers' suggested price would jeopardize their amicable relations with their supplier, which itself is of considerable importance when the dealer is one of a few authorized dealers in a market. And certainly a literal interpretation of the escape clauses lends credibility to these hearsay reports. Surely any court would find it difficult to refuse a defence that a manufacturer had reason to believe that a retailer who sold his products for less than the suggested retail price did so mainly to attract customers to his store in the hope of selling them other articles or that the retailer was not providing the level of servicing that customers might reasonably expect.

The obvious intention of this general ban is that consumers should enjoy the presumed benefits of price competition among retailers. And a ban on refusal to sell as the means to enforcing stipulated retail prices is a necessary condition for the emergence of price competition in many branches of retailing, given the structure and practices prevalent in the Canadian economy. But a ban on the enforcement of resale price maintenance is far from being a sufficient condition for the safeguarding of the consumers' interest in price competition. In particular, a manufacturer is not required to accept the trade of a retailer who has not been his customer, so the ban on the inducement and enforcement of resale price maintenance does little to guarantee supplies to distributors who are known to be price cutters.

In the absence of positive measures designed to induce retailers to engage in price competition, and of measures to strengthen the position of those who charge low prices as their main competitive tactic, it cannot be said that the presumed intent of the provision has been realized to a significant degree.

CONSIGNMENT SELLING

It is apparent that the objectives of resale price maintenance can be realized by various departures from the usual arm's length dealing between manufacturers and retail dealers. In particular, consignment selling transfers control over the retail price to the manufacturer who, in law, becomes the retailer. The adoption of consignment selling by all the major competitors in a market has on occasion eliminated price competition in that market as effectively as could the most rigorous enforcement of resale price maintenance. In the North Star report the Restrictive Trade Practices Commission found that "though the letter of the Act is not violated, its spirit and intent are frustrated by the device of consignment."[16] The commission also referred to its *Report on an Inquiry into the Distribution and Sale of Automotive Oils, Greases, Anti-Freeze, Additives, Tires, Batteries, Accessories and Related Products* (1962) and to the recommendation made in that report that agencies and consignment sales be included in the definitions of exclusive dealing and tying arrangements that should be subject to scrutiny. No legislation has resulted from the latter report. This prickly problem was thrown to the Economic Council in the government's Reference of July 1966 concerning, among other things, combines, mergers, monopolies, and restraint of trade.

The only reported instances of resort to consignment selling by all the major suppliers serving a market deal with the resort to consignment by the major oil companies in response to the challenge of jobbers and medium-sized distributors. The aim of the oil companies was not the usual objective of resale price maintenance, namely, the prevention of price cutting by the manufacturers own retail dealers. Therefore, it is a reasonable conclusion that manufacturers have not made extensive use of this potential escape route from the ban on resale price maintenance. One is left to speculate whether the defences against charges of resale price maintenance enacted by the 1960 amendments have made it unnecessary for manufacturers to resort to this cumbersome device in order to confine price competition at the retail level to modest proportions.

OTHER TRADE PRACTICES

There are two constraints upon the firm's refusal to deal in addition to the ban on refusal to sell in order to enforce resale price maintenance. A monopolist may be required to sell to more retail distributors than he might wish, and the ban on collusion that restricts competition unduly covers collusive agreements among competing manufacturers to engage in a group boycott. The right of the manufacturer to choose his wholesale distributors and sales agents and his retail dealers, to adopt franchise arrangements, and to build an elaborate distribution and sales promotion system is therefore almost complete.

Similarly, there is no jurisprudence on the use of exclusive dealing and tying arrangements and, indeed, no law regulating them, even where they constitute the extension of monopoly power into distribution.

Summaries of intent and effects

INTENT

It would be tidy and gratifying if one could conclude that the clear intent of the Combines Investigation Act could be briefly stated in a summary of two parts. The first part would refer to combines, mergers, and resale price maintenance. It might be assumed that the intent of the regulations in these matters was that the consumer is entitled to the presumed benefits of *price* competition. The free enterprise system is based on price competition; with it there will be endeavours to produce better products at lower costs and prices, but without it there is no such assurance. Price competition is the guarantor of the consumers' interest; consequently, overt acts which restrict price competition are unlawful.

Despite the complications mentioned earlier, this remains the most attractive rationalization of the broad intent of the legislation. However, in similar statements of interpretation, other writers have used the word *competition* unmodified by any adjective. This makes the matter very ambiguous, since competition in one form or another is rarely absent. There is nonprice competition even between products of some small companies, let alone between divisions of a large company producing a variety of differentiated products. Also, when all companies agree to fix prices they still compete actively; nonprice competition among them may even increase. Similarly, resale price maintenance may result in an increase in nonprice competition; this is one of its defects. Moreover, it would be forcing a particular interpretation upon the legislation to assume that the legislator's and layman's concept of competition coincided with that of the economist. Nonprice competition is not viewed by the former with the almost unalloyed disapproval of most economists.

An assumption that the intent of the legislation is that the consumer is entitled to the benefits of price competition encounters the additional difficulty that, in the view of the courts, more competition is not superior to less; the distinction made is solely between some competition and none. Further, the interpretation would be based on the unrealistic assumptions that there will be price competition among manufacturers if only formal and perhaps also obvious tacit collusions are prevented, and that there will be price competition among retailers if only the enforcement of resale price maintenance by manufacturers is prevented.

If so much is conceded, it becomes impossible to formulate any brief summary of what the intent may plausibly be assumed to be. For example, it might be said that the intent is that the public should be protected from restraints upon competition that impose detriment on the public. But this statement is either circular to the point of lacking meaning or so ambiguous that it is implied that the legislators had and have no idea what restrictions upon competition result in public detriment.

The second part of our attempted summary of intent would refer to price discrimination and predatory trade practices. It might be assumed that the provisions respecting these matters indicated that competition among companies should abide by fair rules of the game. A person in business is entitled to be protected from unfair practices that violate his rights to compete on an even footing. No firm should possess a privileged position and there should be no compulsion upon firms to adhere to noncompetitive practices. For example, price discrimination that favours one company to the disadvantage of a rival violates the accepted rules of fair play.

This interpretation encounters the difficulties that only the grossest violations of the neutrality rule are banned, and such bans as there are fall on the form rather than on the substance.

In consequence of these difficulties, we are forced back to the conclusion mentioned at the start of this chapter: it is unrealistic to assume that Parliament ever has had specific intent or is capable of having it now. Only those charged with working out policies in practice can have such intent—or an expert committee which frames rules in advance of their imposition in the knowledge of all important practices and circumstances and the knowledge of how the rules will affect behaviour.

EFFECTS

A proper discussion of the economic effects of any economic policy measure should end in a numerical estimate of the improvement in the operation of the economy. Such estimates are usually expressed as a percentage of national income. However, to attempt such an estimate in the present case would be foolish in the extreme. The most precise conclusion justified by the information available is that the improvement in efficiency has been minute. The most significant finding of this brief overview is that the law and its operation have had little effect upon the most important forms of economic waste cited in chapter 2 as being attributable to imperfect competition. This conclusion holds even if one assumes that the total effect of the legislation is greater than the sum of the effects of the individual provisions because of subtle effects on the mores of the business community.

This is not to say that the legislation is unimportant and not worth all the bother it is to companies. On the contrary, it is an indispensable part of any more effective national competition policy. The main defect of present policy is that it is defensive and punitive and conduct-oriented, rather than positive, corrective, and performance-oriented. It imposes penalties on "wrongdoing" rather than seeking to induce "rightdoing." In short, it has the structure one would expect to find under criminal law. The constitutional powers of the federal government permitting, it would clearly be more effective if the philosophy, approach, and procedures of the civil law were adopted. In fact, most of an effective Canadian competition policy should be neither criminal nor civil law, but rather an integral part of overall economic and commercial policy.

4
Analysis of the issues

An introduction to the problems

ASSUMED OBJECTIVES

The general objective of a national competition policy is, of course, to increase income per capita by increasing productivity. The role of a competition policy is to force change and efficiency upon industries.

To make the objectives specific, I have adopted two general rules which are also criteria of business performance: the rule of consumers' sovereignty and the rule of fair competition among companies. The consumers' sovereignty rule is that the consumer is entitled to be provided with the goods and services of his choice at the lowest attainable cost, to be offered his choice of as much or as little service with a commodity as he wishes to buy, and to be accurately informed.

But consumers' sovereignty and the pursuit of efficiency will not offer guidance in all the problem situations. Rules of fair competition to protect one company from certain actions of another are also required. Specific rules can be worked out only with reference to specific practices and circumstances. The basic rules are familiar: no party should have a privileged position, and each person should be free to engage in the business of his choice (if he can secure the capital) subject only to the constraints needed for the efficient operation of the price system. For example, bankruptcy due to a firm's being less efficient than its competitors is a necessary constraint; the exclusion of firms from entering an industry by most forms of price discrimination is not necessary. Competitive advantage should rest solely on superior efficiency.

More specifically, the aim of the national competition policy should be to achieve greater productivity by a reduction of the avoidable wastes discussed in chapter 2. In the production of commodities, these economic wastes include some part of the high costs attributable to short runs of multiple lines and models and of plants too small to realize most of the economies of scale and some part of the costs of excessive reserve plant capacity. In distribution, the avoidable wastes include some part of the excessive expenditures on sales promotion and much of the costs of chronic excess capacity in many lines of retailing and in many service industries.

The specific goals actually chosen must be refined even further, however. A precise statement of the objectives requires that we first discover the degree to which and the means by which the wastes mentioned can be reduced. The objectives then become the realization of the improvements in performance which are concluded to be attainable.

COMPETITION POLICY AND INTERNATIONAL TRADE

Throughout this study, it is assumed that tariff protection of secondary manufacturers is continued. The assumed objective of the national competition policy is to maximize real income per capita without recourse to the full economic integration with the United States which would follow from free trade.

Stated differently, the goal is to minimize the price paid by Canadians for choosing to retain the moderate degree of independence of economic and political action still open to us. The most recent and first comprehensive estimate of the gain which might reasonably be expected from free trade in manufactured goods between the United States and Canada is about 10 percent of GNP.[1] One way of viewing the aim of the competition policy advocated in this study is the reduction of this cost of maintaining an economy, the manufacturing industries of which are not integrated with their United States counterparts, as well as the reduction of avoidable wastes in the service industries. Free trade in manufactured goods between the United States and Canada would result in the integration of most secondary manufacturing industries in the manner of the rationalization of the Canadian automobile industry that has resulted from the automobile agreement. It would not matter greatly whether the free trade were solely with our neighbour to the south or part of a North Atlantic or even worldwide common market agreement. The north-south intracompany integration would be the means to the higher productivity forecast to follow. Integration would be the purpose of the exercise and would be the means to the elimination of the higher Canadian costs attributable in particular to short runs.

Canadian companies in the tariff-sheltered industries would have to adjust to selling in the continental market. The adjustment would be the least difficult for Canadian companies which were subsidiaries of United States corporations. These companies would simply convert to branch plant operations. Some Canadian companies which are very large by Canadian standards might also find the adjustment manageable without changing their identity. To do so most would have to overcome the legacy of their having served the domestic market almost exclusively: a location which was right for serving the domestic market but wrong for serving a continental market, the high costs of short runs of a full line of differentiated products, and the higher-cost multipurpose equipment suited to those operations. Specialization could be sufficient for companies producing certain semiprocessed materials. But manufacturers of consumers' goods would have to continue to produce and market a full line and establish a marketing organization throughout the United States. This would require a great increase in their operations. Briefly put, such a company would have to emerge from the adjustment to free trade as a multiplant international corporation, and in doing so, it is not very likely that the Canadian owners would retain control. The specialization of plant operations on a few grades or lines, with plant locations ignoring the international boundary, would constitute as great a continental integration as would result from the branch plant specialization of the giant corporations owned by nonresidents.

While it is possible to imagine a large Canadian company making an adjustment of the kind described, it is hardly conceivable that a small company could do so. The obvious course for the latter is absorption by a large United States corporation. If it is taken for granted, therefore, that, other things the same, Canadians would prefer that companies doing business in Canada should be owned by Canadians rather than by nonresidents, it would be the part of wisdom for a Canadian government to encourage mergers among Canadian companies as the precursor to the negotiation of free trade, should that policy decision ever be made.

There is no ground for questioning the expectation that the path of free trade in manufactured goods would increase specialization and productivity far more than any alternative open to Canadians to choose. However, the almost complete intracompany economic integration which would ensue would reduce the scope of independent Canadian economic policy—and of political policy in many spheres such as international relations—almost to the nominal level. And the implications for the maintenance of a feeling of Canadian national identity are almost self-evident.

The purpose of these remarks has not been to argue adequately the case against free trade with the United States, in contradiction to the Economic Council's endorsement of that path.[2] The most important consequences lie within the purview of the sociologist and the political scientist and, in the final analysis, what one concludes will be determined by his value judgements, particularly by how much and why he cherishes a Canadian national identity. The digression was necessary to make clear the essential nature of the assumption that existing Canadian tariff policy will be continued. Free trade with the United States would greatly reduce the need for a vigorous Canadian competition policy. Indeed, the obvious course would be to copy the United States combines and monopoly law. With economic integration, Canadian companies would have to comply with the American law in any event, and it would be extremely difficult, if at all possible, for the Canadian government to impose regulations upon the commodities-producing industries which went beyond the provisions of United States law.

Confronting the issues

It is self-evident that there cannot be an effective competition policy unless a number of basic issues are decided. The first among them is whether the interests of the citizen as consumer should take precedence over the interests of the citizen as producer.

THE CONFLICTS OF INTEREST
BETWEEN CONSUMERS AND PRODUCERS

Though faith in Adam Smith's "hidden hand" is by no means dead, it is no longer fashionable to pretend that there can be an easy harmony between the interest of the owners, managers, and employees of an industry and the consumers of the commodities and services produced. The former want an ever-rising real income in the form of greater take-home earnings; both owners and employees want to retain the gains from increased productivity. They want security and stability of employment, a high return to their capital, and a comfortable life. Many assert a right to exploit whatever bargaining power they may possess. Above all, owners would like to avoid bankruptcy and employees the permanent loss of their jobs; economic change is a danger against which they must hedge and to which they must adjust. In contrast, the citizen as consumer wants productivity-increasing change, the gains from productivity passed on to him in lower prices, and commodities and services at the lowest possible cost—which is incompatible with the exploitation of bargaining power based on monopoly of any degree.

It has been stressed by some writers that company owners in service industries, most members of labour unions, and all government employees enjoy much security. The greater part of the gross national product is produced by industries which are either government-regulated or exempt from combines law. It has been argued that, in consequence, it is inequitable to deny to the minority to which combines law applies the right to screen themselves from the insecurity of unstable prices.

The policy question is whether the security afforded by a right of an industry to avoid price competition should be generalized or exposure to price competition should be increased to the maximum practicable degree in all parts of the economy (with a concomitant reduction in the bargaining power of some trade unions if this were possible).

In this report it is assumed that the latter course is to be adopted. It would be tragic if we facilitated the rigidities which cause economic stagnation. The interests of the citizen as consumer should be put ahead of the interests of the citizen as producer because, if this were done, there would be a net improvement to many even if those who gained had to compensate those who lost. We must give priority to the consumer's interests because that priority is a necessary condition for efficiency and an increasing real income per capita. Excessive security breeds inefficiency, especially in the form of resistance to change.

THE STATUS OF THE TRADITIONAL RIGHTS
OF COMPANIES

If it is accepted that the interests of the consumer take precedence over those of the producer, a reexamination of the status of several of the traditional rights of the company is implied. Among these rights, which are actually privileges, are the right of refusal to sell, that is, the right of the firm to choose its customers, especially when these are distributors or retail dealers; the right to use conventional pricing practices, such as basing-point pricing; the right to practise price discrimination; the right to merge; and, in general, the right to adopt whatever practice and to follow whatever course maximizes the firm's profits and size.

It is thought by many that such "rights" are so integral a part of the free enterprise system—which, correctly interpreted, means the freedom to be enterprising—that no separate defence is needed; to justify the rights is to justify the free enterprise system itself. But this view cannot be correct; if it were, the concept of free enterprise would be internally inconsistent. The unconstrained actions of one firm could restrict or destroy the freedom of others to be enterprising. Like all other freedoms, it can only be that the freedom to be enterprising means freedom of action consistent with the welfare of others, whether they be competitors or consumers. Consequently, the freedom to be enterprising implies only the freedom to pursue one's economic self-interest so long as the course followed does not, in the generality of cases, result in detriment to the consumer. Thus interpreted, free enterprise is quite consistent with the consumers' sovereignty rule postulated at the start of this chapter.

If this reasoning is correct, it follows that whatever the claims companies have of the kinds just listed, they are squatters' rights only. For example, companies have always been allowed to merge, so it is reasoned that they must have a right to do so. Or, basing-point pricing has never been called into question in Canada, so companies must have a right to use that conventional pricing practice. However, although squatters' rights to land have often been recognized eventually as outright ownership, there is no such tradition concerning general privileges or vested rights in a society. Governments have always asserted the power and right to rectify past errors. Retention of a customary right is subject to repeated justification in terms of the public interest.

Sometimes the reasoning relating to conventional pricing practices follows a different route. Great confidence is expressed in the unrestrained operation of competition in the market. It is said that a practice which has emerged "naturally," that is, in the absence of government direction, must be the most efficient. For example, f.o.b. pricing is the general practice of some industries, basing-point pricing of others. So it is reasoned that each must be the most appropriate and efficient for the industries in which it is practised. Little analysis is required to expose the fallacy of this reasoning. Cartels which corner the market and charge prices which, by any reasonable standard, are exorbitant, have on occasion emerged "naturally." But who would assert that they are the most appropriate and efficient? A pricing practice cannot be concluded to be efficient or appropriate without reference to criteria and without making use of economic theory, whether explicit or implied.

Of the four specific rights listed above, refusal to sell is the most likely to be taken for granted. But, far from being recognized under common law, refusal to sell was contrary to the principles of open markets in England of the seventeenth and eighteenth centuries. Recognition of a right of refusal to sell crept into United States law, starting with certain commercial law decisions of the lower courts in the nineteenth century.[3] Possibly, the United States practice flowed across the border unobserved some decades ago. However, the propriety of a government curtailing whatever right of refusal to sell may have been sanctified by usage was not even raised as an issue when the refusal to sell to a retail dealer who refused to comply with suggested minimum retail prices was made unlawful. The 1952 amendment to the Combines Investigation Act may, by itself, be taken as sufficient evidence that whatever rights to customary practices companies may possess, those rights are conditional only and are subject to withdrawal by Parliament in the public interest. The London Dry Dock and the CIL ammunition cases are also precedents indicating that no unfettered right of refusal to sell is recognized. In fact, the passage of the original combines act in 1889 carried the same implication since it set limits upon the freedom of companies to adopt the most profitable behaviour. And contractual rights, notably the rights to merge and to enter price agreements, were curtailed.

Accordingly, it is assumed in this report that companies have no vested rights to any of their traditional or customary privileges; all are conditional upon their being consonant with the public interest, and particularly consumers' sovereignty, and may be taken away without compensation. This strong conclusion has important implications. For example, Parliament must choose between two rules concerning mergers: (a) companies have the right to merge unless a tangible net public detriment is demonstrated, and (b) companies have the right to merge only if no net public detriment is demonstrated. The locus of the onus of proof is an important matter. If it is thought that companies possess a right to merge, rule (a) is clearly the appropriate one; if companies possess no such right, and if there is a presumption that, when generalized, mergers of the kind in question probably lower the efficiency of the operation of the economy in inconspicuous ways impossible to document, rule (*b*) is appropriate. More generally, the retention of any customary right is contingent upon the demonstration of a net gain in the sense that those who gained would be better off even if they were required to compensate fully the losers for whatever detriment they suffered.

ARE DOWNWARD FLEXIBLE PRICES INDISPENSABLE?

The next basic issue to be resolved is whether a national competition policy can be effective without inducing the pricing behaviour observed in an industry of pure competition. Is it crucial to the efficient operation of the price system that prices rise and fall with changes in demand in relation to supply? This is an important question because most Canadian industries are oligopolies that act on the recognition of their mutual dependence, that is, follow cooperative pricing strategies, and therefore prices rise and fall less than they would do if the firms were not collectively able to stabilize prices by curtailing output. It is not a question of prices moving only upward. Prices do fall when led down by one or more members of an oligopoly, usually either because costs have decreased or to meet or preclude the competition of an intruder.

Since profit rates are fairly stable from period to period, it can be reasoned that cooperative pricing behaviour increases the rate of creeping inflation only if costs rise more rapidly than they would otherwise. Money costs might be higher because the resistance to labour union wage demands is reduced by administered pricing. This issue must be set aside, because the evidence adduced in support of the contention is equivocal. However, real costs may be higher because an industry which adopts a cooperative pricing strategy is less efficient than it would be in the presence of price competition. The substantive issue reduces to whether the determination of prices by the free play of supply and demand is the only variant of price competition which effectively induces efficiency.

This issue was examined in chapter 2. The rule of consumers' sovereignty would be met at the distribution and retailing level if a substantial share of the market were occupied by firms which used the strategy of high volume and low margin. It is not a necessary condition that prices bob up and down in response to temporary shifts in demand. The issue is more complex with respect to the pricing behaviour of manufacturers and is the focus of discussion of the next section.

The remaining aspect to be considered is the effect of relatively stable prices upon the stability of employment and output. It is my view that a convincing case can be argued that the business cycle as we know it would disappear if all prices of commodities and services moved freely up and down relative to wage costs, in sensitive response to changes in demand in relation to capacity. However, this is not a view which is held by a majority of economists. In any event, the behaviour of prices in the manner required is not attainable; mutual dependence is much too strongly realized. Moreover, there is reason to believe that fully flexible pricing would not be viable for all industries. If prices were to drop below average cost whenever demand is less than the capacity of an industry, capacity would have to be matched up with demand very closely. Otherwise, the losses suffered when any excess capacity existed would exceed the profits made when demand exceeded capacity and prices were bid up well above average cost. However, such close matching of capacity to demand would be impossible to achieve when the least-cost addition to capacity was large in relation to the total output in the market in question. If the market served were a large international one, or even the total national market, and regional markets were separated only by transportation costs, the indivisibility of plant could be overcome. However, this condition prevails only for the commodities-producing industries—and not for all of them.

The conclusion that emerges is that the gains to be won from an effective national competition policy relate almost exclusively to increased productivity through increased efficiency. One must look to other measures to attain the goals of a high and stable level of employment and output and a stable price level. Secondly, fully flexible prices downward is not a necessary condition for distribution, retailing, and the service industries in general to satisfy the consumers' sovereignty rule of prices being driven down toward lowest attainable costs and the reduction of the wastes listed at the start of this chapter to minor proportions. The next section is devoted to the discussion of the best attainable behaviour in the commodities-producing sector of the economy.

MUTUAL DEPENDENCE VERSUS FORMAL COLLUSION

The existence of some reserve capacity is the normal condition for most of the commodities-producing industries, and it is not suggested that this condition could be and should be changed. Also, it is reasoned that pricing by oligopolies in defiance of their mutual dependence would drive prices below average costs whenever there is reserve capacity. It is apparent, therefore, that there is some validity in the contention that price competition can be too severe; in fact, it is implied that price competition is likely to be undesirably severe whenever the recognition of mutual dependence breaks down completely. And it follows that there is a case for an industry seeking to achieve some degree of security against unstable prices. But it does not follow that a price agreement is likely to be beneficial. Observation of the behaviour of Canadian oligopolists indicates that their almost unfailing tendency to prefer cooperative pricing strategies, and in particular the strategy of never increasing or decreasing prices except on the expectation that the price change will be followed by all competitors, gives more than adequate protection against price breaks which could result in large losses for most of the companies in the industry for long periods of time. On the contrary, the pressing need is for policy measures which lean the other way and diminish the security now enjoyed. The only exceptions to this assertion are the industries suffering from excessive ease of entry.

The grounds for asserting the superiority of the independent determination of prices by firms on the recognition of mutual dependence over collusive price fixing are sufficiently various that it is convenient to array them as a list:

1. In general, prices are likely to be lower when there is action on the recognition of mutual dependence than they are when set by formal collusion. The former affords the consumer the protection that prices are effectively set by the large company which is the least inclined to raise and the most inclined to lower prices. Second, with formal collusion, prices hold firm even when reserve capacity becomes quite excessive, but large excess capacity often precipitates a break in the price level when there is only action on the recognition of mutual dependence. Third, when mutual dependence is recognized, firms may still adopt tactics which are profitable to them but not to the rest of the industry. Consequently, price competition is not completely absent. For example, a firm might improve its product at increased cost and sell it at the same price as before; it is discouraged from doing so when there is collusion because, to be effective, formal collusion must prevent all unauthorized price changes and an improvement in quality is the equivalent of a price reduction. Similarly, firms are more inclined to try price competition in a peripheral market when the only constraint is the recognition of mutual dependence.

2. It has been observed that formally collusive prices are more rigid both upwards and downwards than are prices set on the recognition of mutual dependence. It is difficult to get agreement around a table; hence collusive prices are even less suited to changing conditions of supply in relation to demand than are prices set on the recognition of mutual dependence.

3. If there is action on the recognition of mutual dependence, the way is not paved quite so much for other tacit or formal understandings which are not desirable—in particular, joint action to exclude new entrants and market sharing so that a firm can relax and still earn acceptable profits. The recognition of mutual dependence does not often screen the very or even moderately inefficent firm from losses; formal collusion is more likely to do so.

4. The recognition of mutual dependence is much less inhibiting of the initiative of the firm than is formal collusion. When there are price agreements, the overriding concern is to prevent their breaking down. This concern channels the energies of management into unproductive lines and requires that the more efficient and more innovative firms accommodate the less efficient and less innovative. For example, banking hours were extended only after the demise of the agreements sponsored by the Canadian Bankers Association consequent upon the 1966 amendments of the Bank Act.

5. Price competition is a goad to efficiency, and collusion removes price competition completely, while action on the recognition of mutual dependence allows some leeway for it. There is probably some validity to the shock theory of managerial efficiency, that is, the notion that managers work harder and more effectively when under the severe pressure of trying to avert losses. At least, the writings and talk of managers seem to indicate that there is some validity to the idea. Certainly, it is no mean achievement to run a tight, efficient shop, and a decrease in profits provides an occasion for top management to apply the "whiplash of adversity" to the backs of junior management personnel.

6. The logical evolution of an economy composed of colluding industries is toward the governmental supervision of industry; action on the recognition of mutual dependence avoids that outcome. With only the recognition of mutual dependence, a modicum of the discipline of competition still prevails. If price agreements were to be explicitly condoned or approved individually by a court, following the precedent set by Britain, they surely must be kept under review, which requires

that there be surveillance. Otherwise, the consumer is robbed completely of the protection which is an integral part of the ideology of the free enterprise system. Since businessmen are the first to contend that governmental surveillance would take the enterprise out of free enterprise, this is one point on which there seems to be agreement by all the interested parties.

The reasoning just given sustains the traditional objection to any and all agreements to fix prices. Thus, the anomaly of the exemption of the service industries from the ban on conspiracies to fix prices is emphasized. To the best of my knowledge, the extensive writings on this complex subject contain no reference to conditions prevailing in the service industries which are not shared by the commodities industries and which make price fixing desirable by the former but undesirable by the latter. Neither can I imagine what those circumstances might be. On the contrary, if it is accepted that consumers are entitled to the protection of price competition among retailers of commodities, one fails to discover reasons why consumers should not also have the protection of price competition among barbers, realtors, and insurance companies. The recent amendments to the Bank Act may be taken to be evidence of an increasing realization that the case against price fixing is applicable to all industries.

SETTING PRICES INDEPENDENTLY

The corollary of a ban upon agreements to fix prices is an insistence that each firm must determine its prices "independently." But it is not obvious what this statement means when applied to an oligopoly industry in which each firm must take into account the reactions of its competitors whenever it makes a competitive move. Even the economist refrains from offering advice to the oligopolist concerning how to behave. However, if action on the recognition of mutual dependence is to be condoned while formal agreements are forbidden, there should be no equivocation when faced with the assertions that a cooperative pricing strategy is usually more profitable than a competitive one and that following a cooperative pricing strategy is most easily achieved by the observance of a pricing convention, notably price leadership. The fact is, however, that there is much equivocation, which apparently arises from a reluctance to condone such pricing conventions and an inability to prescribe an alternative.

The difficulty is inherent, because sometimes the only viable course is adherence to a decision not to engage in price competition or, at a minimum, not to precipitate price cutting. Accordingly, the difference between setting prices independently and tacit collusion inheres in intent. If a firm in an oligopoly industry decides to match a price increase or to refrain from lowering its prices because it has concluded that, in the circumstances and taking account of the probable reactions of its competitors, the most profitable act is to do so, the chosen action must be accepted as setting prices independently. But if a company follows the actions of others because there exists a mutual understanding among the firms in the industry to follow signals as the means to exploiting the monopoly power which the established firms possess when acting in concert, there is tacit collusion.

Thus, the line between noncollusive action on the recognition of mutual dependence and tacitly collusive behaviour is tenuous in the extreme. It is rarely possible to distinguish between the two by observation from the outside. If, on occasion, a large firm negates a price increase instituted by others or leads prices down, there is a presumption —but it is only a presumption—of independent, noncollusive pricing behaviour; when neither occurs, a presumtion of tacit collusion is justified pending further investigation. Therefore, when it is accepted that pricing by oligopolists on the recognition of their mutual dependence is the best that can be achieved in the circumstances, one must be reconciled to a considerable amount of tacit collusion. The conclusion for government policy, then, is to seek to weaken the tendency to follow cooperative pricing strategies by preventing established firms from putting obstacles in the way of companies seeking to enter an industry and by creating situations which bring the interests of companies in an oligopoly into conflict.

THE GENERAL VERSUS THE CASE-BY-CASE APPROACH

The Canadian Chamber of Commerce, speaking for the business community, has often argued that there should be a rebuttable presumption in trials concerning price agreements; the accused should be allowed to plead the defence of no detriment to the public interest. When this plea is made with reference to a particular case, it sounds very reasonable. But can it be generalized?

The objection to the case-by-case approach which has won the widest acceptance, even within the business community, is that it leads inevitably to the oversight of companies by an agency of government. Whenever the discipline of the market is suspended, an administrative procedure for consumers' protection must take its place, because there is no guarantee that the price agreement or other restriction on competition will continue to operate to the consumers' benefit. There must be either continuous oversight or a periodic review. A finding of no detriment or even net benefit is good at most for only five years. The United Kingdom Restrictive Practices Court has sought guarantees in some cases, for example, that parties to an approved agreement continue to use an independent cost accountant and that specific, objective formulae continue to be used for calculating prices on the basis of costs. It is clear that these safeguards are insufficient; the court must repeat its examination periodically and must on occasion order industries to behave in specified ways, as the United States courts and Federal Trade Commission do.

Policy must be based on general tendencies. Thus, speed does not always cause accidents, but it often does; hence a maximum speed limit is imposed. On this reasoning, it is irrelevant for a firm to make the reasonable-sounding plea: "Let us defend our record and prove that our profits were reasonable and that we are as efficient as can be expected in the circumstances. Do not condemn us for what we might do but only for what we are doing." If a court with the required expertise were asked to judge whether companies which were party to a price agreement had performed as well as could reasonably be expected in the circumstances, it is likely that the answer would frequently have to be, "Yes—in the circumstances." But this answer would not mean that there was no public detriment. The pertinent question is, "Detriment as compared to what alternative or reference situation?" The emphasis should be on the positive, not the negative. Instead of asking, "Was the performance reasonably good?" we should ask, "If circumstances were altered, would performance probably be better?" The latter question suggests the remedy, if one is needed and is attainable; the former suggests none. Thus the two weaknesses of the case-by-case, pragmatic, or performance approach are that it poses the wrong question and it does not indicate a remedy for defects.

If agreement can be reached concerning what performance will be under different sets of rules and different market structures, there should be little difficulty in deciding which performance is superior. If the government cannot reach such agreement, an effective competition policy is precluded.

The decisive consideration which dictates that competition policy be based on precise rules of general application is that there is no other way of implementing any of the measures ever proposed as the means to greater efficiency and productivity. For example, price agreements and resale price maintenance would preclude the operation of the available techniques for ending the perpetuation of excess capacity, whether in production or distribution, and the reduction of the costs for short runs. For this reason, the proper test for deciding whether a trade practice confers a net benefit or is neutral is not a comparison with the competitive behaviour likely to take place in the absence of the practice; it is a comparison with the competitive behaviour likely to be induced by the positive measures to be included in a national competition policy.

Similarly, it seems reasonable to say, "Don't judge the effects of resale price maintenance in general, but do so with regard to particular circumstances of each trade." But it is not evident why restricting competition among the retailers of, say, chocolates and confections would be beneficial, while restricting competition among the retailers of, say, men's clothing would not be. The effects of the restriction are the same. If it is agreed that consumers are entitled to the protection afforded when each retailer of clothing decides his markup himself, why would the reasoning differ with respect to the retailing of confections? The policy question to be decided is a general one: Does the market work best when there is price competition among retailers in the particular sense that there are present some retailers who use the strategy of high volume and low markup?

When applied to resale price maintenance, the case-by-case approach reduces the two contentions. The first is that markups would be driven so low that the number of outlets would be reduced to the extent that the customer would be inconvenienced; he would prefer more convenience and be willing to pay for it, but the supply is not forthcoming. This situation has never been observed. On the contrary, it can be said that only when the consumer has a full choice of combinations of product and services, ranging from almost zero to a great deal, is convenience provided in the amount most preferred.

The second contention rests on the assumptions that the manufacturer retains some rights respecting his products even after he has sold them, notably the right to protect the "product image," or that he possesses the right to conduct his business in a particular way, such as by selling only to retailers who will promote the sales of his products in the way he wishes. The effect of the exercise of such rights by companies can and should be argued out with reference to all cases at once, because the circumstances of the different industries and products do not differ in any relevant aspect. The case-by-case approach is neither required nor efficient. It amounts to going over and over the same ground.

There is only one respect, therefore, in which the businessman's plea for the case-by-case approach might be soundly based. That approach at least assures him of his day in court to plead that a particular trade practice is in the public interest. It might be contended that, otherwise, a particular practice is not assured of a proper hearing. For example, when amendments to the Combines Investigation Act are being considered, the hearings given to the defenders of a customary practice by a committee of the House of Commons may be claimed to be inadequate. If this contention is considered to have some validity, the appropriate remedy is the reform of the committee and its procedures or its replacement with a more appropriate deliberative body.

The last point suggests a related one. In a sense, the contrast between the case-by-case approach and general rules is misplaced. It would make little difference to the outcome which technique were used if the court or quasi-judicial agency hearing the cases possessed the required expertise, were given clear governing rules and criteria, and were told the economic theory they must follow and the economic generalizations they must accept as proven. If such instructions were those suggested as optimal in this study, all price agreements and like restraints of competition would have to be ruled to be contrary to the public interest, no matter how many particular instances were accorded a hearing. Consequently, the substantive difference in view does not really concern procedure; it relates to theory and criteria.

REFUSAL TO SELL

Perhaps the most cherished of all privileges enjoyed by companies is the freedom from any obligation to sell to a person or firm not of the company's own choosing. Nevertheless, refusal to sell *is* a privilege, conditional upon serving the public interest; it is not a vested right. But it is in direct conflict with the consumers' interests, and its removal is a necessary condition for increased efficiency and reduction in the major forms of economic waste. The extension of the monopoly power of producers into marketing by the franchise system, by their absorption of the wholesale function, and by all other marketing methods by which conditions are attached to the contracts with which wholesalers and retailers must comply facilitates the avoidance of price competition at the wholesale and retail levels and enables manufacturers to pursue nonprice competition to a degree which is wasteful of economic resources. Control of distribution enables producers to act on the recognition of mutual dependence in their marketing practices.

Removal of this right would be a drastic reform. The objective would be to approach as closely as possible the reference case proposed in chapter 2. There it was assumed that independent wholesalers and jobbers whose major competitive strategy was one of high volume and low margin held a substantial share of the market in every industry and market and that independent retailers pursuing this strategy held substantial market shares in every retail market.

REFUSAL TO SELL TO RETAIL DEALERS

It is unlawful for a manufacturer to withhold supplies from a retailer in order to enforce suggested minimum retail prices. This ban has probably decreased substantially the resort to formal policing of resale price maintenance, although the effects of the 1960 amendments are not clear. However, the ban is less than a halfway house. It does not require that a manufacturer sell to all stores which want to handle his products; it requires only that a store which has been a customer should not be cut off on account of refusal to abide by the suggested minimum prices. In particular, the ban does not compel a manufacturer to sell to a retailer who is not already handling his products and who is known to be a price discounter. Consequently, the dealers who are the most likely to inject price competition into a retail trade have no assurance of supplies at competitive prices. Existing law does nothing effective to end voluntary resale price maintenance.

The aim of the ban on the enforcement of resale price maintenance is to assure the customer of the protection of price competition among retail dealers. Since this objective is not in question, the adoption of the only measures which can attain it should not be either.

There are only two rational reasons for a manufacturer to use a franchise system. One is that he wishes to extend the action on the recognition of mutual dependence to the retail price; the other is to induce the retailers to perform functions which he would not otherwise perform. Otherwise stated, the alleged beneficial operation of a franchise system is that it enables the manufacturer to induce the retailer to act as his sales agent. To this end the manufacturer limits the number of dealers handling his products in order to confer some measure of monopoly power upon them. The monopoly power enables the franchised agents to make profits high enough to induce them to act as his agent and perform the functions he wishes them to in the way he dictates.

The use by the manufacturer of the retailer as his agent is, of course, a matter of many degrees. In the absence of the franchise system, the agency function may degenerate into little more than the willingness of the retailer to handle a product, which at least serves the objective of maximum exposure to the market. Often, protection of the product image by not cheapening it with a lower price is also an objective. The sales effort sought includes various combinations of demonstration of the product, conveying of information about it, staff time to induce customers to buy, persuasion concerning its real or alleged superiority, and services such as delivery, the extension of credit, and the provision of repairs and replacements in accordance with the manufacturer's warranty.

All these forms of the agency function are cost-increasing, nonprice competition. Of course, most have some value to some customers. But so long as the consumer has no alternative to buying the package of product plus service, he often has to pay for services he does not want and consumes more of them than he would choose to if he had a choice. Usually, the most expensive part of the service is the convenience afforded by a large number of retail outlets and the maintenance of retail capacity which is not taxed even at rush hours during busy seasons.

It is sometimes contended that a marketing scheme that induces retailers to act as a manufacturer's sales agent is the most effective way of ensuring that the retail function is properly performed, that consumers are provided with adequate information about the qualities and correct use of products and are shown how to operate mechanical products. For example, it is argued that oil companies must have some control over service stations to ensure that gasoline is properly handled, that pharmacists must have an attractive markup to compensate them for the care they should exercise in the filling of prescriptions, that the number of stores handling sportsmen's ammunition must be restricted so that they will be able to afford to exercise proper care in the handling of a dangerous product, that booksellers must have an attractive mark-up to induce them to carry a large stock, and that the number of stores handling cameras, automobiles, washing machines, and other durable consumer goods must be restricted and retailers assured high markups to induce them to demonstrate how to operate mechanical products. Even if these arguments were correct, however, the use of retailers as manufacturers' agents would be a second-best system because of its very high cost. And it is doubtful that the objectives just cited either have been achieved to a significant degree or could not be realized at much less cost. There is a conflict of interest between the manufacturer and the retailer. The manufacturer's objective is to maximize sales effort on his behalf per dollar of the retailer's margin; the retailer's profit objective dictates that he minimize the sales effort beneficial to particular manufacturers. It is arguable that the most effective way for a manufacturer to convey information about the quality and operation of his products is to staff his own demonstration stations and the best way for him to infuse his warranty with full value to the consumer is to perform the warranty function himself.

There remains to be discussed the contention that no-service retailers eliminate high-service dealers. It is true that price competition between the two types of outlet reduces the number of outlets and causes many high-service dealers to convert into low-service ones. This is the necessary condition of providing the consumer with services and commodities at their lowest attainable costs. But to say that services which cannot be separated from the sale—convenient location, credit terms, delivery, prompt service, courteous sales clerks, wiping windows and checking the oil level of automobiles, and the like—cannot exist in the presence of low-service, low-price competition is to say that there is an insufficient number of consumers who want these services sufficiently to be willing to pay their cost, so that the high-services outlets cannot survive. But if this is so, there is no reason why the service should be provided. It all boils down to whether one has confidence in the operation of the competitive market system.

It may be concluded that whatever gains may be thought to be derived from the right of the manufacturer to refuse to sell to retailers, they are small in relation to the gains to be derived from the introduction of price competition among retailers. The latter is the means to the reduction of the economic waste in the form of far more resources devoted to retailing than the consumer would choose if he had a free choice.

Removal of the right of refusal to sell to retailers, however, would not always be sufficient by itself to stimulate price competition among retailers. Supplies at competitive prices would be assured for price discounters who confined their activities entirely to retailing. Very often, however, the most aggressive price cutters are distributors or operate a number of retail outlets and also perform the wholesale function for themselves. The assurance of supplies to these companies and the manufacturers' right to choose his distributors are incompatible.

REFUSAL TO SELL TO DISTRIBUTORS

Why have manufacturers taken over the wholesale function? Why do so many producers of differentiated products sell directly to retailers? And when they do not sell directly, why do manufacturers restrict distribution to authorized distributors, jobbers, or wholesalers —an application of the franchise system at the jobber level? In short, why have firms integrated marketing with production? The obvious answer is that integration provides the most efficient and least costly way of carrying out the marketing strategy they have chosen. But this is true only when that strategy places primary emphasis on product differentiation and sales effort. Integration enables oligopolies to avoid price competition with one another at the wholesale and retail level, as well as with respect to the manufacturer's price. Integration of marketing with production is a necessary condition for voluntary resale price maintenance, that is, the adherence to suggested retail prices voluntarily by retailers without an overt threat of the withdrawal of supplies. If manufacturers sold their products on equal terms to all distributors, those who were "professional price-cutters" would quickly impose price competition upon the prices which retailers paid and thus also upon the prices they charged. Consequently, the existing right of refusal to sell at the wholesale level is actually a right to engage in nonprice competition to the exclusion of price competition. It is therefore incompatible with the objective of providing consumers with products at the least attainable cost.

The least-cost objective requires not only the increase in productivity by retailers but also the elimination of the waste of nonproductive sales effort by manufacturers' sales agents (whether they be employees or authorized distributors). The excessive use of resources by producers' sales agents in the pharmaceutical industry has received considerable attention recently in consequence of investigations in the United States as well as in Canada. There is much evidence that this industry is not an isolated, nontypical example—the exception that proves the rule. Despite the changes in methods and the increase in productivity of the last few decades, there is evidence that much fat remains to be sweated off. Even the rather quaint custom of salesmen calling frequently on retailers to take orders and chat awhile, just to make sure they do not begin to favour competing brands, is still fairly common.

The right of the producer to choose his distributors is even more entrenched than the right to choose retailers. There is nothing in Canadian restrictive trade practices law which requires that a manufacturer sell to a wholesaler who wants to handle his products, even if the latter is not a price-cutter. However, either that right must be withdrawn or its retention must be given priority over the objective of maximum attainable productivity. The conflict between the interests of producers and those of consumers is irreconcilable.

Withdrawal of the right would not be a simple matter. It would not be sufficient to require that manufacturers admit all qualified applicants to their list of authorized dealers. It would be necessary to require that producers be willing to sell to wholesalers who apply to them even if they now perform all the wholesale functions themselves, selling only to retailers, other manufacturers, or the final consumer. Otherwise, the firm which did not want to see its controlled marketing system broken down could simply convert its recognized distributors into sales subsidiaries. Moreover, assurance of supplies is an empty privilege unless the supplies are available at competitive prices. And it appears that the only way to accomplish this objective would be to empower a quasi-judicial agency to establish a uniform manufacturers' selling price so that there would be no price discrimination. If the greater part of the manufacturers' output were sold to authorized distributors, it would suffice to require that there be no price discrimination. But where there was no authorized distributor, or if sales to them were only a small part of output, the agency would have to calculate a manufacturer's selling price by deducting distribution costs from the price to retailers. There would be many controversies concerning the dividing line between distribution and other costs. Unfortunately, no way of avoiding these difficulties comes to mind. The problem would be reduced by a ban on price discrimination on sales to retailers, so that there would at least be a uniform wholesale price on which to base calculations. Even so, the problem could not be solved by a once-for-all-time calculation, on the basis of costs in a base period, of a discount to be applied to the wholesale price. The discount would have to be kept current by its recalculation at least every few years. The best of calculations might still be inaccurate because, ideally, the discount should be based on the distribution costs of the current rather than of a prior period. But precise accuracy would not be needed to attain the objectives. Consequently, controversies over the items of cost which should be taken into account when calculating the discount could be minimized by a small bias in favour of understating the discount.

There would be additional complications where a manufacturer sold both nationally advertised brands of his products to wholesalers and almost identical unbranded articles to firms which were both retailers and wholesalers, for example, department and grocery store chains. These problems are examined under "Different Classes of Buyers" in the section below entitled "Price Discrimination on Sales to Firms Which Compete with Each Other."

Another difficulty concerns the establishment of jobber status. Obviously, the manufacturer could not be required to sell at a manufacturer's price to every party who represented himself as a jobber. Consequently, the quasi-judicial agency would have to rule whether an applicant was a bona fide jobber, and it would be appropriate that such status should be denied where the applicant did not possess the appropriate facilities or otherwise failed to demonstrate competence to perform the jobber function.

It is apparent that the law appropriate for withdrawal of the producer's right of refusal to sell to wholesalers should not take the form of a general rule. Rather, a right should be conferred upon bona fide wholesalers/jobbers to apply to a quasi-judicial agency to order that a manufacturer supply him and, if necessary, to calculate a constructed manufacturer's price.

For the avoidance of doubt, it is appropriate to emphasize the nature of the means to increased productivity in distribution being proposed. It is nothing less than the suggestion that manufacturers who have built up an extensive marketing structure should be told that they must sell to jobbers who are professional price-cutters at prices which would enable the jobbers to march immediately around to the manufacturer's best retail dealer customers and try to take them away by offering price concessions. Such a suggestion would doubtless strike most manufacturers of differentiated products as bizarre, to say the least. But there is no other route to the adopted objectives.

Among the wastes which might be avoided in the future, to some extent, would be the higher costs resulting from the existence of so many plants in a particular regional market that none achieve most of the economies of scale. An example is the four oil refineries in Vancouver; a single refinery could produce refined products at lower cost. If some of the companies had been willing and able to buy supplies from their competitors already in production, and if the cost of that supply had been less than their own production—which it could have been, in view of the unrealized economies of scale—there could have been only one refinery. The actual situation is an instance of the adherence to trade name marketing and the maintenance of a greater appearance of product differentiation than actually exists, resulting in the violation of the consumers' sovereignty rule of prices equal to least attainable costs. That the suggested situation of one refinery is not fanciful is indicated by the fact that the major oil companies now buy and swap considerable quantities of gasoline from each other. The optimal performance of the petroleum products industry could be achieved only if the production and marketing operations of each company were conducted entirely separately from each other, the former selling to the highest bidder and the latter seeking out the cheapest source of supply. A tendency to this condition would result from an increase in the number of companies which were primarily chains of retail outlets which searched for their supplies in the cheapest markets. Given the existence of that type of company, the potential competition of imports would keep the domestic producers' prices close to the least attainable. For this reason it is unfortunate that the many take-overs by major oil companies of smaller companies that were marketers/jobbers have been allowed rather than found to be mergers to the detriment of the public interest.

The changes in the structure and marketing arrangements of industries required to achieve the maximum attainable productivity are so sweeping as to appear alarming in a country noted for its conservatism. Nevertheless, even in Canada, a gradual transition to a more competitive economy might be acceptable. This could be accomplished by the withdrawal of the refusal-to-sell privilege, industry by industry, as an appropriate agency recommended that temporary exemptions be granted to those which would suffer the greatest revisions of their marketing structures—the automobile industry, for example.

The automobile industry is singular in the degree to which marketing is integrated with production. All the manufacturers sell directly to franchised retail dealers. Withdrawals of the refusal-to-sell privilege would bring an end to the franchise system as more and more dealers opted for handling more than one manufacturer's products. Owing to the circumstances of the industry, there would be no need and no point in trying to intrude jobbers between the manufacturer and the retail dealer. But conversion of what the British call the *solus* system, with a dealer selling only one manufacturer's products, into the more usual situation with retail dealers handling several manufacturers' products, and with no price discrimination by manufacturers permitted, the path would be open for the rapid growth of the price-cutting dealer who adopted the large-volume, low-margin strategy. Another result would probably be that the manufacturer would find it desirable to separate the contract concerning the discharging of warranty obligations from the sales contract. There would then be specialization by function in the larger cities. The same result would no doubt emerge with respect to the wholesaling of parts and accessories. Finally, manufacturers would probably find it profitable to operate demonstration and information centres separate from sales outlets.

THE RIGHT TO USE CONSIGNMENT SELLING

It is apparent that a manufacturer can achieve all the objectives of resale price maintenance by selling exclusively on consignment. Since dealers act solely as agents receiving a commission for their services, the manufacturer retains the right to decide the retail price. However, it is not apparent that much use has been made of this avenue of avoidance of the ban on resale price maintenance. In any event, any such tendency would be precluded by the suggested withdrawal of the right of refusal to sell. A manufacturer selling either to a limited extent or exclusively on consignment would be required to make outright sales to dealers who made application to the suggested quasi-judicial agency.

At the conclusion of their report on the North Star and Shell consignment selling plans, the Restrictive Trade Practices Commission expressed the view that consignment plans, "the primary purpose and obvious consequence" of which was "the control of prices and the stifling of competition at the consumer level," were detrimental to the public interest.[4] But that enquiry overlooked the primary objective of the consignment plans used by the major oil companies in the period

1959 to 1965. This objective was to demonstrate to the private-brand dealers and the jobbers who used them as their agents that a differential between the pump prices of major-brand and private-brand gasoline of more than a nominal amount would not be tolerated. The consignment system as the means to engaging in a price war was seen by the major oil companies as an undesirable but unavoidable measure to protect their major-brand dealers and preserve their very large investment in service stations, as well as their shares of the market. Consignment was incidental to the campaign undertaken to end the price cutting by the private-brand stations. Stifling price competition on the part of major-brand dealers may not have been an objective at all, although it certainly was a result.

It is somewhat surprising that the United States Supreme Court also emphasized the lesser evil of the consignment selling plans of the oil companies. When upholding the ban on the use of consignment selling as a means of preventing price competition among retail dealers, the Court stated:

> By reason of the lease and "consignment" agreement dealers are coercively laced into an arrangement under which their supplier is able to impose noncompetitive prices on thousands of persons who otherwise might be competitive. The evil of this resale price maintenance program . . . is its inexorable potentiality for and even certainty in destroying competition in retail sales of gasoline by these nominal "consignees" who are in reality small struggling competitors seeking retail gas customers.[5]

The *Nello Malo* v. *Shell Oil* case brings to light an additional aspect of the gasoline consignment-selling plans.[6] Malo was an independent dealer selling a major brand of gasoline. He chose to use the low-margin, high-volume strategy and operated a "gas bar" offering the minimum of services to his customers. Since his margin was lower than that of his competitors, he was completely dependent upon a much larger volume of sales. When consignment selling was imposed upon all the major-brand dealers in his district, the competition which Malo brought to bear upon other major-brand dealers was eliminated, and with it went the motorist's option of choosing to buy less service with gasoline. A consignment contract was offered to Malo. If he had accepted it, he would have been forced into offering his customers less service than his competitors did for the same price. If he refused the consignment contract, he would have had to continue to pay the previously prevailing wholesale price of gasoline, while his competitors enjoyed a lower net price (the pump price set by the oil company minus the commission paid to the dealer). Since he would have had to pay more for his gasoline than his competitors did, he would have been unable to cover total costs if he maintained the same differential between his pump price and that of his major-brand competitors in order to sell as much gasoline as he had done before the introduction of consignment selling. The only course open to him, therefore, was to drop his gas bar operation and convert to a high-service, high-cost low-volume gasoline service station. He would have to conform.

In the event, the court did not make a finding of unlawful price discrimination, partly because the gas bar had been offered the same consignment contract as its competitors, and unlike the Supreme Court of the United States, it did not find that consignment selling on the scale used by the oil companies lessened competition to the detriment of the public interest. Surely, the case is a prime example of judgement on the basis of form rather than substance. The case also indicates that an offer of the same terms to all dealers is an inadequate test of whether there is disadvantage comparable to that resulting from price discrimination.

The gasoline retailing industry is cited at some length several times in this study, solely because that industry offers convenient examples of many situations to which reference is made. However, one swallow does not make a spring, and one should be on guard against assuming that any industry is representative of many others. So far as I am aware, gasoline retailing is the only documented instance of the use of consignment selling on such an extensive scale that many of the results were identical with those of the enforcement of resale price maintenance by all the manufacturers of a commodity.

On the other hand, consignment selling is often a convenient and efficient business practice free of that defect. It can even be the method whereby manufacturers introduce some price competition at the retail level.[7] A general ban of the practice is therefore not desirable. The appropriate remedy is contained in the rule already suggested. Any dealer would have the right to apply to the suggested quasi-judicial agency, which would order that he be supplied with the product in question at a constructed manufacturer's price, which would place him in the same competitive position as his rivals who accepted consignment contracts. This measure would have prevented the major oil companies from inducing all of their service station dealers in particular markets to accept consignment contracts, a system which, although unpopular with many, was viewed by them as the least of the evils with which they were confronted. The consignment choice was a Hobson's choice since, in effect, the alternative was to pay more for their gasoline than was paid by their competitors.

REGIONAL PRICE DISCRIMINATION
TO MEET COMPETITION

Price discrimination is the charging of different prices for identical commodities or services to different classes of buyers, and the charging of the same price to different customers when the cost of the product-service package to one group is greater than the cost of that sold to others. The issue which must be resolved is which of the very many forms of price discrimination must be proscribed to make a competition policy effective. Some forms are innocuous or beneficial, for example, theatre tickets sold to students at a price lower than tickets sold to adults. Also, some forms of price discrimination are unavoidable for particular firms within some industries. For example, since it is probable that the components of total costs will differ among the various firms in an oligopoly industry, it is also probable that the differentials between the costs of a high-service commodity/service package and a low-service commodity/service package will differ among the firms in an industry. But the firm which is a price-taker has no control over the market prices; it must meet whatever prices are charged by its competitors. Consequently, it is inevitable that some firms will be found to be charging discriminatory prices.

The first variant of price discrimination to be examined consists of the right of the firm to protect its share of the market in the manner least unprofitable to it by meeting a lower price charged by a competitor in a regional market while keeping the prices charged in all other markets unchanged. On the strict definition of the term, such action is clearly price discrimination, because the differences in prices in the various markets do not equal the differences in costs in serving them. Nevertheless, this kind of price discrimination is explicitly permitted by United States law and is implicitly lawful under Canadian law. And this state of affairs is apparently an instance of a law being supported by a consensus. It is even argued that the freedom of action in question increases price competition. This contention is examined in the following paragraphs.

If a firm could protect its market shares only by lowering prices in all the markets in which a commodity is sold to the levels that yield the same net revenue as the lowest price which must be charged to meet competition in any of the markets served, the firm may still decide to meet the competition. In that event, the effects of the price competition are spread throughout the firm's entire market area, and they may even provoke additional price cutting by competitors. Alternatively, the firm in question may decide not to meet the competition of a rival who cuts prices in a regional market. If so, the latter's share of the market will increase, and the consumers in that market will still have the benefit of buying the product at the lower price. Also, in the likely event that the company which initiated the price cut were small in relation to the established companies which dominate the industry, and assuming that its price cuts are never met, it must eventually win a substantial share of the regional market. If so, the number of major firms serving the regional market would be increased, and therefore the facility with which the major firms pursued a cooperative pricing strategy would be somewhat reduced. Price competition would be either unaffected or increased.

This analysis is not complete. The story should start with the circumstances which induced the firm that initiated the price cut to do so. We may ask, Which rule would be the more likely to induce such initial price cutting—banning or permitting price discrimination to meet a rival's lower price? The answer is surely the former. If the price-cutter knows in advance that his larger competitors can meet his price cuts with a minimum loss of revenue and hence are likely to do so, his incentive to cut prices is reduced. The conclusion that permitting regional price discrimination to meet a competitor's price reduces price competition is reinforced.

However, the discussion is still not complete. It has so far concerned only the price cutting by a small new entrant and has left out of account the price competition among the established firms of an oligopoly. It is often contended that competitive price cutting among the established companies, that is, price concessions which are in violation of the generally cooperative pricing strategies, is the rule rather than the exception and is of greater importance than the competition introduced by new entrants. This contention is a complete contradiction of my assumptions that cooperative pricing strategies are the rule and departures from them the exception and that, in the absence of a threat from new entrants, the competitive price reductions which established oligopoly firms do make are limited in scope or duration. They would not be undertaken if they had to be generalized or even if there were thought to be any danger that the limited excursions into price cutting would lead to a decrease in the general price level of their industry. Consequently, such price cutting confers slight benefit upon consumers and exerts negligible pressure upon prices to tend to the least attainable cost.

The policy conclusion to be drawn is determined by the interpretation one makes of contemporary competitive behaviour. In my view, the main hope for inducing a steady pressure upon the price levels of any oligopoly lies in the strengthening of the position of the small company, whose only effective competitive strategy consists of undercutting the prices of its established rivals. Since the small firm will not often be selling in more than a few regional markets, the rule that it may not engage in regional price discrimination is not likely to deter it from following a price-cutting strategy. It is my conclusion, therefore, that the gain from encouraging price cutting by new entrants would outweigh several times whatever diminution might result from the discouragement of established firms from engaging in price competition among themselves.

We must now consider whether the danger lies not in the discouraging of price competition but rather in the opposite outcome. It may be feared that the tipping of the scales of the competitive struggle in favour of the price-cutting firm and against the established companies in the way suggested (and several additional ways are proposed later in this chapter) would make price competition too severe and/or result in an uneconomic increase in the number of firms too small to realize the economies of scale. The latter fear is the easier to dispel. The small new entrant is no threat to the established firms if it cannot produce at a cost almost as low as their own. Even if the new entrant could find the financing required to enable it to start operations by charging less than the established companies while suffering from higher costs, the established companies need pay no attention to it since there would be almost no possibility that the new entrant could expand to the size required to achieve most of the available economies of scale before it went bankrupt under the weight of accumulated losses.

It is, of course, conceivable that the new price-cutter might win a predominant share of a local, somewhat isolated market and become profitable without ever realizing the economies of scale of plant. In that event, to survive, the firm must enjoy some offsetting cost advantage. For example, the freight cost from the closest competitor may exceed the higher production cost due to the diseconomies of small size. But then, the proliferation of plants too small to realize the economies of scale is not uneconomic. On the contrary, the lowest cost of producing and delivering the commodity is not achieved by the distant plant of "economic" size but rather by the plant in the vicinity which is of "uneconomic" size.

This conclusion leaves us with the objection that tipping the competitive scales in favour of the small price-cutting firm would make price competition too severe. Earlier in this chapter, too-severe price competition was given the precise meaning of prices being driven down below average cost much of the time. Excepting industries to which entry is too easy, prices are bid down below average cost in only two sets of conditions. One exists if the tendency of the established firms to follow cooperative pricing strategies is so tenuous that any disturbance brings on a rash of competitive price cutting among them, as happened in several Canadian industries during the depression of the 1930s. But it is a central thesis of this study that the commitment to action on the recognition of mutual dependence is at present undesirably strong rather than so fragile as to warrant protection.

The other set of conditions is usually referred to as a price war. Most price wars are precipitated by the competitive price cutting which follows the matching or bettering of the lowest price in a market by one or more of the large companies which are on the defensive against the inroads being made into their market shares by smaller companies. And it has already been reasoned that such price wars would occur less frequently than they now do if there were a ban on regional price discrimination, because the cost to established companies of heading off competition in a single regional market would be very high because they would have to lower prices in all the markets they served from the plant which shipped to the regional market in question. Consequently, a ban on regional price discrimination to meet price competition would reduce rather than increase the danger that price competition might be too severe.

There is a final objection to a ban on regional price discrimination to consider. It may be that the real objection to such a ban is that, coupled with rules with similar effects, it might make the game of free enterprise not worth the candle. The rewards held out for the efficient are profits and the growth of the firm. But it may be reasoned that if the successful firm is so hedged round by rules that it cannot beat off others who invade its markets, the assumed rewards are denied it. In the writings of the late Joseph A. Schumpeter, the poet laureate of capitalism, free enterprise is likened to a race for prizes which few win and which are retained only briefly by those who do win them. Schumpeter has inspired more spirited defences of the freedom of business activity from public regulation than any other writer in our generation, and probably in any other. However, this is one part of his vision of capitalism which the business community has not adopted. Rather, the feeling seems to be that few will want to play the game if the rewards for efficiency are illusory.

This discussion raises a fundamental issue. It has frequently been remarked that, provided there is no barrier to growth of the firm in the form of increasing costs,[8] the logical evolution of an industry is through stages from a fairly large number of firms to a smaller number as the most efficient survive, and finally to a very small number with considerable monopoly power. Thus, it is said that the natural development of an industry is toward monopoly and to take away the monopoly power is to take away the reward for striving to be efficient. Despite the fact that this is a fundamental issue, all the argument revolving around it has been speculative. It is assumed that the profits and sizes of firms to which we are accustomed are a necessary condition of the urge to efficiency; but it is an assumption only. There is no tangible evidence which justifies a prohibition of changes in the rules governing competition which would erode the privileged position of successful firms (some of which, of course, achieved their present position by merger rather than by internal growth). The existence of a very large number of firms which continually strive to increase their size and efficiency in the face of profit rates and market shares much less than those of firms which enjoy some measure of monopoly power indicates that the latter would not pick up their marbles and withdraw from the game if their prizes were reduced by the introduction of more price competition. If a contrary conclusion is drawn, an effective competition policy is precluded.

PREDATORY PRICING

It is extremely difficult to distinguish predatory pricing with the intention of destroying a competitor or disciplining him so that he will refrain from price cutting from the defensive act of simply meeting the competition initiated by a rival by lowering prices to be identical with his. It might appear that there should be no difficulty in deciding that the pricing was not punitive so long as the larger firm in the battle did not initiate the price cuts but only reacted to them, and when reacting, did not go below the smaller company's prices but only matched them. However, the difficulty is not so easily resolved; it is not always a simple matter to determine whether the prices charged by different companies for different packages of products and services are equivalent or whether, all things considered, one is lower than the other. There is little question that identical nominal prices are in fact different prices in the simple case in which two commodities are to all intents and purposes physically identical but one is a much-advertised, trademarked product and the other is not. But what does one conclude when, no matter what price the marketer of a nonbranded gasoline sets, the major companies set their prices only one cent higher? Are they in fact undercutting him? The package of services sold at major-brand stations is worth more to most customers and costs more than does the package sold by the nonbrand dealer. Whether different nominal prices charged for different product/service packages are equivalent prices cannot be determined by reference to their value to the consumer. Those who pay the higher price presumably consider that the extra service is worth the additional cost. The only recourse is to compare the spread between the two prices with the cost of providing the additional services.

At present no effective protection is offered by Canadian law against punitive pricing. But the situation is not much better in the United States, and there are good reasons for not following the United States lead. First of all, there is the danger that a preoccupation with the prevention of cutthroat competition as the means to achieving or preserving monopoly power may impede the elimination of inefficient firms which happen to be small. It would surely be wise to guard against making large firms apprehensive that they might be charged with predatory pricing if they lowered prices following adoption of an improvement in the methods of production or distribution which offered cost reductions only to large-scale operations or which they were the first to adopt. Consequently, an allegation of predatory pricing should be subject to inquiry by a quasi-judicial agency with discretionary power to determine whether the alleged aggressors engaged in a deliberate campaign. But to say so much is only passing over the problem. Intentions and objectives are secondary issues; it is the results that count. Neither is it decisive whether larger companies accused of predatory pricing by smaller ones are on the defensive and trying to preserve their shares of the market or on the offensive and trying to enlarge it. The actions that a company must take to meet competition are similar to or identical with those taken to eliminate a competitor. Competition is a rough-and-tumble game. While it is desirable, and on my reasoning a necessary condition for efficiency, that the rules of the game be made as fair as possible, it has to be recognized that one company's gain is usually another company's loss, unless all are content to grow at the same rate as the demand for the products of their industry.

Finally, if the defence of a small company against predatory action of its large competitors must rest upon a finding by a court or commission, as seems unavoidable, that recourse must surely be the defence of last resort. The battle is often likely to be over before the case is completed unless provision could be made for pretrial injunctions. And, although a few precedents could discourage imitators, there remains the preference for a self-regulating market over judicial arbitration.

In the light of these difficulties, I am much attracted by the alternative indirect attack upon predatory pricing in the form of a ban upon all regional price discrimination. This solution operates by raising the cost of predatory pricing and requires less complex enforcement machinery. More generally, attempts should not be made to erect defences against one company trying to put another out of business. Rather, defences should be erected against all advantages which enable one company to drive another out of the market except the advantage which accrues from superior efficiency. On this reasoning, the status of some of the actions of the aggressor company in the matches case[9] becomes ambiguous, while the zinc oxide case[10] remains clear-cut. In the former case, the defendant company excluded competitors by flooding the market with fighting brands at low prices just as new firms began production. In the latter case, one firm was able to put all new entrants out of business by the lower prices it could charge because it paid a secret low price for the raw material which was the major constituent of total cost. A general rule designed to prevent a company from slashing its prices to saturate the market to block entry of a new firm would inhibit price competition. But price competition is likely to be enhanced by a ban on price discrimination on sales to firms which compete with one another, especially if there are particularly heavy sanctions when the discrimination is secret.

If primary reliance were placed upon indirect measures to cope with the problem of predatory actions, it would still be desirable to empower the quasi-judicial regulatory agency which is proposed later in this chapter to make a finding that a particular instance of established companies lowering prices in all markets had or would have the effect, and must be assumed to have the intent, of bankrupting or disciplining a competitor, and therefore that it was predatory. However, once small companies had the protection of a ban on regional price discrimination and on all other forms of price discrimination on sales to firms which are competitors, it would be desirable that regulation err on the side of competition. The regulations governing the regulatory agency should contain very specific instructions relating to the evidence to which it may give weight. It is suggested that no finding of predatory action be made and no damages awarded to the complainant company unless the actions of the defendant companies left no ground for reasonable doubt that the activities over the period in question constituted a punitive or predatory campaign.

DELIVERED PRICE SYSTEMS

Basing-point pricing and regional price discrimination are not quite identical. We usually think of basing-point pricing as a pricing practice consistently adhered to over a long period of time, while the regional price discrimination discussed in the section above entitled "Regional Price Discrimination to Meet Competition" referred to the departure from the normal relationship among prices in different regional markets, made to meet competition in a particular regional market—the price being lowered in one market while prices in all other markets remain unchanged.

Nevertheless, basing-point pricing always entails some price discrimination, and we now inquire whether an effective competition policy requires that this practice be prohibited even as a regular, nonpredatory pricing practice. Only the variant of basing-point pricing which has won the support of a substantial number of economists is examined. If it is concluded that this form should be banned, it follows that all others should also.

The least objectionable form of basing-point pricing uses multiple bases. Each production point is a basing point for pricing; no other point is. To facilitate the discussion, a condition rarely met in practice is assumed—that the delivered price at every location within each basing-point zone is always the mill-door price at the point of production plus actual freight costs to the point of delivery. Thus, multiple-base basing-point pricing is identical to f.o.b. pricing with the crucial exception that there is freight absorption on shipments from mills outside the zone; under f.o.b. pricing, no shipment originates outside a zone. Under basing-point pricing, when a mill outside the zone in question sells inside the zone, it usually charges the same price as its competitors located inside the zone, that is, posted price at the basing point plus freight from that point (a fictional calculation for mills outside the zone). There is therefore freight absorption and cross-hauling to the extent that mills sell outside their zones. On occasion, however, companies in some industries which use basing-point pricing undercut the posted prices in other zones.

For this discussion, it is not necessary to review the controversy concerning why basing-point pricing is practised. Instead, the discussion proceeds directly to the pros and cons of permitting it. The pros are not consistent; that is, different ones are argued by different writers. For convenience, the counterargument is placed after each point in favour.

BASING-POINT PRICING: PRO AND CON

1. It is contended that price competition would be too severe in certain industries in the absence of basing-point pricing.

Counterargument. This argument has already been discussed under the heading of regional price discrimination. If it is considered that the recognition of mutual dependence by Canadian oligopolies which use basing-point pricing is so tenuous that, in its absence, any small disturbance to the prevailing level of prices would induce the large companies to undercut one another's prices so much that prices would be driven down below average cost much of the time, the contention might be accepted. But it is a basic contention of this report that the recognition of mutual dependence by Canadian oligopolies, especially those using basing-point pricing, is so strong that the protection of a mutually understood pricing convention is not needed. On the contrary, the objective should be to reduce the resort to cooperative pricing strategies.

2. Most economists who choose multiple-base basing-point pricing as the best of attainable pricing practices are not worried about price competition's being too severe. Rather, they reason that permitting freight absorption increases price competition. It is asserted that companies observe the prices posted for their own zones but not those prevailing in other areas. Poaching in other zones by offering secret price concessions to undercut the prices charged by mills inside those zones is said to be a regular occurrence, and it constitutes the only price

competition in the oligopoly industries in question. Therefore, if freight absorption by mills outside a zone were barred, there would be no poaching and the only price competition likely to occur in the industries would be ended.

Counterargument. In some industries which use basing-point pricing, for example, newsprint, there is no such occurrence as a secret price cut. Every order won by a company is the loss of an order by another company, which always finds out why it lost the order. Consequently, the only price reductions made are those taken in the knowledge that all competitors will follow. There is much crosshauling, but only at the established prices for each zone. In other industries which use this pricing convention, for example, wire rope, there is poaching accompanied by price cutting. Since the production centres are separated by high transportation costs, however, it would be unprofitable for a company continuously to sell a large proportion of its output in another zone. Poaching is profitable only on a sporadic basis, and then only when there is excess plant capacity and there exists slight danger that the retaliatory poaching by competitors located in other zones will undermine the general price level in the home zone.

In the first type of industry, since there is no price-cutting poaching, there would be no reduction in price competition consequent upon a ban on freight absorption which would make it unprofitable to poach. In the second type of industry, the price-cutting poaching would be made unprofitable and terminated. But such price cutting is only sporadic and does not exert the strong pressure on prices required to drive them down toward the least attainable cost. Consequently, the decrease of price competition resulting from the ban on freight absorption would be more than offset by the increase induced. The latter is discussed below as a con point.

3. It is claimed that mandatory f.o.b. pricing would turn each zone occupied by one or two producers into local monopolies.

Counterargument. The opposite is claimed in the con argument below.

4. It is claimed that f.o.b. pricing would turn each zone into a self-sufficient supply area, sealed off from the outside, so that periods of excess demand and excess supply would follow each other in a cycle. This situation would result from f.o.b.'s making it unprofitable for companies outside a zone to lower the price level in their own zone in order to obtain a few sales in an adjoining zone. Of course, during a period of tight supply in one zone, accompanied by excess supply in an

adjoining zone, customers unable to obtain sufficient supplies in their own zone could always import at their own initiative from an adjoining zone—at a higher cost. This is considered unfair to firms which would be low on waiting lists.

Counterargument. The reasoning is based on the assumption that the boundaries of the various zones would change very infrequently under f.o.b. pricing. However, the opposite result is predicted. With f.o.b. pricing, the only way for a mill to increase output is by lowering its mill door price. Granted that there is a strong incentive for them to act on the recognition of their mutual dependence when there are only a few companies located in the same centre, but such cooperative pricing would be under much greater pressure under f.o.b. than it would be with basing-point pricing. If one firm, possibly the most recent entrant, suffered a low operating rate while the others enjoyed fairly high outputs in relation to their capacity, there would be a considerable incentive for the first firm to lower its mill door price even though this would mean a decrease in revenue from its existing sales. The objective would not be to take sales away from the other mills in the same location, since it could expect that they would match its price reductions. Rather, the objective would be to take sales away from firms located at other centres, by undercutting their prices near the boundary of the zones tributary to each centre. It is this conflict of interest that is relied on to weaken action on the recognition of mutual dependence, thereby increasing price competition. It is fairly easy for firms to act on the recognition of mutual dependence, so long as there is considerable freedom of action for the firm which is under greatest pressure to increase its sales. Such an outlet is provided by basing-point pricing in the form of poaching in adjoining zones without destroying cooperative pricing in the home zone. Under f.o.b. pricing, there is no safety valve. Hence, there is likely to be a conflict of interests between firms with low operating rates who want to increase output even at the expense of lower revenue on existing sales and firms with high operating rates who prefer the higher revenue from existing output and existing prices.

The conflict of interest would be greatest when demand was low in relation to capacity in one zone while output was pressing against the physical maximum capacity in an adjoining zone. Then, the temptation to some firms in the first zone is likely to be irresistible, and they can be counted on to lower their mill door prices in order to sell in the area just beyond the initial boundary line between zones. Thus, the boundaries between areas served from different centres would be continually shifting in response to the strength of demand in relation to capacity in the different zones. Consequently, there would be no cycles of feast and famine in adjoining zones. Imports and exports between zones would be accomplished by the shifting of the boundaries between them. In fact, price cutting by a firm in the famine (of orders) zone is not required to cause the desired shift in boundaries. All that is necessary is that the mill door price in the feast zone be raised relative to the mill door price in the famine zone. This can be accomplished either by raising the former prices or lowering the latter. In either event, the boundary of the feast zone would move in, and the boundary of the famine zone would move out. Thus, all customers would be served at the least attainable freight cost.

5. It is claimed that the system just described might work for industries that produce homogeneous products such as steel and cement, but that it is not viable for differentiated products such as gasoline or automobiles. The reasoning is that a consumer who has a marked preference for a particular brand that is not produced in the zone in which he is situated should not have to pay the penalty of the full freight cost from the distant centre where it is produced. This does not strike one as very cogent reasoning; there is no reason why other consumers should bear part of the freight cost entailed in catering to his preference. However, it is claimed that the adverse consequences for producers are much greater. It is said that the firm that markets a trademarked product should have equal access to the entire national market, and this is possible only if a considerable amount of freight absorption is permitted. With mandatory f.o.b. pricing, and when there are several production centres, each firm's sales would be heavily concentrated in the zones closest to the factories.

Counterargument. There is no presumption of detriment to a firm from having its sales concentrated in the areas closest to its factories. How the total market shares of different firms would be affected by the f.o.b. rule cannot be predicted. If there is a defect, therefore, it can only be that the nonprice competition which is stressed by makers of trademarked products would induce them to continue to serve most parts of the national market by meeting the prices charged by their competitors, and to do so, they would have to build factories at every major production centre. It might be claimed that the end result would be a proliferation of plants too small to realize most of the economies of scale. It could then be contended that the cost of providing the consumer with the variety of products which he prefers would be artificially raised.

To analyse this conclusion, one must distinguish between commodities which are physically dissimilar—automobiles, for example—and those which are only superficially different, such as automobile tires and gasoline. In the latter instance, there need be no increase in the cost of product differentiation due to f.o.b. pricing. It would be open to the firm to serve a market in which it had no plant by the simple technique of buying its supplies for that market from a competitor. There is already extensive intercompany swapping and buying of gasoline among the major oil companies, the bought gasoline being refined according to the specifications of the purchasing firm, so that whatever real product differentiation exists is preserved. The same system is feasible for automobile tires and a considerable range of other trademarked products which possess very similar physical properties. When this course is followed, the shipping point relevant for the observance of the mandatory f.o.b. rule would be the company's warehouse, which would of course be in the same centre as the competitor's factory from which supplies were drawn.

Industries which produce physically dissimilar close substitutes are another matter. The number of industries of this type which are relevant for our examination is not great, since freight absorption is not of much consequence unless freight costs are large relative to the price of a commodity. For this reason, it is suggested later in this chapter that mandatory f.o.b. pricing be made applicable only where the freight cost exceeds 5 percent of the wholesale price. There are nonetheless some physically dissimilar differentiated products to which the rule would still apply, and automobiles are a convenient example to consider. It is immediately apparent that in most instances the decision facing a company would not be between allowing itself to be priced out of a regional market and establishing full production facilities there, but rather between being priced out of the regional market and assembling the product there. It is also clear that, for purposes of establishing a base point to comply with the f.o.b. factory rule, assembly can be reduced to a nominal function such as putting on the wheels of an automobile. For this reason, there would be no interference with the company's decisions regarding the optimal number of plants to serve a national market. On the contrary, it appears that the mandatory f.o.b. pricing rule would not require any reduction in the usually partial freight absorption practised by this type of industry. The rule would not, for example, preclude partial freight absorption on shipments of automobiles from Oakville to Halifax if nominal assembly were conducted in Halifax. However, a cost would be imposed upon predatory pricing in some circumstances. If at least nominal assembly were not already being done regionally, the firm which wanted to escape the f.o.b. rule in order to cut prices regionally would have to incur the expense of some decentralization.

These complications must, of course, be kept in mind when a mandatory f.o.b. pricing rule is proposed. Nothing is gained and something lost when regulations impose a compliance cost to no tangible effect. The motto to be followed should be (with respects to former Prime Minister W. L. Mackenzie King): Regulation if necessary but not necessarily regulation. Consequently, a mandatory f.o.b. pricing rule should be confined to more or less homogeneous products where, in any event, freight absorption is of the greatest consequence.

ARGUMENTS FAVOURING F.O.B. PRICING

Most important, as argued above, mandatory f.o.b. pricing would create conflicts of interests among the members of an oligopoly industry, which would tend to weaken the adherence to cooperative pricing practices and thus introduce some degree of price competition. A firm could not increase its sales except by decreasing its milldoor prices.

The second argument in favour of mandatory f.o.b. pricing is non-controversial. All forms of basing-point pricing result in wasteful cross-hauling. This is a violation of the consumers' sovereignty rule, which requires that competition drive prices toward lowest attainable costs.

The third argument is almost equally noncontroversial. Basing-point pricing often imposes obstacles in the way of the attraction of additions to plant capacity to their least-cost locations. When the demand in a region reaches a certain size, the saving in transport cost is often greater than the increase in production costs incurred by producing the commodity in the region, provided production is carried out in a single plant. But basing-point pricing robs the plant of this natural locational advantage. The new plant must find its customers throughout a much larger area than that tributary to it and other centres retain the larger share of the market in that area. There is therefore no incentive, and indeed a substantial impediment, to the establishment of plants in their least-cost location.

SUMMING UP

The potential gains to the economy justify the limitation of the freedom of action of firms by the imposition of a mandatory f.o.b.

pricing rule. It is suggested later in this chapter that an f.o.b. rule be imposed subject to the discretionary power of a quasi-judicial agency to grant exemption and that the agency be instructed to grant exemption freely except where the economic gains just discussed would be realized. In general, industries would be subject to the rule only if the product is fairly homogeneous and where freight costs are a substantial proportion of the wholesale price excluding sales taxes—say, 5 percent. In other words, the rule would apply to such commodities as cement, steel, other metals, lumber, newsprint, woodpulp, sugar, and gasoline. There would be no harm done by including industries which already follow f.o.b. pricing, for example, lumber.

To have any effect whatever, a mandatory f.o.b. pricing rule must be accompanied by a ban on price discrimination; there must be a single mill door price to each of the class of customers in question. For example, assume that a company wishes to poach outside its zone by quoting the same delivered price to customer A, who is outside the zone, as it is charging to customer B, who is inside the zone. Assume, of course, that freight cost to A is considerably greater than it is to B. If there is no ban on discriminating between A and B, the f.ob. rule would have no effect. Instead of quoting the same mill door price to A and B and overtly absorbing freight to A, as it might do in the absence of all rules, the company need only quote a lower mill door price to A, plus actual freight.

It will be apparent from the discussion in the following section that there are many circumstances in which it is not feasible to require that a company charge the same price to all classes of customers. The suggestion made later in the chapter, therefore, is quite restricted, namely, that no price discrimination be permitted on sales of a commodity or service to a single class of customers which consists of firms that compete with one another. The appropriate definition of *class of customers* restricts the application of the f.o.b. rule even further; that definition will also emerge in the subsequent discussion.

The proposed ban on price discrimination would not require that a firm charge the same mill door price for shipments from mills located in different regional markets.

This discussion of f.o.b. pricing has had exclusive reference to sales in the domestic markets. Nearly all Canadian firms that sell in export markets are price-takers. They must meet the prices established by their competitors, adopt the pricing strategy dictated by the competitive manoeuvres of others in the particular markets, and comply with the laws and cope with the dumping duties of the countries of destination of their exports. Anomalies in the world structure of prices of commodities exported by Canadian firms in competition with other members of an international oligopoly are beyond the power of any single country to change.

Resolution of the problems posed by imports into Canada is not so easily accomplished by their exclusion from a regulatory rule. For example, a non-resident company may absorb its domestic freight in order to poach in a Canadian market near the international border. The earliest point at which an f.o.b. pricing rule could be imposed would be the point of entry of imports. However, Canadian tariffs and dumping duties usually provide more than adequate protection against any tactical advantage importing firms might gain in consequence of an f.o.b. rule. It should be sufficient safeguard to permit allegations of competitive disadvantage to be lodged with the quasi-judicial agency proposed in the final part ("Means to the Ends") of this chapter.

PRICE DISCRIMINATION ON SALES TO FIRMS WHICH COMPETE WITH EACH OTHER

There is some ambivalence in attitudes toward price discrimination practised against final consumers. When one group of customers is charged more for an identical product or service than another group, there is a loss of consumers' surplus; other things being the same, the gain to those paying the lower price is assumed to be less than the loss suffered by all others. The ambivalence arises from the proviso that other things be the same. It is desirable, therefore, that one be precise concerning the ground for complaint by those who are disadvantaged by price discrimination. One falls into an equivocal position if the grievance rests upon an allegation of unfairness on the assumption that all consumers who are the same in all relevant respects are entitled to buy a commodity for the same price, because one is then faced with the task of identifying which of the two prices charged, if either, is the correct price. And the correct price is identified by the consumers' sovereignty rule. In the simple case of price discrimination between two groups of consumers, therefore, the firm ground for complaint by those paying the higher price is that the price exceeds the least attainable cost. This being so, there is no need for an independent rule of fair pricing relating to prices paid by final consumers.

In certain unusual circumstances, for example, in the pricing of an electricity-distributing utility, the best attainable solution may require some form of price discrimination on sales to final consumers. However, no separate rule is required to provide for these exceptions; the rule that prices equal least attainable cost is sufficient.

On the other hand, both the rule of least attainable cost and the rule of fair competition among companies require that no firm be disadvantaged in its competition with others. The competitive struggle guarantees the survival of the fittest only when the outcome of the contest turns solely upon the efficiencies of the contestants. It is desirable, for example, that chains of supermarket grocery stores displace independent stores when the former perform the retailing function at lower costs. But the lowest cost is not necessarily attained when the sole advantage of the larger firms results from the price discrimination practised by supplying companies. In the latter event, not only is efficiency not served, but there is a violation of the fairness criterion.

Some may argue that price discrimination should be countenanced if the large firms which receive discounts in excess of cost savings are also the more efficient, because the elimination of the less efficient firms is thereby accelerated. There is a bonus to the virtuous, so to speak. But neutrality, which is almost always coincident with fair rules, is preferable. Enterprise should not require an assist in the form of biased rules. In any event, it is the proper function of the market system to identify the efficient more accurately than would any generalization that firms that benefit from price discrimination are likely also to be the more efficient.

What is remarkable is not that the case for no discrimination among firms which are competitors is decisive, but rather that it has not been accorded more importance than it has. Deciding to accord the matter a higher priority and implementing the decision are, unfortunately, of unequal difficulty.

The simplest case of discrimination of the type in question consists of discounts on the basis of the volume of single shipments when the discounts exceed the cost savings. Clearly, there is a bias in favour of large companies. Again, the most promising remedy would not be an overall ban, but rather the right of appeal by the injured party to an appropriate quasi-judicial regulatory agency. And the onus should be on the supplier to demonstrate that the discounts do not exceed the cost savings, since only he possesses the required information. It should not be a defence that small accounts require or are accorded more sales efforts than large accounts are per dollar of orders received. To do so would undermine the rule entirely. In any event, it is questionable that the sales effort is always welcomed or valued by the smaller customers.

Discounts based on cumulated sales during the year are similarly discriminatory. If the discount is based on total sales, there is a bias in favour of the large buyer. If the discount is on the basis of the absolute increase in sales over a prior period, the same bias is present. But if the basis is the percentage increase in sales, there may be a bias in favour of smaller dealers. The case against such discounts may appear to be coloured if it appears that their objective is to induce dealers to compete by cutting their margins. However, the measures being proposed are more effective means to that end.

Obviously, any ban of the type under discussion should apply not just to discounts and lower prices, but also to any other consideration which would not be given in the absence of the supply contract. However, all the forms of discrimination other than straightforward discounts or lower prices involve complexities and occur most frequently when there is some form of integration between manufacturing and marketing. These complications are sufficiently severe that the protection afforded by any practicable ban on price discrimination on sales to firms which are in competition with each other would be much less than might at first appear. It is convenient to distinguish five aspects: sales to some retail dealers accompanied by a consideration not available to other retail dealers; jobbers' discounts and jobbers' status; major brands v. house brands of chain and department stores; different classes of buyers—manufacturers v. distributors; and long-term supply contracts.

SALES TO SOME RETAIL DEALERS ACCOMPANIED BY A CONSIDERATION NOT AVAILABLE TO OTHERS

It is not unusual for some retail dealers, especially franchised ones, to receive larger considerations, such as advertising or warranty allowances, than are received by others. Such discrimination should not be permitted, because it violates the rules of fair dealing and because competition does not ensure the survival of the fittest unless the only source of competitive advantage is superior efficiency. Enforcement of the rules could be sufficiently accomplished by the right of a disadvantaged competitor to take his case to the quasi-judicial agency.

Sometimes the circumstances of the discrimination are quite complex. Perhaps the best-known instance is the competitive disadvantage to the independent major-brand service station dealer resulting from the subsidization of lessee stations by the major oil companies. Independent service station dealers own their stations, though most are fairly heavily mortgaged, while lessee dealers rent stations from their oil company suppliers. It can be reasoned that there is no discrimination when a consideration in the form of a rental of a service station for less than cost accompanies the offer of the sale of gasoline at a posted price to some dealers but not to others, because the rentals charged for the lessee stations are approximately equal to their market values. Immediately they are built, and for most of their useful life, most lessee stations are worth less (to anyone except the oil company) than they cost. Nevertheless, disadvantage to the independent dealer is clearly present. If an independent dealer's sales increase sufficiently to make his operations profitable, it is only a matter of time before a rival is established close by and is provided with facilities for a rental which is as little as one-half the annual cost which the independent dealer would have to pay to acquire them. The obvious result is that the return to the independent's capital and the return which would accrue to his years of effort in building up a clientele are much less than they would otherwise be. On the strict definition of the term, there is also price discrimination because there is no differential between the price paid for gasoline by the independent and that paid by the lessee dealer. Neutrality requires that the difference in the cost of the package of commodity plus facilities be matched by an equal difference in price.

It might seem that the consumer should not complain, because the oil companies build and rent service stations for less than their cost. Neither should he, if the result were lower prices of the commodity and the services which go with it than would otherwise be the case. But the evidence is to the contrary. The cost of service stations in excess of the net rental revenue derived from them reduces the revenue available from the margin between the cost of the refined products at the refinery door and the selling prices to service station dealers and other customers. On the reasonable assumption that the established companies endeavour to make as much profit as they can, given the constraints within which they operate, the prices charged for gasoline sold to service station dealers are higher by the amount of the lessee station rental subsidy.[11]

JOBBERS' DISCOUNTS AND JOBBERS' STATUS

It is customary for discounts to be granted to tradesmen that are not available to final consumers, even though the amount of a particular purchase is the same. When such discounts are not passed on to the consumer, they constitute a source of income for electricians, plumbers, carpenters, painters, and automobile repair garages, among others, additional to the payment received for their services.

This variety of price discrimination would not be affected by conclusions reached so far concerning the undesirable forms of price discrimination which could, to advantage, be subject to prohibition. It would be stretching the concept of parties who are in competition with one another to a ridiculous extreme to rule, for example, that the professional house-painter was a competitor of the do-it-yourself householder. Moreover, disadvantage to the householder is not obvious because it is improbable that the retail prices paid by householders for materials and supplies would be lower in the absence of the customary discounts granted to tradesmen.

The variety of price discrimination just discussed is rarely a contentious matter. The alleged disadvantages of the small store in competition with the large company operating chains of stores lie at the other extreme. But the difficulties facing implementation of the rule that survival in the competitive struggle should depend solely upon relative efficiency are severe when some companies have absorbed the wholesale function into their retail operations while others have not. Then, the rivals buy at different price levels; the former pay the manufacturer's price (to wholesalers) and the latter the wholesale price (to retailers). Price discrimination is present when the difference between the two price levels exceeds the cost (to the manufacturer) of the wholesaling function absorbed by the retailer-wholesaler. Such price discrimination clearly offends the rule.

It would be possible to implement the rule by allowing independent stores to apply to the proposed quasi-judicial agency for a finding of discrimination and its removal. Since the administrative difficulties of this remedy are severe, however, the indirect route appears all the more attractive. If the producers' right of refusal to sell to wholesalers were withdrawn, and if the differentials between the prices paid by the retailer-wholesalers and those paid by the retailers substantially exceeded the costs of distribution, price-cutting jobbers would appear and would drive the differential down toward the lowest attainable distribution cost.

MAJOR BRANDS VERSUS HOUSE BRANDS

On the strict definition, there is price discrimination when the difference between the price of an article bearing a much-advertised trademark and the price of an article which is to all intents and purposes physically identical except that it bears a little-advertised trademark exceeds the difference in the costs of production, including the cost of investing a trademark with a market value.

The situation is similar to the one in the preceding section, because the department store that markets clothing, hardware, furniture, electrical appliances, automobile tires, et cetera, under its own house brand names also either performs the wholesale function for itself or eliminates it and has the bargaining advantage of very large-scale purchases. The major oil companies which are paid commissions on the sale of tires, batteries, and accessories sold under their house brand names to their service station dealers are also in a similarly advantageous position.

The house brands of the department stores and supermarkets are frequently a boon to the consumer, if casual observation has any evidential value. It is a widely-held conviction that the house brand of the department store is the best bargain available in many durable goods —at any rate, in the absence of full-fledged discount houses. Also, the impression gained for casual observation is that a substantial increase in the share of the market won by house brands drives down the marketing margin of the competing major-brand commodities.

Nevertheless, the lack of neutrality between the very large and the small retailer remains, and the only hope for its diminution, other than interference with the potent pressure on prices imposed by the house brands, lies in the further reduction of the marketing margin taken on the major-brand commodities. And that further reduction would be accelerated if the right of refusal to sell placed the highly advertised, trademarked lines in the hands of price-cutting jobbers and jobber-retailers.

DIFFERENT CLASSES OF BUYERS: MANUFACTURER VERSUS DISTRIBUTOR

There is often price discrimination when identical commodities, including the trademark, are sold to other manufacturers and also to distributors or retail dealers. An extreme example is to be found in the automobile tire industry.[12] The automobile companies buy major-brand tires for very much lower prices than do retailers or even firms which combine retailing and wholesaling.

Since the classes of buyers involved compete only at the final remove (they both compete for the consumer's dollar), only a determination to root out all manifestations of price discrimination wherever found would be cause to try to end this form of discrimination. It can be reasoned that little contribution is made to overhead costs by the revenue from the sale of initial equipment tires to manufacturers, and therefore almost all the fixed costs are borne by the consumers of replacement tires. However, a requirement that a single price be charged both classes of customers would very probably result in the loss to the tire companies of the initial equipment tire business, because the automobile companies have the alternatives of producing tires for their own use and of buying control of a tire company. Consequently, there might be an increase in the number of tire plants and a resulting increase in the total costs of production of all tires taken together. As it is, the Canadian tire plants produce too many lines to be able to realize most of the economies of scale. A gain to the consumers of tires as a body seems very doubtful. The only promising avenue to reducing the cost of replacement tires is by an increased productivity of the industry, through greater economies of scale in production and a reduction in the resources devoted to marketing.

The tire industry is an extreme case. But less striking instances are very common. Large commercial and industrial firms are frequently able to buy commodities at negotiated prices, or even call for tender bids, while retail dealers and firms which use small quantities of the commodity must buy at posted prices. There is active price competition on sales to the former, but action on the recognition of mutual dependence concerning the latter.

Little need be added to what has been said already concerning similar situations to be able to conclude that this variety of price discrimination is beyond the reach of general rules regulating business behaviour. Frequently the large company is able to buy at negotiated prices because it can turn to a source of supply alternative to the oligopoly domestic industry. If a company in the supplying industry were required to sell its total output at the lowest price won by any of its customers, total revenue might be less than its total costs and it would cease to supply customers who had access to alternative sources of supply at low prices. On the other hand, if the companies that bought at negotiated prices had no source of supply alternative to the domestic industry and discrimination were banned, the practices of selling at negotiated prices and at tender would have to be terminated. Negotiated prices are typically embedded in contracts running for fairly long periods, and the prices won vary from week to week. Consequently, negotiated prices and prices bid at tender are inherently discriminatory.

To comply with a ban on price discrimination, companies would have to post a single price to be charged to all members of a single class of customers, and the uniform price would probably be set by all firms in an industry acting on the recognition of their mutual dependence. The uniform price would very probably be higher than the average of the various prices charged when some sales are made at negotiated prices and some at posted prices.

This discussion brings to light a difficulty that would be encountered in the enforcement of a mandatory f.o.b. pricing rule. Because an f.o.b. pricing rule would be without effect in the absence of a uniform mill door price to all members of a given class of customers, it should not be applied to sales at prices arrived at by competitive bidding.

When companies buying large quantities have the benefit of negotiated prices while companies buying small quantities have to buy at uniform prices set on the recognition of mutual dependence, a regulatory agency could issue an instruction requiring that the spread between the lowest price and the price charged for a standard volume be no greater than a stipulated percentage. But such instructions are appropriately issued only after an investigation of the pricing practices of an industry.

LONG-TERM CONTRACTS

Sometimes a mutual benefit is derived from a long-term contract, stipulating prices, between a producer and a marketer; for example, between chicken farmers and supermarkets, vegetable growers and canners, and large department stores and small manufacturers. It is sometimes said that the gains are not always unalloyed, especially to the producer who courts the danger of becoming a "captive supplier." Nevertheless, in general there must be a presumption of gain, since there is an arm's-length contract freely entered and the contract provides a hedge against risk for both parties. Also there is a presumption that the marketer may post lower prices if the long-term contract provides him with lower merchandise costs.

Efficiencies may also be achieved by long-term contracts stipulating prices when investment decisions are complementary. For example, it might not be profitable for a coal mine to be developed in the absence of an assured market for a large proportion of its output, and the demand for its output might be insufficient to justify the investment in the absence of the construction of a thermal power plant or a steel mill.

Conversely, the construction of the latter might not be profitable in the absence of an increase in the supply of coal in the market in question at a predictable price. Thus, the simultaneous investment in the coal mine and in the plant which will consume most of its output is profitable, while investment in either in the absence of the other is not. A long-term supply contract stipulating prices becomes the catalyst.

Such long-term contracts should be free of interference from any of the rules proposed concerning price discrimination and the withdrawal of the right of refusal to sell. It would not be feasible to require the producer to supply other customers at the price stipulated in a contract with the major customer to whom he is tied.

PRICE DISCRIMINATION: SALES TO CONSUMERS

The first general question to be examined is whether it would be desirable to ban a general practice of price discrimination in the form of marketing two brands of what is, to all intents and purposes, the same product, with one brand being much advertised and the other little advertised and priced much lower. By the strict definition, price discrimination is present wherever the price difference exceeds the difference in cost. However, this is another instance in which an attempt to realize an ideal condition would result in more harm than good. For one thing, it would be very difficult for companies to comply with such a rule more than approximately. More important, the most probable effect would be to induce a company to discontinue the less expensive brand—which could scarcely be called a gain for the consumer.

In the circumstances described, not only is there price discrimination, strictly defined, but there is also a violation of the right-to-be-informed part of the consumers' sovereignty rule. It is in the consumer's interest that he know when two brands serve his purpose equally well. But if he were so informed, the company would very probably drop the less expensive brand.

The second issue to be explored is that of the standard price discrimination of the textbooks. The first condition is that there be a single commodity sold in two different markets, usually classes of customers, which can be kept separated (buyers in the cheaper market cannot resell to persons in the dearer market). The second condition is that sales must be less sensitive to price in one market than in the other. There is a violation of the consumers' sovereignty rule because customers in the higher-priced market are not supplied with the commodity at lowest attainable cost. The loss by these consumers is matched by the producer's gain, possibly shared to some extent with consumers in the lower-priced market.

It is claimed that in some circumstances this form of price discrimination results in a net benefit, because total costs could not be covered without price discrimination and the commodity or service would not be produced. There is reason to doubt that this circumstance is more than the rare exception. But if it were the only complication it would not be a sufficient reason for not banning standard price discrimination, because the defence of inability to cover costs without discrimination could be allowed, with argument being heard by a suitable court. Unfortunately, there is a much more difficult complication to overcome.

If standard price discrimination on the sale of physically identical products were banned, it would be open to firms to use different brand names or attach different grade ratings to the products sold in the different markets and to claim the commodities were not identical. To give support to the claim, it would be a simple matter to create a slight difference. For example, oxygen sold to hospitals could be slightly purer than oxygen sold to welders. This avenue of avoidance of a general ban could be closed only by a rule that price differences between different products must not be greater than differences in average costs. And that rule has just been examined and rejected.

It would be feasible, however, to confer a right upon consumers to appeal to a quasi-judicial regulatory agency, which would be empowered to order a discontinuation of the practice and perhaps also award damages. The defence of net benefit could be allowed, with the onus of proof resting on the accused parties, since they alone would possess the information required to determine that issue. Such a procedure would reduce the task of enforcement to manageable proportions. It would also meet the difficulty mentioned earlier since the net benefit defence might take the form of evidence that the lower-priced market would not be served if price discrimination were not permitted. If such a procedure were followed, it would seem desirable to clothe the quasi-judicial agency with the power to set aside a defence that the products sold were not identical if the difference was a spurious one undertaken to mask the price discrimination.

Another variant of price discrimination which warrants attention occurs when the mill net from sales of a commodity in the domestic markets exceeds the mill net from export sales. Some of the major

Canadian export industries follow cooperative pricing strategies with respect to sales in the domestic markets but must meet the prices set by world competition in their export markets. It is possible for price discrimination to occur because transport costs afford a natural protection of the domestic market. Our criteria require that the domestic consumer have the protection of price competition or the closest attainable equivalent. This condition could be realized without resort to a general ban on this form of price discrimination. It would suffice to grant buyers a right of appeal against higher discriminatory prices as just suggested with respect to standard price discrimination. A right of defence of net benefit should be permitted but it is difficult to imagine grounds on which such a defence might be based. Minor differences in mill net yields should be ignored, and it should not be necessary to allege a deliberate practice of discriminating but only a pricing practice which resulted in discrimination and substantial disadvantage.

HORIZONTAL MERGERS

It was reasoned earlier in this chapter that companies do not possess an inherent right to merge, to sell themselves to the highest bidder, or to take over another company. These privileges are conditional upon their being in the public interest. Ideally, then, no merger should occur unless there is a net public benefit or at least no net disadvantage.

If these statements are accepted, the policy issue to be decided is one of technique only. And only two general procedures are possible. The first implies an assumption that a net benefit results from most mergers. Accordingly, there would be no rule banning mergers in general, but the Director of Investigations and Research for the Combines Investigation Act would be empowered to challenge proposed and past mergers. If a net detriment were found by the proposed quasi-judicial agency, the merger would be proscribed or dissolved. If no detriment were found, the merger would be allowed to proceed.

The alternative procedure would be to require all mergers large enough to be of much consequence to receive authorization from the quasi-judicial agency prior to their implementation. The mergers which must receive prior authorization might fall into either of two categories: those in which any of the companies involved are nonresident or nonresident-controlled; and those in which, on the one hand, any of the companies to be party to the merger possess, or would possess after the merger, a share of any large domestic market greater than a given percentage (a large domestic market might be defined as a market in which sales of the product in question exceed a certain percentage of the sales in the national market) or, on the other hand, any of the companies involved have assets or sales exceeding a given absolute amount.

It is at once apparent that, in practice, the two procedures would be almost identical, provided that the same rules were rigorously applied and enforced. There is no substantial difference between allowing all mergers to go forward provided that they are not successfully challenged and allowing only those mergers to go forward which pass a screening test. However, the latter would be the easier to enforce and should be preferred by companies because it would provide certainty concerning the legality of a contemplated action and would protect them from an order of dissolution. The former procedure is superior only if it is expected that most mergers—say over 70 percent—yield a net benefit and therefore would be permitted.

The issue of horizontal mergers is difficult because the effects on company behaviour of a reduction in the number of firms in an industry, even when the number of companies is already small, are not clear and it is surely desirable that the high costs of short runs, too many plants and too many firms, be reduced. The latter can be accomplished only by the reduction, by competition, of the number of firms producing a given line or by mergers or intercompany agreements.

Uncertainty concerning the effects of increased concentration upon pricing practices stems both from the empirical findings and from a priori reasoning. Correlations between profit rates and concentration ratios have proven indecisive.[13] The difference in profit rates of unconcentrated industries as a group and concentrated industries as a group is persistent and substantial. But concentration ratios do not account for an impressive proportion of the variance of profit rates among industries which are concentrated. Nor should this finding be very surprising. The investigations rest on the assumption that oligopolists practice limit pricing; that is, they are assumed to endeavour to earn the highest rates of profit consistent with the constraint of discouraging entry. And it is also assumed that the more concentrated is the industry, the easier it is to practise limit pricing (because the recognition of mutual dependence is the greater) and the more effective is the limit pricing likely to be (because entry is likely to be more difficult). These assumptions leave out of account the observation that some concentrated industries have low-profit preference price leaders, for example, aluminium and steel in the United States, and others have high-profit preference price leaders, for example, automobiles. Also omitted is the observation that profit rates of most of the pure monopolies that have been investigated, such as the United Shoe Machinery Company and the Aluminum Company of America when it was a monopoly, have been substantially less than those in several concentrated oligopolies.

Another defect of simple correlations between profit rates and concentration ratios is that the latter do not capture all of the constraints upon increasing profits by limit pricing, namely, the differing heights of barriers to entry and the existence or absence of a fringe of small companies, of overseas sources of supply, and of poor substitutes. Consequently, concentration ratios do not adequately measure the monopoly power of oligopolies when they practise limit pricing.

The low correlation between profit rates and concentration ratios lends some support to the basic tenet of this study, namely, that firms in most oligopoly industries act on the recognition of their mutual dependence and adopt cooperative pricing strategies, whether the number of competitors in the particular market is only three or is more than twenty. Of course, one does not expect identical behaviour regardless of the number within that range. When there are only three and all have a substantial share of the market, a price-cutting tactic is unthinkable. But when there are as many as twenty it is likely to be profitable for at least one to play the role of the maverick. Nevertheless, the relation between the number of firms and pricing behaviour is a loose one.

Although it is a simple matter to explain away the low correlation between concentration ratios and profit rates, the assumption that a decrease in the number of competitors by merger will probably result in higher profit rates and therefore higher prices is nevertheless left without strong empirical support. It must be accepted, therefore, that consumer detriment from a general presumption of decreased competition should not be given a heavy weight. But this does not mean that the effect of a particular merger upon competition should not be a matter of inquiry. It would obviously be appropriate to inquire whether there has been a history of mergers in the industry or whether the merger in question is likely to start a trend. It might be that an immature oligopoly in which cooperative pricing strategies occasionally broke down was in danger of being transformed into a mature oligopoly able to practise cooperative pricing more successfully. Second, it might be that the company to be taken over has been or is likely to be a maverick endeavouring to grow under the umbrella of the stable prices of its larger rivals. Third, it might be that the merger would increase the integration of marketing with production and thus, on the reasoning of the section entitled "Refusal to Sell" above, result in public detriment.

Moreover, a decrease in competition is not the only public detriment which may result from mergers. There is surely a loss when a vigorous and efficient independent company is absorbed by a moribund large one. It is also possible that a merger may decrease research and development and other innovative activity. Also, the only substantial reason for many mergers is the desire of one of the companies to increase its share of the market. But if the consumer is presumed to have a preference for a range of choice not just of differentiated products but also of suppliers, there is a detriment to the consumer. In any event, product differentiation is more likely to be substantial when the products are produced by different companies than it is when they are produced by the same company. Finally, if the take-over bid is made by a nonresident company for an independent Canadian company, the preferences of many members of the Canadian public are likely to be adversely affected.

Taken together, these reasons seem sufficient to justify placing the onus of proof on companies wishing to merge that a net benefit will accrue. And if this is accepted, it is relevant to ask what kind of benefits may be claimed and what alleged benefits should be rejected.

Considerable guidance in this matter can be gained from recent discussions of the problem by American economists.[14] Some suggest the rejection of all purely pecuniary gains; for example, the fact that a merged company can buy television time more cheaply by a pooling of advertising. Similarly, an increased payoff per dollar of any sales effort costs is not considered to be a real economy but only a pecuniary one, without benefit to the consumer. Increased financial strength and increased access to the capital markets are other examples of purely pecuniary gains. Second, increases in efficiency should not be counted if they are expected to be temporary or could be obtained in any way other than by merger, such as the raising of the calibre of the management of one of the companies. Finally, lower costs that could be obtained by internal growth of the companies within a reasonable period of time should also be inadmissible.

The benefit which is left as an admissible claim on behalf of a merger consists of reductions in real costs. And this benefit nearly always requires the integration of production facilities or an increase in the specialization of plants within the firm. In general, of course, the greater the probability that the reductions in costs will result in lower prices, the stronger the case for the merger. In addition, there are circumstances when a merger or even a series of mergers will enhance competition, notably the combination of many small firms into an aggressive challenger to the dominant companies. For example, the emergence of a fairly large company making automobile replacement parts is likely to increase competition substantially, since its interests would be in sharp conflict with those of the automobile companies.

Finally, if a merger is likely to increase productivity but also to reduce competition, it should be allowed to proceed, provided that a change in the competitive environment is made which offsets the defect. The major policy variable by which the environment can be made more competitive is, of course, the tariff.

It is apparent that there is no conflict between the desire to reduce the cost of short runs and inadequate plant size by fostering mergers and a rule that all mergers of substantial size must pass through a screening test to demonstrate net benefit. Not many mergers result in the merging of plant facilities or an increase in the specialization of plant operations.[15] The real economies achieved are therefore hard to discern, and one would not expect many of them to be able to pass the test. On the other hand, there are numerous instances of high costs of short runs and plants too small to realize most of the economies of scale in industries in which the companies show no disposition to merge. These are the industries in which mergers and production agreements should be encouraged. However, if the companies are subsidiaries of United States parents, there is little prospect that the sponsoring of mergers would meet with success. A merger or a production agreement between a Canadian subsidiary of a United States corporation and any of its competitors in the Canadian market would probably be struck down by the United States courts. The main hope lies with companies controlled by Canadian residents.

VERTICAL INTEGRATION OF PRODUCTION

The logical starting point for the discussion of the issues of vertical integration is the rule developed in the previous section. Companies are not entitled to merge unless the merger is consistent with the public interest. Sometimes that screening test should be easily passed because substantial reductions in costs are effected by the physical integration of some of the stages of production. Perhaps the most striking instances consist of the integration of plants producing semiprocessed materials with plants producing fabricated products. The transportation of molten metals directly from the mill to the foundry avoids the cost of cooling and reheating the metal. Transportation of woodpulp in sludge directly from the pulp mill to the paperboard mill avoids the costs of drying and bailing the woodpulp and its mixing and beating to restore it to a sludge.

However, any other vertical integration by merger or any other vertical tie between producer and customer would be in conflict with the objective of marketing and distributing commodities at the least attainable cost. Vertical integration sometimes increases monopoly power and usually extends it to another stage of production.

Discussion of this matter is most easily conducted in terms of an hypothetical example. Let us assume that there are six paperboard companies and thirty paper box companies and that no cost reductions are to be had by the integration of the production of paperboard and boxes (a realistic assumption). Absorption of the thirty by the six would replace the uneasy action on the recognition of mutual dependence by the thirty with the much easier cooperative pricing by the six. If, additionally, the paperboard companies already produce boxes in competition with their customers, the box companies, competition between the two would be eliminated by the integration; a substantial decrease in competition is likely, because the interests of the box companies often conflict with those of their supplier-competitors.

In these circumstances, it would be necessary to ban mergers altogether, to prevent a trend to complete integration. If for any reason one of the six decided to buy out one of its customers or one of its competitor's customers, the others would feel constrained to do the same; otherwise they would be in danger of losing their markets.

It is maintained by some economists that vertical integration does not increase monopoly power and therefore does not result in detriment to the consumer, even though monopoly power is extended from one stage of production to another. Accordingly, in our hypothetical example, nothing would be changed when the six absorbed the thirty except the structure of the industry. The reasoning is that the thirty would be price-competitive and therefore earning only normal profits and the six would either be engaging in price competition (and would continue to do so after they had absorbed the thirty) or would be formally or informally colluding. If the latter, they would be acting in concert to maximize their profits collectively. To do so they must calculate the most profitable prices for paperboard boxes, having regard to the competition faced from containers of other materials. From these prices they would deduct the average cost of the fabrication of boxes, including only normal profits. This calculation would indicate the most profitable monopoly price for paperboard. Hence the six would be taking the maximum monopoly profits available before they absorbed the thirty box companies, and integration would not increase their monopoly power. Hence there would be no detriment to the consumer from the vertical integration; improvement could be effected only by dissolution of the six or some similar drastic measure.

However, this reasoning is open to the criticism that it assumes only two polar alternatives: the six paperboard companies either engage in price competition or collude to maximize their collective profits. But neither behaviour is likely. Even when there are six companies or fewer, it is unusual for companies to be willing to give up their independence of action to the extent required to maximize collective profits. The only agreement that can usually be reached and sustained is the convention not to engage in price competition among themselves. Within this constraint business is solicited from competitors' customers. The most likely behaviour is that the six independently determine their prices on the recognition of their mutual dependence. Consequently, prices are effectively set by the company which is the most concerned to discourage new entrants, to avoid public inquiry and regulation, to discourage its competitors from cutting prices, and to discourage the box companies from trying to find alternative sources of supply. Pricing is also subject to the constraint of the price leader's notions of fair pricing and it is unlikely that capturing monopoly profits available to the capital employed by the box companies would be considered to be admissible conduct.

Even if the six were colluding, however, the monopoly profits available to them would be increased by the absorption of the box companies. Entry to the paperboard industry would be made more difficult by the disappearance of the box companies; a new entrant would lack that market. In the extreme, if box companies were the only market for paperboard, entry to the paperboard industry would be possible only for an integrated company which was able to take away from the established companies some share of the market for paperboard boxes.

It may be concluded, therefore, that vertical integration between a semiprocessed or raw material stage and a fabrication stage of production extends the monopoly behaviour of the more concentrated stage to the less concentrated stage and makes entry to the industry more difficult at both stages. Consequently, such vertical mergers should be required to pass the test of demonstrating net benefit to the public. And when considering such cases, the proposed quasi-judicial agency should particularly consider whether a single merger which seemed without effect by itself could begin a trend which was undesirable. And it follows from the argument concerning withdrawal of the right of refusal to sell that any forward integration from production into marketing should be deemed to result in a net detriment; mergers between production and distribution companies should be subject to a general ban, since there is no real economy available from integration.

CONGLOMERATE MERGERS

By definition, conglomerate mergers do not result in the physical merging of production facilities, so there is no increase in productivity. There may be pecuniary gains, such as an improved access to the capital markets or an increased effectiveness of sales promotion. But by the rules developed in the previous two sections, such gains should not be counted in a calculation of net benefit to the consumer unless resource allocation is improved or overall productivity of the economy enhanced. It may be claimed that management is strengthened in a way which could not otherwise be achieved. However, such a contention is frequently almost impossible to judge. It is negated if the smaller company being taken over is the more efficient, as indicated by comparative rates of profits and growth. In the more usual case, clear evidence is lacking, and there is a presumption that any gain is likely to be temporary but no presumption that the improved management could not be attained except by the merger. Indeed, this issue would not even arise in many cases, since it is not unusual for the acquiring company to make no change in the management of the company taken over.

Usually merger proposals are given the benefit of the doubt; it is assumed that a gain will result, at least to the shareholder. But there seems to be an increasing tendency to identify corporation managers and the groups who promote a merger as the primary beneficiaries. The presumption that mergers usually increase profit rates is being challenged both in and out of academic circles.[16] For example, a recent study of the major industrial firms of the United States found that corporations which had been involved in few mergers returned a higher profit rate to the original stockholders than did firms that had been involved in many mergers.[17] Paradoxically, the performance of conglomerate merger firms was found to be better than that of horizontal and vertical merger firms.[18]

It is nevertheless possible for real gains to result. On occasion, real economies in distribution may be achieved—for example, in warehousing. Also, common sense suggests that if the company being taken over is in financial, production, or marketing difficulties, so that bankruptcy is likely, its acquisition by a conglomerate firm (or any other) would probably yield a gain to some with no offsetting loss to others. Similarly, if the firm taking over another has a history of aggressive competitive action, has reduced its costs below those of its rivals, has forced the rationalization of an industry, or has cut prices, there is likely to be a net gain by allowing it to expand by absorbing companies which lack these virtues.

A reversal of these situations identifies mergers which common sense suggests will result in a net detriment to the consumer, that is, when the firm being taken over has a better record of profit and growth rates, and more importantly, when it is an independent company which has a history of aggressive competitive action, has reduced its costs below those of its rivals, has forced the rationalization of an industry, or has cut prices while the acquiring firm has not.

In general, there is a presumption against conglomerate mergers because large firms tend to be conservative in all their activities, including their pricing behaviour. At least insofar as their large competitors are concerned, they prefer action on the recognition of mutual dependence.

The appropriate policy with respect to conglomerate mergers is therefore the same as it is for horizontal and vertical ones. They should pass through the screening test of approval by the proposed quasi-judicial agency, which would exercise judgement in the application of the specific criteria and instructions given to it.

THE ADVERTISING DILEMMA

There are two basic problems that stand in the way of a reconciliation of advertising with the consumers' sovereignty rule. The first is that anything less than the whole truth can be misleading and often is. But to require the whole truth would be too exacting a rule to apply; that ideal has not been approached in the political arena and is not fostered by our tradition of the adversary approach to the establishment of the truth. The difficulty is inherent in the coupling of sales promotion and the dissemination of information; the conflict of interest between the producer and consumer is complete. The producer's objective of selling his product requires that superior qualities be stressed or invented, preferences created, and defects concealed; the consumer's objective is precise and comprehensive information.

The second basic problem stems from the volume of messages aimed at the consumer; from his point of view, the volume of advertising has surely run into negative returns. But, short of quantitative curbs on persuasion advertising, there is no way of enabling advertising to perform its informative function. The consumer is inundated with such a welter of conflicting claims it is impossible for him to sort out the wheat from the chaff. One claim negates another, and the consumer has neither the time nor the competence to sort them out. The volume of messages is so great that a statement of the whole truth could not get through.

However, if the reformation of advertising to have it perform efficiently the information function on which its utility to the consumer rests is a lost cause, something less might be achieved. If it is too much to expect the producer to tell the whole truth, it might still be a considerable gain if he were required to disclose information indispensable to a comparison with competing products. Withholding such information, on the ground that disclosure might damage its competitive position, is a privilege to which the company is not entitled. For example, the octane ratings of gasoline are treated as confidential information. Yet it is the only precise and common measuring rod. Since octane ratings are not posted, much premium gasoline is used by owners of older cars to no purpose. It is true that the manufacturers' handbooks state whether standard or premium is to be used, but the standard-grade gasoline of today has as high an octane rating as the premium-grade had a few years ago. Without precise information, which can be conveyed only by using numbers, the consumer cannot buy to the maximum advantage. Similarly, many consumers would be pleased if the regulations which require that weights or volumes be stated were also to require that they be stated in at least eight-point type and if a uniform system of weights and measures were to be used—either our clumsy pounds, ounces, and inches or a complete conversion to the metric system.

These are the simple and obvious examples of information indispensable for satisfaction of the consumers' right to be informed. But once we leave products for which there is some common, relevant measuring rod (though no implication is intended that weight and volume are always the most important information), the difficulties pile up. The policy aspect of the matter, however, does not relate to the difficulties. Rather, it is the need to decide once and for all time that companies do not possess a right to withhold, or indeed not to advertise, relevant information which is easily conveyed. If this policy decision had been affirmed and firmly adhered to in the past, the consumer would have a great deal more information easily available to him than he now has.

To say that much is probably not straying far from a consensus. It would be otherwise once one moved out of the realm of regulations which were fairly readily complied with and into the realm of government activities. Thus, it is a popular view that the Department of Consumer and Corporate Affairs would perform a valued service if it sponsored a watchdog and information agency with a budget large enough to enable it to run radio and television programs reporting tests of product qualities and even filling in the pieces missing from manufacturers' advertising messages, to turn the truth into the whole truth. If the agency were private it would need a large appropriation to fight the many law suits which would ensue. If the agency were an arm of a government, it would be considered unfair that a private company should be unable to undo the damage done to its business by an error in a testing program which gave its products a low rating. However, damage of that sort could be largely undone by subsequent reporting. What many manufacturers fear most, of course, is that their products would have to stand or fall solely on the basis of quality and price, and the value of their investment in trademarks would be much reduced. It can be concluded that the absence of such government-sponsored dissemination of information is conclusive evidence that the producers' interests are accorded priority over consumers' interests, and it seems unlikely that it will be otherwise in our lifetime. A contrary view would no doubt be based on the arguments that it is not possible substantially to supplement the information already made available by manufacturers, those who make a contrary assertion simply not knowing much about the products in question, and that, to the extent that it is possible to do so, the function is already being adequately performed by the American publication *Consumer Reports* and others like it.

Similarly, it is a recently popular idea that there should be an ombudsman to fight for the consumer's interests in opposition to provincial government practices and policies when these clearly conflict; for example, one provincial government's one-price policy for all brands of beer throughout the province and its prevention of price cutting by a small brewery. Unfortunately, the constitutional and political obstacles to this perfectly sensible proposal are formidable.

Finally, the idea that a valuable contribution to consumer welfare could be made by a government agency which undertook to push selected industries away from grossly wasteful behaviour toward the goal of prices equal to the least attainable cost is attractive at the general level. An example, mentioned earlier, is the sponsoring of real estate information centres. However, a government agency of that sort might prove no more efficient than the employment offices of the Department of Manpower and Immigration. Some means of improving performance while still leaving the function in the private sector is therefore more attractive.

EXCESSIVE EASE OF ENTRY

Several times throughout this study, reference has been made to industries which are chronically "sick" in the sense that most of the capital and labour do not make average profits or wages. They could be put to more profitable use elsewhere. And it was reasoned that the root cause of the sickness is that entry is too easy and exit is not fast enough. Since firms are usually family-sized and numerous, there is normally active price competition. This keeps returns low, which exerts great pressure on surplus capacity but, given the attraction of the activity to many persons, even that pressure is insufficient to drive out the excessive commitment of resources to the industry. The firms that comprise the Greater Ottawa Truckers Association are a classic instance of entrepreneurs caught in this dilemma.

It appears that no wholly satisfactory solution has been contrived. Sometimes an improvement for the entrepreneurs is effected by a licensing curb upon entry accompanied by legally collusive pricing or the regulation of prices by a government agency. But security provided against unduly severe price competition is by itself insufficient to cure the excessive commitment of resources to the industry and the low returns to capital and labour. In the absence of a capital cost or other barrier to entry, excess capacity drives the return to capital below normal, and in the absence of a union to restrict the entry of labour, wages are driven down below those available elsewhere. Consequently, an exemption from the ban upon price agreements, as requested by the Greater Ottawa Truckers Association,[19] would not by itself improve matters substantially. On the other hand, if a change in technology were to increase the minimum size of the firm large enough to realize most of the economies of scale, thereby erecting a capital cost barrier to entry, the "natural" and sufficient remedy would emerge.[20]

The remedy most frequently proposed by economists is that entry be rationed by a periodic auction of licenses. However, even under ideal conditions, at least three difficulties face a licensing system: first, a unit of capacity has to be established and kept current with technical advances; second, companies already in the business lack security of tenure; and third, the prices of licenses are bid so high that few companies earn normal profits.

Consequently, the most effective remedy is likely to be the simplest and most direct one. Since the problems of these industries are all due to too-easy entry, the obvious corrective is to increase the costs of entry somewhat. As mentioned, a natural corrective would take the form of higher capital costs for the smallest firm large enough to realize sufficient of the economies of scale to survive. An unnatural remedy, then, is the imposition of a capital cost barrier. But the auction of licenses which are good for all time and transferable is not the best approach; the optimum number of licenses would still have to be calculated. Instead, the minimum capital cost required to prevent competition from being too severe should be discovered by trial and error. Let us assume that this sum is found to be $10,000 in excess of the minimum capital expenditures. Then, a new entrant should be required to post $10,000 as a condition of receiving a license, the $10,000 to be refunded as follows (with interest paid in the meantime): to the company at the end of, say, five years, if it is still solvent; and to creditors of the company at any time before then, if the company becomes insolvent.

This simple scheme would impose no cost or penalty upon the companies in the industry; it could allow them to make normal profits and could prevent the absorption of excessive resources into the industry. The scheme is obviously not feasible for the rationing of the exploitation of natural resources, because it would not capture any of the rent for the Crown or other owner.

Such a scheme would be criticized on the ground that there would be a detriment to those who were excluded from the industry; but no improvement is possible without limiting entry. The scheme would also be subject to the charge that it turned entry into the industry into a privilege, and that privilege should not be rationed on the basis of the possession of capital. But this is how the free enterprise system operates.

Means to the ends

For easier reference and to avoid misunderstanding, the various conclusions concerning the measures to be taken in order to realize the objectives cited in the first part of this chapter are repeated below with elaboration where necessary.

Implementation of these regulations would require that the present Restrictive Trade Practices Commission be converted into a quasi-judicial agency charged with the task of applying the rules to particular cases. And it is clear that the new agency (for convenience, let us call it the Competitive Practices Commission, or CPC) could not perform its functions if appeals were to be allowed to the courts on findings of fact. The courts would simply set aside the commission's findings and substitute their own judgement, regardless of their lack of expertise, and they would disregard the regulations and instructions which should be binding upon the CPC.

The courts' jurisdiction in the new national competition policy should be confined to points of law only. Accordingly, the only cases to be heard by them should be those in which the sole issue is whether there is evidence, admissible under the rules of evidence employed by our courts, that an offence has been committed. These offences would be violations of general rules which would apply in any or all circumstances. They would therefore be few in number: a conspiracy to agree on prices, collusive agreements to allocate markets or prevent the entry of new competitors, patently false statements concerning prices, and refusal to comply with a directive of the CPC.[21] The courts would, of course, also hear appeals from rulings by the CPC on points of law only: whether, contrary to the instructions of the new act, that tribunal had acted improperly by refusing to entertain evidence, whether it had exceeded its powers, and whether the legislation was *ultra vires* the federal government.

Little comment is required concerning the deliberate and complete exclusion of the courts from any role in the enforcement of the new competition policy, except for offences where the economic effects are not at issue. Unlike the courts of the United States, the Canadian courts have followed the British procedure and refuse to look through the form to the substance. They follow the doctrine of statutory interpretation which considers only the plain meaning of the words, and they absolve themselves of any responsibility for determining the objective of the statutes in order to further the intentions of Parliament. They have insisted that they are not competent to understand reasoning founded on economic theory. Finally, the Canadian legal fraternity has not developed an effective cooperation with economists similar to that which has been developed in the United States. Having insisted that they are able to distinguish between only pure black and pure white, the Canadian courts have left the government no alternative to referring matters of infinite gradations of grey to quasi-judicial administrative tribunals.

However, if all questions of fact, for example, whether a merger would result in detriment to the public, are to be decided by the new CPC, appeal to some other authority should be permitted. It is contrary to our traditions that any agency possess the power to act arbitrarily. The only practicable safeguard would be to allow appeals on findings of fact to a second quasi-judicial agency, which we shall call the Competitive Practices Appeals Tribunal (CPAT) to distinguish it from the Competitive Practices Commission. As mentioned, appeals should be allowed to the courts on points of law. This restriction would have little effect, of course, if it were true, as it is often said to be, that any competent lawyer can convert a question of fact into a point of law. However, the statute should lay out the terms of reference and the procedure to be followed, such as what evidence must be given due consideration, so that there would rarely be occasion for challenging whether the CPC or the CPAT had proceeded improperly or exceeded their powers. Appeals from their rulings should therefore be infrequent.

The per se rules, namely, the bans on agreements to fix prices, allocate markets, and exclude new entrants and on misleading advertising concerning prices should be enforced by the taking of cases, by the Director of Investigation and Research, directly to the courts for conviction and the issuing of restraining orders. To facilitate this procedure, the Combines Investigation Act should be amended to stipulate precisely the practices which are violations. Section 33C(1), concerning misleading advertising regarding normal prices, already has the required precise wording. Where the combines investigation branch obtains evidence admissible by the courts of a violation of the law, nothing would be gained by having a preliminary hearing before the CPC. However, even though the need for the courts to develop some expertise would be at a minimum, there would still be an advantage in taking all such cases directly to the Exchequer Court. In such open-and-shut cases, there should be no argument concerning public detriment or extenuating circumstances and no opportunity afforded magistrates or judges of the lower provincial courts to indulge themselves in lengthy *obiter dicta* concerning the nature of the defendant's actions and the economic effects they have had. It should be a cut-and-dried matter of the Exchequer Court's judging, on the evidence, whether an offence had been committed.

It is suggested that, in addition to whatever fine is imposed by the court, it be mandatory that all price agreement cases in which an offence is found to have been committed be referred to the CPC. The latter should be required to discover what measures, if any, would improve the performance of the industry. In the event that the commission's proposed remedy requires action by the cabinet, notably a change in the tariff, it should be mandatory that the appropriate minister report to Parliament the action taken, and he should do so within a reasonably short period of time, for example, ninety days.

It is suggested further that all cases investigated by the combines investigation branch in which no conclusive evidence, admissible by the courts, of an offence is discovered, but in which there is evidence of tacit collusion by conscious parallel action or even of an absence of price competition, should be referred to the CPC for an investigation of whether there are any feasible measures, within the constitutional powers of the federal government, which would improve performance. Recommendations of remedial measures made by the CPC in these cases might well be referred to the CPAT, which would provide for hearings so that the companies involved would have the opportunity to defend their record. If the measures proposed by the CPC were endorsed by the CPAT and required that action be taken by the cabinet, its report should be submitted to the appropriate minister, and as before, he should be required to report within, say, ninety days the action taken. It is contemplated that the measures recommended would consist mainly of tariff changes, the sponsoring of mergers, and the issuance of cease-and-desist orders.

Additional details concerning how the various measures of the new competition policy might be administered are contained in the elaboration of the summary of these measures given below.

If the CPC were charged with a set of duties and functions without precise guidelines, there would be a danger that its rulings would not differ significantly from those of the present Restrictive Trade Practices Commission. It has been stressed several times in this study that several policy decisions must be made by Parliament as the prerequisites for an effective competition policy. In keeping with our democratic traditions, these decisions should first be set out in a White Paper and then incorporated into the statutes. The rules laid down in the act and regulations should detail the circumstances in which the CPC shall find a public detriment and those in which it may find a net public benefit. The judgement to be exercised by the CPC would therefore be narrowly constrained.

The proposed course of action would bring to the fore disputes concerning the jurisdiction of the federal government over matters which might be thought to fall under the trade-and-commerce clause of the British North America Act but might also be contended to be within the provincial jurisdiction over property and civil rights. However, since these jurisdictional disputes must be faced in any event, it would be as well to have them tested at the outset. It is assumed that it would be within the competence of the federal government to impose most of the regulations suggested in this report by proscribing practices, whether they be mergers, pricing practices, or the restriction of sales to franchised dealers, with authority conferred upon the CPC to grant exemption whenever, upon investigation, it found that the exemption would result in a net public benefit. The power to grant exemption would apply to all except the general bans.

Under the proposed procedure, the role to be played by the combines investigation branch of the Department of Consumer and Corporate Affairs would be much reduced. All matters involving any degree of judgement concerning economic effects would be the responsibility mainly of the CPC and, to a much smaller extent, the CPAT—the latter on appeals from the CPC only. Thus, all references for investigation, such as that concerning the drug industry, would go to the CPC. This commission would, of course, require a large staff. It would be a negation of any policy decision if the CPC were not provided with the required funds and staffed with persons who not only possess the required training and experience but also are in sympathy with the policy decisions. The staffing problem could be made less acute by the availability of some of the present staff of the Director of Investigation and Research.

THE REGULATIONS

1. The ban on conspiracies to set prices should be applied to the service industries.

2. There should be a ban on all regional price discrimination on homogeneous products sold to a given class of customers and on all price discrimination on sales to firms which are competitors. These rules would be general, subject to rulings by the CPC that a particular practice constitutes discrimination, that a product is differentiated and hence exempt, that a group of customers is or is not a single class, and that firms are or are not competitors.

3. There should be mandatory f.o.b. pricing on sales of all homogeneous commodities sold by a company to a single class of customers when total freight costs exceed 5 percent of the revenue derived from sales of the commodity (calculated at the wholesale price excluding sales and excise taxes and duties). Interpretation and supervision of this rule would be performed by the CPC. On application by injured parties, the CPC would also order that the prices charged on sales in domestic markets for a commodity which is also exported should yield the same milldoor revenue as sales to export markets.

4. There should be a complete elimination of the refusal-to-sell privilege with respect to sales to retailers and to wholesalers. The manufacturer should retain no property rights in the product or its image once it is sold. The existing ban on resale price maintenance would thus be superseded and the defences of section 32(5) removed. Where manufacturers sell only to retailers, this withdrawal of the firm's right to choose its distributors would require the calculation of a constructed manufacturer's selling price to wholesalers. Applications for orders to manufacturers to comply with the rule would be made to the CPC, and it would rule whether the applicant is a bona fide distributor and would hear charges that a manufacturer refused to sell on uniform terms to companies lodging complaints, for example, by making shipments of defective articles, by frequently shipping to the wrong address apparently in error, and the like. The CPC would also hear defences by manufacturers of refusal to sell on the sole grounds of insufficient capacity or stocks.

5. There should be a ban on consignment selling which the CPC, on application by persons or companies who allege detriment, finds to be practised in an industry or market to the extent that price competition among retailers or other traders is substantially reduced and therefore the consignment selling is the equivalent of manufacturer-sponsored resale price maintenance.

6. Persons and companies who consider themselves adversely affected by specified practices should have a right to lodge a complaint with the CPC, which could order that the practice be discontinued and might award damages. The specified practices should be the following: predatory pricing or the predatory use of fighting brands, where the entire history of a series of competitive moves leaves no reasonable doubt that the objective was to bankrupt the complainants or prevent them from cutting prices; and standard price discrimination by the segregation of markets by all firms in an industry, that is, when a company sells identical commodities, or commodities which differ in an inconsequential way, to more than one class of customers at substantially different prices, those paying the higher prices would complain to the CPC.

7. An appropriate department of the federal government should sponsor intercompany agreements and horizontal mergers that would achieve specialization in fewer lines and models, thereby reducing the costs of short runs. The department should take the initiative in encouraging such mergers and agreements, but only the CPC should have authority to grant exemption from the ban on mergers. In the normal course, obviously, the department would discuss and clear a prospective agreement or merger with the CPC before encouraging it.

8. Tariffs should be made subservient to the national competition policy. Canadian tariffs should be unilaterally reduced to the minimum required for normal profits after the protected industry has been rationalized. It would not matter if rationalization reduced the number of firms to one, provided there were sufficient competition from imports.

9. The CPC should scrutinize all vertical, horizontal, and conglomerate mergers involving sales or assets above specified amounts or involving nonresident or nonresident-controlled companies. No merger should be authorized except where a reduction of costs or other increase in efficiency would be effected by the merger and could not be obtained in any other way.

10. On a petition by an industry or on a reference from the cabinet or as a result of its own investigation, the CPC should have the authority

to make a recommendation that an artificial capital cost barrier be imposed upon entry to a sick industry suffering from excessive ease of entry. Such recommendations should pass a screening test in the form of a reference to the CPAT, which, if the recommendation were endorsed, would request the appropriate minister to take the required action. (If that action lay outside the federal power, the minister should seek the cooperation of a provincial government.)

11. When the CPC finds during its investigations, however initiated, that price competition among the major companies of an industry is absent, it should have the authority to recommend that it supervise the activities of the trade associations of the industry, with the objective of reducing the contacts which the executives of the companies have with one another for whatever reason, because the participation in common endeavours reinforces the recognition of mutual dependence and thus increases the ability of the companies to practise co-operative pricing. (This measure has not been discussed previously.)

POSSIBLE GAINS

Whenever changes from the established order are advocated, it is appropriate that an estimate of the magnitude of the probable gains be attempted. If such a magnitude could be estimated in the present case, it would be the correct measure of the economic waste attributed to imperfect competition, on the reasoning that a comparison with an ideal performance has no practical relevance; the operational definition of economic waste is the shortfall of the actual below a specified best attainable performance.

Obviously, and unfortunately, the gains to be expected from the competition policy suggested in this study cannot be forecast with any precision. Nevertheless, it can be asserted with considerable confidence that the gains would be many times greater than the loss attributable to the existence of monopoly in the writings of economists over the past decade. These measures indicate a loss of a fraction of 1 percent of the Gross National Product.[22] But the only waste measured in those studies is the so-called deadweight loss of consumers' surplus. In contrast, in this study, that loss is considered to be negligible and is left out of account altogether.

In chapter 2, the economic wastes attributable to the absence of price competition were listed as follows:

1. In the production of commodities, some part of (a) the high costs of plants too small to realize most of the economies of scale, (b) the high costs of short runs of too many lines, styles, and models, (c) the fixed costs of multiple designs and styling, and (d) excessive reserve plant capacity.
2. Much of the amount of resources that are in excess of those that would be devoted to sales promotion by manufacturers if sales promotion were subject to a strong constraint imposed by price competition.
3. Much of the amount of resources that are in excess of those that would be absorbed by retailing if there were always price competition among retailers.

Waste falling under item 1(a), the diseconomies of plants and firms too small to realize most of the economies of scale, overlaps item 1 (b), the high cost of short runs, to such an extent that it would be extremely difficult to disentangle the two, even by arbitrary estimates. Much the same comment applies to item 1(c), the fixed costs of multiple designs and styling. Consequently, no figure will be set down separately for either 1(a) or 1(c).

The magnitude of gains relating to item 1(b), the high cost of short runs, depends crucially on the number and size of industries for which rationalization by specialization is feasible without economic integration with the United States. The Wonnacotts' full cost estimate of the potential gain from United States-Canada free trade is 10 percent of Gross National Product (GNP).[23] If it is assumed that one-half of the potential gain from free trade could be realized by rationalization within the domestic market, the potential gain indicated is 5 percent of the GNP.

An arbitrary estimate can also be made concerning item 1(d), waste due to excess plant capacity. If the new competition policy undermined pricing by oligopolists on the recognition of their mutual dependence, the penalty for adding substantially to capacity years in advance of the increase in demand would be greatly increased; periods of low profits attributable to low operating rates would be replaced by periods of very low profits, or losses, due to low operating rates and low prices. But it is not likely that action on the recognition of mutual dependence would be sufficiently weakened to impose this penalty for excessive expansion very often. Breaks in the price level would probably occur more frequently than they do now as a consequence of very large excess capacity, but not with sufficient regularity to improve performance substantially. However, the intrusion of the jobber between the manufacturer and the retailer and the subordination of tariff policy to competition policy would concentrate competition upon low-cost production to a greater extent than now prevails. And one of the ways of achieving lower costs would be by curbing a cavalier lack of concern about the amount of reserve capacity. Given the correct ceiling to prices imposed by imports achieved by the manipulation of tariffs, the reduction of excessive reserve capacity could be significant. If the output of tariff-sheltered manufacturing is set at 15 percent of GNP, the interest cost of plant capacity is equated to the depreciation cost and that is set at 10 percent of manufacturing cost, and it is assumed that the reduction of reserve capacity would be 10 percent of total capacity, then the saving will amount to 0.15 percent of GNP.

The reduction of wastes in item 2, unproductive sales promotion expenditures, might or might not be substantial. One might assume that sales promotion expenditures are about 5 percent of the gross value of the output of the private sector, or about 3 percent of GNP, that the reduction of the integration of marketing with production would reduce sales promotion expenditures by 20 percent, and that the value of that marginal 20 percent of expenditure (that is, what the consumer would willingly pay if he had a choice) is one-tenth of the cost. These assumptions produce a reduction of economic waste equal to 0.54 percent of the GNP. Obviously, other assumptions would yield other estimates.

The gains relating to item 3, the excess of resources devoted to retailing, complete the list. Retailing accounts for almost 6 percent of GNP. If the avoidable excess resources are set at 30 percent, the indicated prospective gain in efficiency is 1.8 percent of GNP.

The total of these various elements of increased efficiency indicates a gain in real income of the order of 7.5 percent of the GNP.

Obviously, these numbers are highly conjectural. The exercise was undertaken solely to determine whether the potential gains were minute or substantial. Despite the highly arbitrary nature of the estimates, it is a reasonable conclusion that the gains to be obtained are far from negligible.

The ban upon various forms of price discrimination and removal of the right of refusal to sell would prevent the most effective punitive and exclusion tactics and remove most of the artifical barriers to entry. Consequently, there would be a great gain in fairness in the competitive rivalry among companies. In my view, this gain, although intangible, would be an important one. In addition to whatever importance is accorded to fairness by one's value judgements, those who are convinced of the superiority of the market system as a technique for maximizing real income will not lightly regard the avoidance of dissatisfaction with its operation, especially when it is seen that that dissatisfaction might lead to the replacement of the system by less efficient techniques in various parts of the economy.

Finally, in relation to both fairness itself and the esteem with which the market system is regarded, there would be a considerable gain if the instances in which market power is used to earn monopoly profits, other than those which are an intentional constituent of the patent system, were eliminated. It has been mentioned that economists usually count only the deadweight loss of consumers' surplus. However, this measure is of slight interest to the consumer. When the infrequent example of a manufacturer's price of, say, $5.00 as compared to a cost of $3.00 is brought to his—or, more pertinently, her—attention, the indignation is not likely to be diminished by the explanation that the $2.00 of monopoly profit did not represent a waste of resources but only a transfer of income from the consumer to the manufacturer. The conviction that profits should be no higher than is required to keep the free enterprise system operating efficiently is strongly entrenched. And the regard with which that system is held depends, in no small degree, upon the impression which consumers gain concerning the prevalence of profits that greatly exceed competitive rates.

NOTES TO THE INTRODUCTION

1 Economic Council of Canada, *Interim Report on Competition Policy* (Ottawa: Queen's Printer, 1969).

2 G. Rosenbluth and H. G. Thorburn, "Canadian Anti-Combines Administration, 1952–1960," *Canadian Journal of Economics and Political Science* 27 (November 1961): 498–508.

3 R. A. Smith, "The Incredible Electrical Conspiracy," *Fortune* 63, nos. 4 and 5 (April and May 1961): 132–137; 161–164.

4 See, for example, Canada, *Report of the Royal Commission on Banking and Finance* (Ottawa: Queen's Printer, 1964), pp. 341–342.

NOTES TO CHAPTER 1

1 The ideal of some economists requires that all industries be compelled by market forces to behave in an optimal way. Other economists, perhaps more realistically, are content when industries do behave optimally whether compelled to by market forces or not; hence they consider that the efficient monopoly should be left alone until it ceases to be so. The point being made here has a somewhat different focus: If all alternatives were attainable, which would perform better in the majority of cases? On this ground, the pressure of low profits is preferred to its absence, on the reasoning that the former is more likely to quickly adjust capacity to demand. The conclusion turns entirely upon the correctness of this judgement. Whether the structure of an existing industry should be changed is a much more complex matter.

2 The formula for calculating the percentage increase in sales required just to compensate for a decrease in the markup is as follows:

$$\frac{\text{increase in sales}}{\text{initial sales volume}} = \frac{\text{change in the markup}}{\text{markup after the price change}}$$

For example, where M is the markup and P the price, if $M_1 = .3P_1$ and $P_1 - P_2 = .1P_1$, then $P_1 - P_2 = .5M_2$, and the required increase in sales is .5. Before the price decrease, gross profits are 30¢ per dollar on a volume of 100; after the price reduction, gross profits are 20¢ per dollar on a volume of 150. Put another way, the new sales volume must equal the old sales volume times the ratio of the old to the new markup: $M_1 \times Q_1 = M_2 \times Q_2$. Hence Q_2 must at least $= Q_1 \times M_1/M_2$ where Q = sales.

3 Canada, Department of Justice, *Report of the Director of Investigation and Research, Combines Investigation Act for the Year Ended March 31, 1966* (Ottawa: Queen's Printer, 1966), p. 14.

[4] *Ibid.*, p. 15.

[5] R. F. Lanzilotti, "Pricing Objectives in Large Companies," *American Economic Review* 48 (December 1958): 921–940.

[6] *Financial Post*, 16 September 1967, p. 1.

[7] According to static thinking, average variable cost should be a floor to any price reduction, because it is less unprofitable for a company to suspend production than it is to produce for prices lower than out-of-pocket costs. Since this consideration is decisive only if there are no costs of reentry, including the costs of regaining lost customers and workers, variable costs rarely set a floor to prices.

[8] Canada, Department of Justice, *Matches. Investigation into an Alleged Combine in the Manufacture, Distribution and Sales of Matches in Canada*, Report of the Commissioner, Combines Investigation Act, 1949 (Ottawa: Queen's Printer, 1949).

[9] But the prices of toothpaste are identical (or so it appears if one can find the small type declaring the weight and can convert ounces into kilograms) despite the fact that one brand is strongly recommended by dentists. In matters of pricing, it seems that every generalization requires numerous qualifications.

[10] In any event, even if the markup is fairly high, say 40 percent, the increase in sales would have to be 14 percent to compensate for the lower margin, even if the added cost of making more sales is neglected. See note 2.

[11] There was one change in the "real" price—a decrease in the form of delivery to the pressroom instead of delivery at dockside; but the quoted price remained unchanged.

[12] Most of the recent studies of Canadian tariff-sheltered manufacturing have remarked upon this practice. A list of these studies is given in note 6 of chapter 2.

[13] See G. J. Stigler, "The Kinky Oligopoly Demand Curve and Rigid Prices," in American Economic Association, *Readings in Price Theory*, [ed. G. J. Stigler and K. E. Boulding] (Homewood, Ill.: Richard D. Irwin, Inc. for the Association, 1952), pp. 427–428.

[14] See L. W. Weiss, *Economics and American Industry* (New York: John Wiley & Sons, Inc., 1961), chap. 5, for an excellent brief account of the United States aluminum industry as monopoly and as oligopoly. It is perhaps significant that Alcoa's profit rate was about the same after the industry became an oligopoly as it was when Alcoa was a monopolist.

NOTES TO CHAPTER 2

[1] See my article, "A Reformulation of the Kaldor Effect," *Economic Journal* 77, no. 305 (March 1967): 84–99.

[2] D. C. Mueller and J. E. Tilton, "Research and Development Costs as a Barrier to Entry," *Canadian Journal of Economics* 2 (November 1969): 570–579.

[3] Useful short articles on the innovation controversy include D. Hamberg, "Size of Firm, Oligopoly and Research: the Evidence," *Canadian Journal of Economics and Political Science* 30 (February 1964): 62–75, and E. Mansfield, "Size of Firm, Market Structure and Innovation," *Journal of Political Economy* 71 (December 1963): 556–576. For other references see E. Mansfield, *Industrial Research and Technological Innovation* (New York: W. W. Norton & Company, Inc., 1968), pp. 222–226.

4 This conclusion is not altered by a finding that firms are experiencing decreasing costs. Even if a doubling of sales would reduce average cost by, say, 25 percent, it is not a defect that the firms do not expand to realize the economies of scale. Demand is not sufficient to absorb sales at that volume. The pertinent point is that the amount of service demanded is being provided by a firm of the size which is optimal for the demand prevailing.

5 Economic Council of Canada, *Fourth Annual Review: Canadian Economy from the 1960's to the 1970's* (Ottawa: Queen's Printer, 1967), p. 149.

6 F. A. Knox, C. L. Barber and D. W. Slater, *The Electrical Manufacturing Industry, An Economic Analysis* (Toronto: University of Toronto Press, 1955); Canada, Royal Commission on Canada's Economic Prospects, *Canadian Secondary Manufacturing Industry*, study prepared for the commission by D. H. Fullerton and H. A. Hampson (Ottawa: Queen's Printer, 1957); H. E. English, *Industrial Structure in Canada's International Competitive Position* (Montreal: Private Planning Association of Canada, 1964); H. C. Eastman and S. Stykolt, *The Tariff and Competition in Canada* (Toronto: Macmillan Co. of Canada, Ltd., 1967); R. J. Wonnacott and P. Wonnacott, *Free Trade between the United States and Canada, The Potential Economic Effects* (Cambridge, Mass.: Harvard University Press, 1967); Economic Council of Canada, *Fourth Annual Review*, chap. 6; Economic Council of Canada, *Scale and Specialization in Canadian Manufacturing*, Staff Study No. 21, prepared for the council by D. J. Daly, B. A. Keys, and E. J. Spence (Ottawa: Queen's Printer, 1968); D. E. Bond and R. J. Wonnacott, *Trade Liberalization and the Canadian Furniture Industry* (Toronto: University of Toronto Press, 1968); W .E. Haviland, N. S. Takacsy, and E. M. Cape, *Trade Liberalization and the Canadian Pulp and Paper Industry* (Toronto: University of Toronto Press, 1968).

7 Eastman and Stykolt, *The Tariff and Competition in Canada*, p. 61.

8 Bond and Wonnacott, *Trade Liberalization and the Canadian Furniture Industry*, pp. 20–21.

9 *Ibid.*, p. 26.

10 *Ibid.*, p. 21.

11 *Ibid.*, p. 29.

12 *Ibid.*, p. 30.

13 Eastman and Stykolt, *The Tariff and Competition in Canada*, table 1, p. 63.

14 The fact that gasoline is one of several joint products of crude oil and, therefore, the average cost of gasoline alone cannot be calculated does not affect the rule. To meet the joint-cost objection, one need only substitute "package of refined products" for "gasoline."

15 The waste takes the form of committing resources to fixed plant and equipment before they are needed. The magnitude of the waste, therefore, is the interest rate times the capital cost of the unused capacity times the number of years it remains unused.

16 Canada, Parliament, House of Commons, Special Committee on Drug Costs and Prices, *Drug Costs and Prices, Second and Final Report to the House*, Proceedings no. 34a (Ottawa: Queen's Printer, 1967), p. 21.

17 See W. S. Comanor and T. A. Wilson, "Advertising, Market Structure and Performance," *Review of Economics and Statistics* 49 (November 1967): 423–440.

18 Additional evidence of very substantial excess capacity is cited in British Columbia,

Report of the Royal Commission on Gasoline Price Structure (Victoria: Queen's Printer, 1966), and in Alberta, *Report of the Gasoline Marketing Enquiry Committee* (Edmonton: Queen's Printer, 1968).

[19] See British Columbia, *Royal Commission on Gasoline Price Structure*, Hearings, 19 May 1965, pp. 26–36 and Exhibit 93 (submission of Imperial Oil Company Limited), appendices C and D.

[20] Saskatchewan, *Report of the Royal Commission on Consumer Problems and Inflation* (Saskatoon: Queen's Printer, 1968), chap. 10.

[21] *Ibid.*, p. 199.

[22] *Ibid.*, pp. 188–190.

[23] Canada, Parliament, *Special Joint Committee of the Senate and House of Commons on Consumer Credit (Prices)*, Proceedings no. 41, 25 April 1967 (Ottawa: Queen's Printer, 1967), p. 3461.

NOTES TO CHAPTER 3

[1] Canada, Department of Consumer and Corporate Affairs, *Report of the Director of Investigation and Research, the Combines Investigation Act for the Year Ended 31 March 1968* (Ottawa: Queen's Printer, 1968), p. 9.

[2] Regina v. Howard Smith Paper Mills, Ltd. et al., O.R. 713; 22 C.R. 205; 112 C.C.C. 108; 4 D.L.R. 225; 25 C.P.R. 27, Appeal (1955). Howard Smith Paper Mills Ltd. et al. v. The Queen, S.C.R. 403; 26 C.R. 1; 118 C.C.C. 321; 8 D.L.R. (2d) 449 (1957).

[3] D. H. W. Henry, Director of Investigation and Research, untitled address to the New York State Bar Association, Antitrust Law Section, New York City, 30 January 1964, mimeographed, p. 19.

[4] Regina v. B.C. Sugar Refining Company Ltd. et al., 32 W.W.R. (N.S.) 577; 129 C.C.C. 7 (1960); 38 C.P.R. 177 (1962).

[5] Rex v. Eddy Match Ltd. et al., 13 C.R. 217 (1952) and 18 C.R. 357, Appeal (1954); and Regina v. Electric Reduction Co. of Canada, Ltd. (Supreme Court of Ontario, Toronto, 12 January 1970, unreported). See also Canada, Department of the Registrar General, *Report of the Restrictive Trade Practices Commission Concerning the Production, Distribution and Sale of Phosphates, Other Phosphorous Chemicals and Sodium Chlorate* (Ottawa: Queen's Printer, 1966).

[6] Canada, Department of Justice, *Report of the Restrictive Trade Practices Commission Concerning the Manufacture, Distribution and Sale of Ammunition in Canada* (Ottawa: Queen's Printer, 1959).

[7] Canada, Department of Justice, *Report of the Restrictive Trade Practices Commission Concerning the Distribution and Sale of Gasoline in the Toronto Area. Alleged Price Discrimination—Texaco Canada Limited* (Ottawa: Queen's Printer, 1961), p. 27.

[8] Canada, Department of Justice, *Report of the Restrictive Trade Practices Commission Concerning the Distribution and Sale of Gasoline in the Toronto Area. Alleged Price Discrimination—Supertest Petroleum Corporation, Limited* (Ottawa: Queen's Printer, 1961), p. 55.

[9] Canada, Department of Justice, *Report of the Restrictive Trade Practices Commission Concerning the Distribution and Sale of Gasoline in the Toronto Area.*

Alleged Price Discrimination—The British American Oil Company Limited (Ottawa: Queen's Printer, 1961).

[10] Canada, Office of the President of the Privy Council, *Report of the Restrictive Trade Practices Commission Concerning the Pricing Practices of Miss Mary Maxim Ltd.* (Ottawa: Queen's Printer, 1966).

[11] Canada, Department of Justice, *Report of the Restrictive Trade Practices Commission Concerning the Production, Distribution and Sale of Zinc Oxide* (Ottawa: Queen's Printer, 1958).

[12] Regina v. Carnation Co., Ltd., 67 D.L.R. 2d 215 (C.A.) (1968); 68 W.W.R. 97 (S.C.) (1969). See also Canada, Department of Justice, *Report of the Restrictive Trade Practices Commission Concerning the Manufacture, Distribution and Sale of Evaporated Milk and Related Products* (Ottawa: Queen's Printer, 1962).

[13] The Queen v. The Producers Dairy Limited (Ontario Court of Appeal, 8 June 1966, unreported).

[14] Canada, Department of Justice, *Report to the Minister of Justice of the Committee to Study Combines Legislation* (Ottawa: Queen's Printer, 1952).

[15] L. A. Skeoch, "The Abolition of Resale Price Maintenance: Some Notes on Canadian Experience," *Economica* n.s. 31 (August 1964): 260–269.

[16] Canada, Office of the President of the Privy Council, *Report of the Restrictive Trade Practices Commission Relating to the Distribution and Sale of Gasoline in the City of Winnipeg and Elsewhere in the Province of Manitoba* (Ottawa: Queen's Printer, 1966), p. 22.

NOTES TO CHAPTER 4

[1] R. J. Wonnacott and P. Wonnacott, *Free Trade between the United States and Canada: The Potential Economic Effects* (Cambridge, Mass.: Harvard University Press, 1967), p. 335.

[2] Economic Council of Canada, *Fourth Annual Review: Canadian Economy from the 1960's to the 1970's* (Ottawa: Queen's Printer, 1967), p. 167.

[3] U.S., Congress, Senate, Select Committee on Small Business, *The Right to Buy and Its Denial to Small Business*, prepared for the committee by Vernon A. Mund, 85th Cong., Document no. 32 (Washington, D.C.: Government Printing Office, 1957), chaps. 1 and 2.

[4] Canada, Office of the President of the Privy Council, *Report of the Restrictive Trade Practices Commission Relating to the Distribution and Sale of Gasoline in the City of Winnipeg and Elsewhere in the Province of Manitoba* (Ottawa: Queen's Printer, 1966), p. 23.

[5] Simpson v. Union Oil Company of California, 377 U.S. 13, 84 S.CT. 1051 (1964), rehearing denied; 377 U.S. 949, 84 S.CT. 1349 (1964).

[6] Nello Olindo Malo v. Shell Oil Company of Canada, Ltd., Superior Court of the Province of Quebec, District of Montreal, no. 557 (12 May 1965), p. 712.

[7] For example, a manufacturer of consumers' goods wishing to break into a new retail market may want to ensure that the retail prices of his products are lower than those of the firms established in the market. Consignment selling is the most direct

way for him to do so and, at the same time, to induce stores to handle his products by eliminating the risk attendant upon failure of the products to find a market.

[8] And increasing costs of the firm are rarely present except in such one-man enterprises as dairy farming and small-scale contracting, where the supervision of the owner-manager is crucially important.

[9] Canada, Department of Justice, *Matches. Investigation into an Alleged Combine in the Manufacture, Distribution and Sale of Matches in Canada*, Report of the Commissioner, Combines Investigation Act, 1949 (Ottawa: Queen's Printer, 1949).

[10] Canada, Department of Justice, *Report of the Restrictive Trade Practices Commission Concerning the Production, Distribution and Sale of Zinc Oxide* (Ottawa: Queen's Printer, 1958).

[11] According to the British Columbia Royal Commission on Gasoline Price Structure, the excess of the annual expenses over the rental income of all lessee stations of the major oil companies in British Columbia in 1963 was 1.8 cents per gallon of gasoline sold to lessee stations, if a return on the capital invested in the stations is excluded from cost, and 3.5 cents per gallon if a return of 10 percent before tax (about 6 percent after income tax) is included. British Columbia, *Report of the Royal Commission on Gasoline Price Structure* (Victoria: Queen's Printer, 1966), pp. 42–44.

[12] See Canada, Department of Justice, *Investigation into Alleged Combines in the Manufacture, Distribution and Sale of Mechanical Rubber Goods, Tires and Tubes, Accessories and Repair Materials, Rubber Footwear, Heels and Soles, Vulcanized Rubber Clothing*, Part III, Report of the Commissioner, Combines Investigation Act (Ottawa: Queen's Printer, 1952), and Stefan Stykolt, *Economic Analysis and Combines Policy: A Study of Intervention into the Canadian Market for Tires* (Toronto: University of Toronto Press, 1965).

[13] J. S. Bain, "Relation of Profit Rates to Industry Concentration: American Manufacturing, 1936–40," *Quarterly Journal of Economics* 65 (August 1951): 293–324, and Erratum (November 1951): 602; G. J. Stigler, *Capital and Rates of Return in Manufacturing Industries*, a study by the National Bureau of Economic Research, New York (Princeton, N.J.: Princeton University Press, 1963), chap. 3; R. W. Kilpatrick, "Stigler on the Relationship between Industry Profit Rates and Market Concentration," *Journal of Political Economy* 76 (May/June 1968): 479–488; W. S. Comanor and T. A. Wilson, "Advertising, Market Structure and Performance," *Review of Economics and Statistics* 49 (November 1967): 423–440; V. R. Fuchs, "Integration, Concentration and Profits in Manufacturing Industries," *Quarterly Journal of Economics* 75 (May 1961): 278–292.

[14] See O. E. Williamson, "Economies as an Antitrust Defense: The Welfare Tradeoffs," *American Economic Review* 58 (March 1968): 18–36.

[15] Economic Council of Canada, *Interim Report on Competition Policy* (Ottawa: Queen's Printer, 1969), pp. 88, 217, 218.

[16] See, for example, "The Art of Blocking That Take-Over," *Newsweek*, 16 December 1968, pp. 84–86.

[17] S. R. Reid, *Mergers, Managers and the Economy* (New York: McGraw-Hill Book Company, 1968), p. 157 and chap. 8, *passim*.

[18] *Ibid.*, p. 189 and chap. 9, *passim*.

[19] Brief to the Economic Council of Canada, dated 10 July 1967.

[20] Unless the labour force is too immobile to be displaced, as is the case with the inshore fisheries, for example.

[21] If the defence allowed by section 34(5) of the Combines Investigation Act against allegations of an enforcement of resale price maintenance were retained, such cases should be heard by the CPC; however, all these defences would be swept away if the proposals made in this study concerning withdrawal of the right of refusal to sell were adopted. The courts would have no jurisdiction except when companies refused to comply with the directives of the CPC.

[22] The pioneer study is Arnold Harberger's "Monopoly and Resource Allocation," *American Economic Review* 44 (May 1954): 77–87.

[23] Wonnacott and Wonnacott, *Free Trade between the United States and Canada*, p. 335.

Index

Advertising: and product differentiation, 48; and sales promotion, 94–97; excessive volume of, 95; and public regulation, 95, 97; and radio and television, 96; offends consumers' sovereignty rule, 96, 186–87; and economies of scale, 97; erects barriers to entry, 97; misleading, 119; information function of, 187–88; negative returns to, 187

Aluminum Company of America (Alcoa), 34; and price discrimination, 34; and monopoly pricing, 61

Ammunition case, 113

Anticombines and restrictive trade practices policy. *See* Competition policy

Arrow, Kenneth, and impossibility theorem, 74

Automobile industry: and integration of marketing with production, 149–50; pricing practices, 150, 173–74

Automobile tire industry: reasons for high costs in, 83–84, 174; and price discrimination, 173–74; economies of scale in, 174

Bank Act: *1967* amendments, 100; *1966* amendments, 137; and price fixing, 138

Bankruptcy, role of in a free enterprise system, 127

Banks, chartered: excessive resources in, 99–100; competition between, 99–100

Barriers to entry, 5, 27, 32–34, 46–52; and economies of scale, 50; and excess capacity, 92-93; and nonprice competition, 97. *See also* Ease of entry

Basing-point pricing, 34

British American case, 115

British Columbia Sugar Refining Company Ltd., merger case, 112

British North America Act, trade-and-commerce clause, 194

Business cycle: and bunching of investment in oligopolies, 92; and pricing behaviour, 135

Canadian Bankers Association, 137

Canadian Chamber of Commerce, 139

Canadian combines law. *See* Combines Investigation Act

Chemical pulp industry. *See* Pulp and paper industry

Collusion, 32, 40–41, 67; and regulation, 5; and trade associations, 26–27; tacit defined, 27, 138–39; formal, 37, 110, 118, 135–38; and tariff protection, 53; and exports, 110–11

Combines Investigation Act: and resale price maintenance, 7, 105, 119–23; and service industries, 9, 26; and Director of Investigation and Research, 29, 106–07, 178; and pricing behaviour, 29–30, 53; intent of, 105–07, 122–24; prohibited practices under, 105–22; section *32*, 107, 110–12; effects of, 109–10, 124–25; section *33*, 111–13, 116, 118–20; 192; and mergers, 111–13; and price discrimination, 113–16, 124; and predatory pricing, 116–19, 124; amendments to, 119–20, 122, 133; and consignment selling, 121–22; and economic waste, 124; main defects of, 124–25; of *1889*, 133; suggested amendments, 192–93

Combines policy. *See* Competition policy

Commodity/service mixture, 68

Competition

imperfect, and economic waste, 65–103 *passim*

monopolistic: and chronic low returns, 25–26; as a model of furniture industry, 86

nonprice, 2, 72, 81–82; prevalent form of intraindustry rivalry, 4; conventional remedies for, 4; by sales promotion, 47–48; and resale price

209